Critical Accla

"This is travel writing at its glorious best."

—*Chicago Tribune*

"The Travelers' Tales series is altogether remarkable."

—Jan Morris, author of *The World: Travels 1950–2000*

"For the thoughtful traveler, these books are invaluable."

—Pico Iyer, author of *The Global Soul*

"Nightstand reading of the first order." —*Los Angeles Times*

"...the popular Travelers' Tales collections offer a perfect fit for just about anyone, with themes of geography, women's travel, and a passel of special-interest titles on topics including shopping, pets, diners, and toilets around the world." —*Chicago Sun-Times*

"These well-edited anthologies of first-person travel narratives are like mosaics: Each piece may add only a single note of color, but combine them and step back, and a rich and multifaceted portrait emerges."

—*San Francisco Chronicle*

"The Travelers' Tales series should become required reading for anyone visiting a foreign country who wants to truly step off the tourist track and experience anther culture, another place, firsthand."

—*St. Petersburg Times*

"This is the stuff that memories can be duplicated from."

—*Foreign Service Journal*

Travelers' Tales Destination Titles

America
American Southwest
Australia
Brazil
Central America
China
Cuba
France
Grand Canyon
Greece
Hawai'i
Hong Kong
India
Ireland
Italy
Japan
Mexico
Nepal
Paris
Provence
San Francisco
South Pacific
Spain
Thailand
Tibet
Turkey
Tuscany

TRAVELERS' TALES

30 DAYS IN THE SOUTH PACIFIC

Travelers' Tales

30 Days in the South Pacific

True Stories of Escape to Paradise

Edited by Sean O'Reilly,
James O'Reilly,
and Larry Habegger

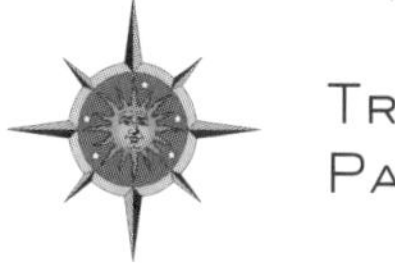

Travelers' Tales
Palo Alto

Art Direction: Stefan Gutermuth
Cover Photographs: courtesy of www.TahitiTourisme.com
Map: © 2004 by David Stanley, *Moon Handbooks South Pacific*
Interior design and page layout: Melanie Haage,
using the fonts Spectrum, Gill Sans, and Voluta Script.

Distributed by: Publishers Group West,
1700 Fourth Street, Berkeley, California 94710.

Library of Congress Cataloging-in-Publication Data

30 days in the South Pacific : true stories of escape to paradise / edited by Sean O'Reilly, James O'Reilly, and Larry Habegger.--1st ed.
p. cm. -- (Travelers' Tales)
Includes index.
ISBN 1-932361-26-X (pbk.)
1. Oceania--Description and travel. 2. Travelers' writings. I. Title: Thirty days in the South Pacific. II. O'Reilly, Sean. III. O'Reilly, James, 1953- IV. Habegger, Larry. V. Travelers' Tales guides.
DU23.5.A13 2005
919.504--dc22 2005021956

First Edition
Printed in the United States
10 9 8 7 6 5 4 3 2 1

Somewhere among the notebooks of Gideon I once found a list of diseases as yet unclassified by medical science, and among these there occurred the word Islomania, *which was described as a rare but by no means unknown affliction of the spirit. There are people, Gideon used to say, by way of explanation, who find islands somehow irresistible. The mere knowledge that they are on an island, a little world surrounded by the sea, fills them with an indescribable intoxication.*

—LAWRENCE DURRELL, *Reflections on a Marine Venus*

TABLE OF CONTENTS

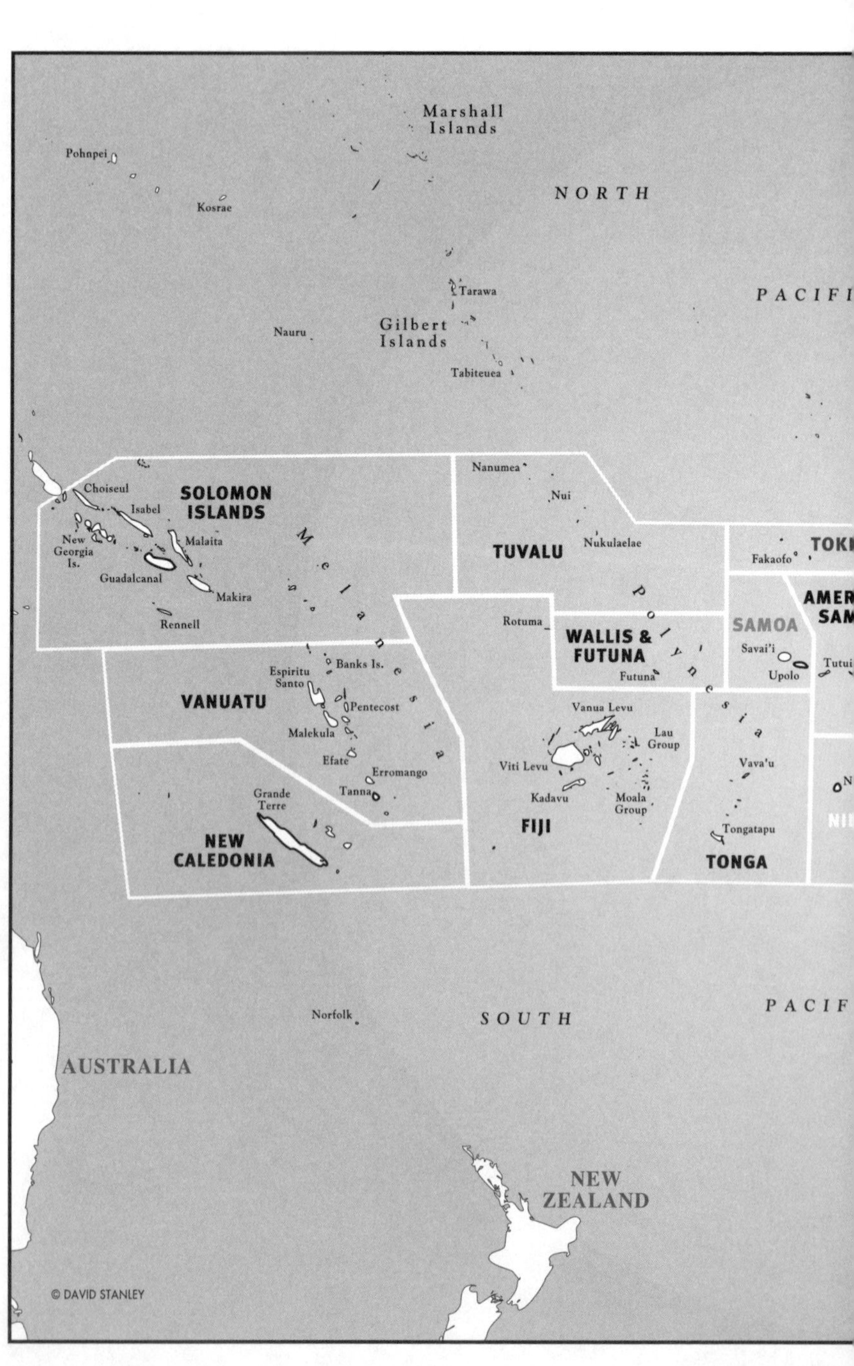

Marshall Islands
Pohnpei
Kosrae
NORTH
Tarawa
PACIFI
Nauru
Gilbert Islands
Tabiteuea
Nanumea
Nui
SOLOMON ISLANDS
Choiseul
Isabel
New Georgia Is.
Malaita
Guadalcanal
Makira
Rennell
Melanesia
TUVALU
Nukulaelae
TOK
Fakaofo
AMER SAM
SAMOA
Savai'i
Upolo
Tutui
Rotuma
WALLIS & FUTUNA
Futuna
Polynesia
VANUATU
Banks Is.
Espiritu Santo
Pentecost
Malekula
Efate
Erromango
Tanna
Vanua Levu
Lau Group
Viti Levu
Kadavu
Moala Group
FIJI
Vava'u
Tongatapu
TONGA
Grande Terre
NEW CALEDONIA
Norfolk
SOUTH
PACIF
AUSTRALIA
NEW ZEALAND

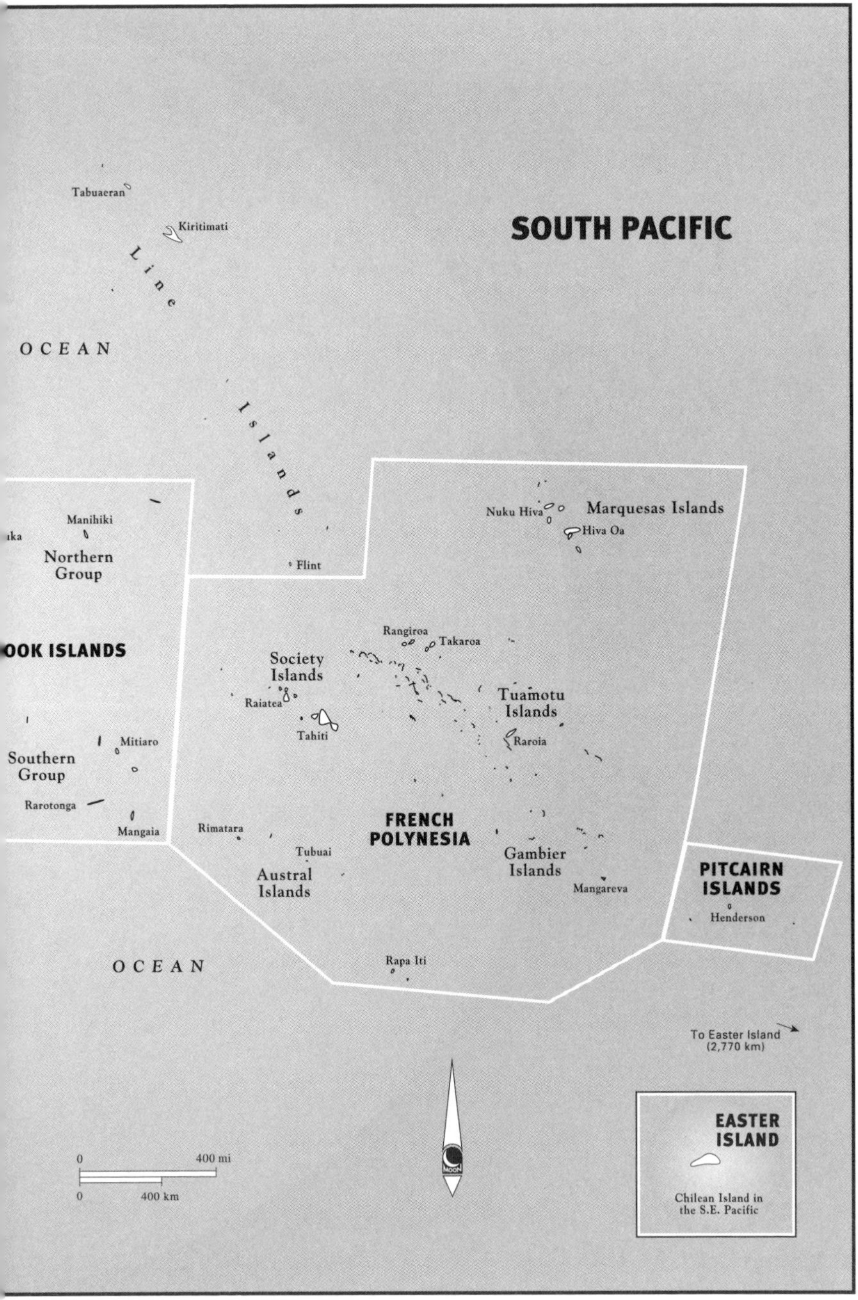

SOUTH PACIFIC

Tabuaeran
Kiritimati
Line Islands
OCEAN
Flint
Manihiki
Northern Group
OOK ISLANDS
Southern Group
Mitiaro
Rarotonga
Mangaia
Nuku Hiva
Marquesas Islands
Hiva Oa
Rangiroa
Takaroa
Society Islands
Raiatea
Tahiti
Tuamotu Islands
Raroia
FRENCH POLYNESIA
Rimatara
Tubuai
Austral Islands
Gambier Islands
Mangareva
PITCAIRN ISLANDS
Henderson
OCEAN
Rapa Iti
To Easter Island (2,770 km)
EASTER ISLAND
Chilean Island in the S.E. Pacific
0 400 mi
0 400 km
MOON

SEAN O'REILLY

INTRODUCTION

I WATCHED THE BEARDED, POT-BELLIED FRENCHMAN IN A black thong, so popular among the European set, amble across the white sand toward the surf. "The savage," I thought, and wondered where his spear was. What is it about the South Pacific that turns Europeans and other Westerners inward toward a state of nature—myself included? Ever since Herman Melville, Robert Louis Stevenson, and others immortalized the simplicity of the native cultures of the region, Westerners have been coming to the South Pacific to become primitively whole. Perhaps it is the stress of living in the machine culture of Western civilization that makes all of us yearn for a simpler and more immediate life. Food, drink, the hospitality of islanders, an undercurrent of sensuality, and the hot sun all conspire to put one in a state of mind that could only be described as loose and open to change.

The Pacific, mother of all oceans, covers more than a third of the earth's surface. It is estimated that there are some 30,000 islands scattered among the commonly designated regions of Micronesia, Melanesia, and Polynesia. Oceania is the term that covers the entire area geographically but nothing can really describe with adequacy the hold that the South Pacific has on the Western imagination. The literary torch ignited by Melville and Stevenson, carried on by Jack London, James Michener, and others attests to this eternal pull. James Michener's imaginary paradise of Bali Ha'i, for example, in *Tales of the South Pacific*, might be thought of as a recasting of Shangri-La in an oceanic setting. Michener's tale was so compelling that even though it was a fictional account, Bali Ha'i was claimed by many island groups as their own. Stevenson, in one of his last books, *In the South Pacific*, best captured these sentiments that the South Pacific evokes:

> No part of the world exerts the same attractive power upon the visitor, and the task before me is to communicate to fireside travelers some sense of its seduction, and to describe the life, at sea and ashore, of many hundreds of thousands of persons, some of our own blood and language, all our contemporaries, and yet as remote in thought and habit as Rob Roy or Barbarossa, the Apostles or the Caesars.

Stevenson may have had little inkling that among these "thousands of persons" scattered across the South Pacific some 1,200 languages were once spoken, a full third of the world's language repository. Unfortunately, many of these languages are no longer spoken or are in danger of dying out. The original Polynesian culture that spread 3,500 years ago throughout the so-called Polynesian Triangle that began, as some have claimed, in Samoa and spread to Hawai'i in the north, Easter Island to the east, and New Zealand and the Solomons to the west, has been significantly affected for the past 250 years by Western civilization. There was, as poet Rupert Brooke noted, something magical about the original Polynesian culture that is a shadow of its former self, although it still lingers in places like Fiji, Yap, and Samoa:

> You lie on a mat in the a cool Samoan hut, and look out on the white sand under high palms, and a gentle sea, and the black line of the reef a mile out, and moonlight over everything...and among it all are the loveliest people in the world, moving and dancing like gods and goddesses, very quietly and mysteriously, and utterly content. It is sheer beauty, so pure that it's difficult to breathe it in.

Contrary to Brooke's rapturous view, guidebook author and South Pacific expert David Stanley notes that: "the modern world is transforming the Pacific more and more. Outboards replace outriggers; Coca-Cola substitutes for coconuts and consumerism has caught on in the towns.... Television is still absent from many Pacific homes; instead attitudes are molded by the tens of thousands of VCRs that play pirated videotapes available at hundreds of corner stores. Villages are trapped by material desires.... The diet is changing as imported processed foods take the place of fiber-rich foods such as breadfruit, taro, and plantain."

Nonetheless, one still sees in Fiji and Western Samoa examples of the "sheer beauty" that Brooke witnessed in Samoa. I had a taste of this in an unexpected way at the local airport in Savusavu, Fiji. I was approached by a crippled man selling necklaces. He was paralyzed from the waist down and walked slowly and courteously towards me, maintaining eye contact as he leaned heavily on his worn, aluminium walker. He entered my personal space with infinite care and self-awareness, and as things go in the South Pacific, he told me his story. Four years ago, he fell from a tree and broke his back, rendering his lower body useless. He had been, from all appearances, a once well-built man whom we might describe from the position of our own cultural perspective as being black. I could tell that his injury caused him much pain. His toes were bandaged and bleeding from being dragged along on the ground in sandals. Twice a day, taking both bus and taxicab, he would take the necklaces he purchased in town out to the local airport to sell to the tourists who arrived twice daily. He had a wife and three sons to support. There was no pleading with me, no whining or wheedling as he showed me his merchandise, just an infinite dignity in his manner.

I purchased two necklaces for my youngest children but the gift he gave me that day was far greater than any gift I have been given by mortal man. I encountered in him a remarkable faith in humanity under circumstances that would cause most of us despair. He was a god in disguise, and I tell you, if you see this man on your journeys give him what you can, for what he has to give you is beyond price.

The man selling necklaces was a Christian but it really didn't matter what religion he was. He had what the old Polynesians called *mana,* or the power of the gods—perhaps akin to what we in the West call faith. The vast hospitality of Polynesian culture, likewise, has much to offer us, and what the West has to offer, in terms of technical expertise, is of clear value to the people of the South Pacific.

As tourism continues to develop, and new social structures evolve from the present clash of cultures, one can only hope that a bright future will emerge. Bear this in mind as you go about your journeys. Observe and tread lightly, but above all, be prepared for the South Pacific to beguile you and change you.

It was Robert Louis Stevenson, master of Vailima and craftsman of *Treasure Island,* who put the ultimate crown on all musings about the South Pacific when he wrote,

> The schooner turned upon her heel, the anchor plunged. It was a small sound, a great event; my soul went down with these moorings whence no windlass may extract nor any diver fish it up; and I, and some part of my ship's company, were from that hour the bond slaves of the isles...

Take this refreshment along with the Tahitian proverb that says, "the palm shall grow, the coral shall spread, but man shall cease." Don't depart this life without visiting the South Pacific.

—Sean O'Reilly
Baie de Kuto
Ile des Pins

Editors' note: *In this book we have included stories from Micronesia, Melanesia, and Polynesia, relying on the idea of the South Pacific rather than literal geography. The "South Pacific" conjures tropical Pacific waters, and thus we've taken the liberty to include some stories on islands that lie north of the equator.*

I

LAURIE GOUGH

LIGHT ON A MOONLESS NIGHT

Where are you the happiest?

I LIKE TO REMEMBER THE NIGHT OF MY RETURN TO THE remote Fijian island called Taveuni. Remembering it makes me smile. Warm winds dried off the saltwater slapped in my face during their earlier tantrum as I beached myself ashore after a thirty-six-hour boat ride on high South Pacific seas. My balance was as off as a tone-deaf minstrel after a night of medieval merriment. I didn't care. I was back in Taveuni.

TAV-EE-UUN-EE. I loved the feel of the word in my mouth, full and rich and ripe like the island itself, about to burst with ancient lava and laughter and secrets from the past. It made me think of jumping from a place up high, like a rock, a tree, or a cliff, into someplace unfamiliar and alive. The mere speaking of the island's name carried its own magic for me, was a way of entering and leaving the world. When spoken during the day, Taveuni was an expansive name for a place containing mirth and light and possibly mischief, but at night the name held its own dark sort of grace. And if whispered at night, or, even worse, whispered in just the right tone, the name caused shivers. Taveuni whispered. Think of it.

Eight months had fallen from the Earth since I'd left Taveuni. Eight months of exploring other places: New Zealand, Australia, Malaysia, Thailand, Indonesia. It didn't feel real, standing on that old Fiji dock again in the hot night, everything familiar in a dreamy kind of way. Even the taxi drivers came on like old friends. They sauntered towards us boat escapees looking as if they'd just heard the world's best joke. Or seen it. Our faces had to be green. One man was puking his boiled-fish dinner into the sea while his wife patted his back. That's true love. New visitors aren't hassled here as in parts of the world where a traveler can be swarmed by a sea of faceless strangers speaking the few words of English they know to conjure up business: "Room, room, taxi, hotel cheap, Miss, Miss, good food, cheap, speak English, please Miss, come, cheap."

Life's gentler on Taveuni.

Like salty fermenting pickles crammed in a jar, six of us shared a taxi ride along Taveuni's one road. The driver sang us a ditty. He was a happy man. As the taxi jerked its way along the bumpy road over hills and too fast around curves into the blackness of the night, I could imagine exactly where we were, what we'd see if it were daylight. Memories spilled over each other like ocean waves: of the two months I'd spent here, of the Fijians and their children I'd taught at the school, of the village that clings to the tropical mountainside, of the other travelers I'd met at the campground by the sea. I wondered if anyone would be awake at this hour. Would the quiet Fijian men and their children with immense eyes still be on the beach, circled around the kava bowl singing South Pacific harmonies? They'd be surprised to see me, of that I was sure.

I was surprised myself. Rarely do travelers return to such remote destinations even if they had the best of intentions when leaving them. I was seventeen when I visited the island of Madeira on a school-sponsored holiday and I vowed to return one day. Over ten years have passed, many of them spent traveling, and my list of secret spots on Earth to come back to is ever growing, with Madeira so far recessed that I don't know when I'll find my way back there.

But Taveuni called me back and I'd listened. I had daydreamed of this countless times over the past sweltering months, lost and bone-weary on noisy diesel-hazed streets, caught in crushes of human traffic in jammed Asian markets, or waiting for trains, buses, or cars with only a series of mangled straw hats between me and the unkind blaze of the equatorial sun. Ideas of returning to Taveuni—hidden so far and so secretly from the rest of the world that I often wondered if it really was of this world—had been growing steadily in my scorched mind.

I asked the taxi driver to stop half a mile or so before arriving where I thought, in the dark, Buvu Beach Campground lay. I wanted to walk the last part of the road as I imagined it. In my daydreams it had always been broad daylight, but I wasn't fussy. The driver didn't even question dumping me in the middle of nowhere at two o'clock in the morning. The other passengers eyed my tent skeptically. They were off to Taveuni's resort. An elderly English woman warned me, oblivious to our native driver, "They were cannibals here, dear, right in this jungle. Whatever are you thinking?"

"That you shouldn't knock eating people until you try it yourself."

O.K., I said that after the taxi roared off and left me standing in the mud. I set off with my backpack through the darkness, hoping I wouldn't veer off the dirt road into the bush. I suppose it was possible that ghosts of cannibals might still be hanging around, suspended in the confusion of trees. Or perhaps underneath the tender ground lay mute bones of half-eaten men carved up for special occasions. If I stepped in the wrong place, the bones would crumble into powder and release terrible secrets. So I looked up instead, into the soft center of the universe. The sky is ancient and the ghosts there don't remember cannibals. The storm had passed back out to sea and a great white sweep of Pacific stars poured down. I tried to find the Southern Cross but couldn't see it. As usual. Instead I spotted Orion directly over me and its familiarity reassured me that I was doing the right thing to return here. It's a consistent constellation.

> The earth is softer in Taveuni than in other places, and darker. It's how the earth must have been millions of years ago, in the world's warm beginnings.

No light of the moon floated down into the world that night. Into an awkward blackness I walked for what seemed like hours, gradually losing confidence that I knew where I was. Not only disoriented, I was dizzy. Landsickness. I wavered back and forth along the dirt road, giddy and excited. I could see no lights shining anywhere, as at the time Taveuni (only twenty-five miles long and six miles wide) had no electricity except for the occasional house with a generator. Most people used oil lamps, all that was needed by islanders who lived naturally with the sun, sea, and land.

I finally came to a hill so I knew I'd passed Buvu Beach just behind me. Exhilaration lifted my load of clothes, books, and gifts as I found my way back to the campground's entrance. I walked barefoot—the only way to walk on a muddy road. The earth is softer in Taveuni than in other places, and darker. It's how the earth must have been millions of years ago, in the world's warm beginnings. My hands remembered their way up a giant tree marking the pathway leading into the wooded beach. I'd arrived.

Heaven owns real estate on Buvu Beach. An extended Fijian family owns it also. They live up a hill across the road. The campground is shaded by towering and twisted trees which drop down leaves large enough to hide overfed cats. Coconut palms, mango trees, ferns, and bamboo shoots jump up everywhere to join the lush green picnic of it all. But it's the flower blossoms that lure people inside. The smells they emit refuse to be shunned. Scent-drenched, the blossoms fill your nostrils, swarm the cracks of your memory until you're inhaling more than flowers. You're inhaling echoes of how the world once was. Three or four little bamboo huts, known in Fiji as *bures*, lie hidden among the voluptuous vegetation. A few tents are always edged away somewhere, too. I like to believe that travelers are blown this way by ancient sea winds. We fall inside the soft air and sleep to the pounding waves of the ocean's heart which beats in time to our own. Only the occasional annoying rooster or thud of a wayward coconut interrupts one's sleep.

Pitch black. The hand extended in front of my face was invisible. This was the kind of utter darkness that falls only in remote places, inconceivable to city dwellers. Nothing but an eight-month-old memory of the place could get me over the preposterous tree roots erupting out of the sand. They were like mutant flora. Last time here I'd broken a toe, twice, on one of these roots. The Fijians made such a big deal about it and laughed at me so much that if I did it again I'd be forced to hop back out to the boat unseen. There's only so much jocularity about my feet I'll tolerate.

I walked in slow motion toward the grass-roofed hut and heard it creaking in the wind. The little hut always reminded me of Gilligan's island, being so makeshift, crafted out of whatever grew on the beach. The hut was our refuge, our hangout, our sheltering haven. Here campers and Fijians would cook, talk, and laugh for hours into the night. It had a sand floor and no walls, a stove and cupboards, a few benches, and a little table that mangoes, coconuts, and pineapples always lay on. We called the little hut our kitchen. Sometimes when the moon was full, the tide was high enough that the sea would slip right up and wet our kitchen floor. We didn't mind.

Beside the kitchen, we would gather on the beach at the end of each day and watch the sun setting over the Pacific. It would spread over us like a mauve shadow. When it grew dark we would sit around a fire, drinking the Fijian elixir of life, kava, out of coconut bowls. Kava isn't alcoholic, but it's something. It slows down time. The Fijian men would sit with us and sing and play their guitars. After a while we'd all be singing. Then we'd tell stories. We'd tell travel stories mainly, since we were all travelers of some sort. The Fijians would tell stories, too, stories of their lives growing up on Taveuni. Storytelling is important in television-free places like Taveuni. It's important anywhere. I remembered all the stories told around those campfires. And now I stood in the kitchen again, remembering these things as if I'd never left.

But I had left. I left because I couldn't stop moving. I couldn't stop searching for the perfect place. That's the thing about travelers. We always have to see what's over the next hill. But someone once wrote that to leave is to die a little. So I came back to the place I left. And immediately I found my heart beating alive inside this strange island's quiet grace, stirred to see into the life of things here. I stood still and listened as moist night air invaded my hair like seaweed. What I heard was a kind of song coming out of the sea, like a drum banging in the waves, but singing too. All that time over in Asia, I'd only remembered the adventures I'd had here—the hiking, the snorkeling, the music, the family, the kids in the school. But now I understood it was the waves that had pulled me back. They'd been here all along like a steady pulse, patiently keeping time for the world. Waves like this never stop rolling inside a person, just beneath one's awareness. The sea has a way of slipping us back to our beginnings, soothing a rusty place inside us, to remind us of something. Like a secret trance, a forgotten calling.

I stood in water as warm as my blood and exhaled a tremendous unconditional breath like the wind itself. The sea washed something out of me, freed me in its imperceptible way of what lay smoldering within: eight months of traveling alone on a road full of startling faces and unfamiliar tongues. I'd been traipsing through too many days and nights of dog-ridden streets and climbing over shaky mountaintops, not always liking what I found on the other side. But traveling is a journey to the center of the soul, a crazy Irishman once shouted at me. One forges through dark mountains and unnamed streets until there's nothing left to see but chiseled pieces of light.

As I walked along the shoreline I thought about how nature overwhelms everything with the sea's pastel painted fish and purple coral, the island's extravagant trees of sweet unrecognizable fruit growing amidst waterfalls and volcanic mountains, rugged and wet. It would be difficult not to be delirious in such a place, a place where nature overpowers people, where people give themselves over to the land and sea. Little bits of phosphorescence, colored dots of fluorescent green, washed up at my feet. Laughter came in on the waves. I was home, as close to home as a traveler can get, and I felt like staying for good.

Laurie Gough has written for the Los Angeles Times, *the* Globe and Mail, Canadian Geographic, *and her work has appeared in several anthologies, including* Wanderlust: Real Life Tales of Adventure and Romance, AWOL: Tales for the Travel Inspired Mind, *and many Travelers' Tales books. "Light on a Moonless Night" was excerpted from* Kite Strings of the Southern Cross, *which was the silver medal winner of ForeWord Magazine's Travel Book of the Year Award and was short-listed for the Thomas Cook Award. Her latest travel book,* Kiss the Sunset Pig, *will be published soon. She lives in Canada.*

2 LAURENCE SHAMES

BLUE WATER DREAMS

Song and myth became reality for this traveler.

For me, it all started with Rodgers and Hammerstein.

Other people, from more sophisticated backgrounds, might have formed their fantasies of Polynesia from the paintings of Gauguin or the writings of Somerset Maugham. I got mine from *South Pacific*, sitting on the living room carpet with my mother, singing along with "Bali Ha'i" and "Some Enchanted Evening."

My daydreams were pretty rudimentary. Being seven or eight and from New Jersey, I had no very clear idea of where the South Pacific was. I'd never seen coral, much less a volcano. Palm trees I could picture—I'd seen them in Miami. Beyond that, I thought of Polynesia as a place where the fruit was always ripe, the breezes always warm, the people always talking happy-talk. I resolved that I would go there someday.

As the years went by, my daydreams grew more specific and more grand. I learned to sail, developed a passion for it. When I went to Polynesia, I decided, it would be as captain of a sailboat.

Amazingly, it happened. A mere forty or so years after the birth of the fantasy, there I was, with my wife, Marilyn, on what was actually my second visit to those islands, hoisting sail in the lagoon of Raiatea.

The water beneath us glinted turquoise; every change of depth shot back a different shade of blue or green. A mile or so to seaward, waves were breaking on the reef; a curtain of spindrift lifted into the air, refracting prisms as it settled down again. The trade winds bent and gathered around Raiatea's volcanic bulk, filling our sails, dipping our hull farther into the ripples.

Above the low whistle of breeze in the shrouds, I could not help singing my personal sailing mantra: *How sweet it is…*

We were heading for Faaroa Bay—a dramatic cleft in a broken mountain, with a river valley snaking away at its head. We nosed between the bluffs, and everything seemed to stop. The wind dropped, the water flattened out, the sea smell of the air was replaced by the musk of damp soil and the punky aroma of burned fields. On shore were small houses, some with tin roofs, some with traditional thatch, surrounded by banana trees. Music broke through the foliage. We heard snippets of high-spirited Tahitian conversation—happy-talk.

We anchored, climbed into the dinghy, and headed up the bay. We slipped behind a point of land and very suddenly, practically without transition, we were navigating a sort of mini-Amazon. The air instantly grew thick; the quiet had a jungle buzz to it. The ocean, just a few miles away, already seemed a distant memory. Tucked in among the tangled shrubbery were rustling birds we knew we'd never see.

Here and there houses hugged the riverbanks. Fishing nets

dangled from ropes strung between breadfruit trees. Small boats were raised out of the water on hand-cranked slings. Dogs barked now and then; a scuffling sound turned out to be a rooting pig. We zigged and zagged; sometimes we saw the mountaintop; sometimes the trees and vines closed in, and we saw nothing more than the next fifty yards of river.

I switched the engine off, and we drifted back downstream on the sluggish current, keeping pace with waterlogged coconuts and fallen hibiscus flowers drifting out to sea. This was my wife's first trip to Polynesia. Like everyone else, she'd had her own fantasies about the place—what Bloody Mary called "your own special dreams."

I gestured at papayas hanging over the river, at cooking smoke rising from a shed in a yard of swept red dirt.

"Is this what you pictured?"

She pondered a moment. "I didn't really have a picture," she said at last. "I had a feeling...and this is it."

The term "Polynesia" is a slightly confusing one, and so a bit of geography is called for. Historically, Polynesia comprised a vast triangle, explored and settled by a seagoing people, that extended from New Zealand in the south to Easter Island in the east to Hawai'i in the north. These days, however, Polynesia usually refers to *French* Polynesia—an overseas territory of the French Republic, consisting of five separate archipelagoes. In all, there are thirty-five high islands and eighty-three atolls. They sprawl across a swath of the South Pacific that's as big as Western Europe yet has a total landmass barely larger than that of Los Angeles County. The central archipelago is called the Society Islands, which is further divided into Windward and Leeward sections. The Windwards include Tahiti—by far the most important and therefore perhaps least Tahitian of the islands. The Leewards, where we sailed, encompass Raiatea, Tahaa, Huahine, and Bora Bora.

This last, of course, has been a hallowed tourist mecca at least since James Michener did it the questionable favor of dubbing it "the most beautiful island in the world." But the others are less frequently visited. Which means that when you get there, you have the ever-rarer pleasure of seeing people living their lives the way they choose, being themselves rather than putting on a show.

Consider the wearing of flowers. My wife and I were won over by this charming custom before we'd even left Raiatea's tiny alfresco airport.

We'd just arrived and were waiting for our bags when we noticed an extremely animated Polynesian family—Mama in a lime-green pareu, Papa in one of those side-vented shirts that's like an oversize bib, a couple of teenage daughters with rubber sandals and magnificently braided hair. The guest of honor, it soon became clear, was a son who was waiting for an outgoing flight, most likely to Papeete for university or work.

Every member of the family was bedecked with flowers—and the son, since he was the one departing, was the most lavishly garlanded of all.

He was around twenty, broad-shouldered and thickly muscled. He wore Ray-Bans and a Nike t-shirt. It conflicted neither with his masculinity nor his hipness that he also wore a triple-tiered crown of *tiare*—a species of gardenia and the emblematic flower of Polynesia—as well as an elaborate lei of white and lavender orchids. This was not a show for tourists; this was a contemporary Raiatea family wearing flowers because it pleased them to wear flowers.

On Raiatea, *everyone* wore flowers. Flowers were offered, for free, at the supermarket checkout counter, the way American businesses might offer toothpicks or mints. Flowers were worn by children, ancient women, men grown fat as sumo wrestlers on too much coconut milk, and even the scraggly guys who sat around the docks at the island's main town, Uturoa, fishing with enormous bamboo poles and swilling Hinano, the local brew. In other places these wharf-rats might have seemed vaguely sinister; in the Leeward Islands they smiled, said, "*Ia orana*" (a particularly warm version of hello—more like a Pacific "shalom"), and gave off the aroma of a florist's shop.

Uturoa, the administrative center for the Leewards, is also Polynesia's yacht-chartering center; it was there we picked up our thirty-five-foot Beneteau sloop from the charter company. But first we spent some time exploring. Uturoa is the second biggest town in Polynesia—but a very distant second, with around 5,000 people (as opposed to Papeete's 100,000 plus). Still, there was a bustle to the place, a purposefulness. Everybody chattered; the word *uturoa*, in fact, means "long jaw"—a reference to the locals' love of gossip. People left the grocery stores with sacks of rice on their shoulders, boxes of Pampers balanced on their heads. Tiny trucks clattered along, carrying a bizarre miscellany in their open beds—spools of wire, live chickens, outboard engines.

> From the working Eden of Raiatea, we sailed to Tahaa, a smaller island that shares the same lagoon and may be thought of as a paradise that has decided to sleep in.

I had been in Uturoa in 1991; since then its waterfront had been considerably spiffed up. There was a new concrete dock with bollards stout enough to hold a cruise ship, and a handsome arcade with shops and restaurants. The chatty locals, God bless 'em, seemed unanimous in deploring those changes.

"Too modern!" said the proprietress of a shop selling everything from candy bars to fishing gear. "Too big!" said a lady at the public market, from behind her pyramid of grapefruits. "Who needs it?" asked a grizzled fisherman with a bamboo pole tucked beneath his arm. He shrugged so emphatically as to displace the flower behind his ear. He took a moment to resettle it before continuing on his way.

From the working Eden of Raiatea, we sailed to Tahaa, a smaller island that shares the same lagoon and may be thought of as a paradise that has decided to sleep in.

Tahaa was quiet, drowsy, unconcerned with time. Insofar as it is known at all, it's known for its vanilla—by reputation the finest in the world. The island, in fact, exuded vanilla; under certain conditions of breeze and mist, a gorgeous and narcotic vanilla smell seemed to blanket the whole lagoon.

Steering a lazy course along the coast, we concluded that everything on Tahaa was beautifully to scale—a decidedly miniature scale. Houses were doll-like. Villages vanished into forest almost before we could see them. We spotted a few small pensions and tiny marinas tucked into coves and bays that would be tough to find without a detailed chart.

When we went ashore, we could see that Tahaa's agriculture was similarly Lilliputian. Most of the island's inhabitants still worked the land, producing bananas, melons, and vegetables, the bulk of which were then "exported" across the lagoon. But what was grandly called a "plantation" was usually a family-owned plot about the size of a tennis court or two. As for the ferries that took the goods to market, a number of them scudded past our bow; they turned out to be brightly painted outrigger skiffs powered by vintage outboards and sitting low in the water under the weight of a couple of Tahaa families, a dozen cabbages, and an armful of pineapples.

If Tahaa was delightfully dinky, it was far from lacking in amenities. Consider the Tahaa Grill—one of the more improbable institutions I had ever encountered.

Marilyn and I were moored in Hurepiti Bay. There was no village there, no restaurants, nothing. One other yacht was anchored near us, but no one seemed to be on board. It was around 7 A.M. The sun was just topping the coconut palms; we were on our second cup of coffee. Suddenly a powerboat sped into the bay. As it got closer, I saw that its driver was waving to us. Nearer still, I could see that the boat bore a sign: Tahaa Grill.

It maneuvered alongside, and a handsome young Frenchman sang out, "*Bonjour! Voudriez-vous des croissants, pain-au-chocolat?*"

In my very best French, I said, "*Excusez moi?*"

My accent, though superb, persuaded him to switch to English, "Sandwiches? Baguettes? Papaya? Roast chicken?"

Roast chicken? I thought. My God, we're in an unpeopled South Seas paradise, and we're also in France. Hell, why not *foie gras*?

"Paté?" he responded.

We stocked up, of course, one gets very hungry on a boat. But it wasn't until the Tahaa Grill had motored off, and I took the first bite of a very buttery croissant, that I truly believed the whole episode was more than a mirage.

My wife has a way of cutting right to the heart of the matter. As we turned our backs on Tahaa and headed toward the reef at Passe Toahotu, she looked at me and asked, "Are we going to die?"

The boat was heeling steeply; an outward current was sweeping us toward the coral. Still, with my usual sangfroid, I said, "I think we're fine."

She shot me a look that every husband knows. It said, to put it gently, *Are you sure you know what you're doing, honey?*

I found it politic to interject: "I see the red buoy. Aha! Now I see the green."

She said, "And *I* see breaking waves. And no gap in the coral."

It was hard to refute her point. Up ahead loomed a seamless swath of boiling foam.

According to the chart, the pass was plenty wide—fifty yards or so. But nature is all rough edges, and a reef doesn't simply *stop*; it tails off, leaving scraps, fringes, booby traps. You've got to pass through at a quite specific angle. I wrestled with the wheel; my eyes flicked back and forth between the compass and the barely submerged coral that was getting ever closer. Current eddied around coral heads, stenciling jade-green paisleys on the surface.

Finally, we got onto the prescribed heading, and sure enough, just as advertised, the gap appeared. Indigo waves crashed left and right; a small green river flowed between. We rode the outflow past the ocher fringes of the reef, and all at once we were in the ocean, heading for Huahine, some twenty-five miles to the east.

It was our first open-water passage, and it engendered in us awe, excitement, and sangfroid or no sangfroid, an undeniable frisson of fear. After all, you don't mess with the Pacific Ocean. It's the biggest thing in the world. Plopped in the middle of it, our plastic boat with its assorted strings and wires suddenly seemed puny to the point of pathos. We had five feet of freeboard, and the water was two miles deep. Our stub of keel sliced through denim-colored swells that had traveled thousands of miles without obstacle or detour, lifting and dropping unimaginable volumes of sea along the way.

Driven by hugely distant storms, Pacific waves seldom come from the direction of the local winds. Which makes for interesting sailing. We had southeasterly breezes and southwesterly swells.

This meant that the wind was in our faces, but we took spray on the backs of our necks. We bounced along, the boom creaking and the jib sheet snapping when we wallowed in a trough.

Marilyn took the wheel. I went below and turned on the CD player. Chet Baker. There was nothing Polynesian about him—in fact, a Polynesian would probably have said, *Yo, Chet, why so depressed?*—but, boy was he good. On the way to Huahine, we sang along. Loudly. Why not? There wasn't another human being within ten miles of us.

Huahine prides itself on being the most authentically Polynesian of the Tahitian islands—and the boast, in fact, seems justified.

Just before sunset, its lagoon, second in beauty only to that of Bora Bora, filled up with outrigger canoes—singles, doubles, and larger craft with teams of six. Weaving among the paddlers, the deep-sea fishermen came roaring through the pass, with their catch of mahi-mahi and bonito. They docked at the main village of Fare, hung their fish from wooden poles, and blew a conch shell to announce that they were ready for business.

I had to remind myself that this was not a show.

When the conch shells blew, locals within earshot of the dock hurried down—some to buy with money, many to trade for produce, fabric, a dented bicycle, some cans of motor oil. On Huahine the barter system was alive and well.

For me it was the key to the culture and it intrigued me. Other people look at temples, ruins, means of warfare. I like to know how people get the stuff they need to live. Accordingly, the thing I was most curious to see on Huahine was a fish trap that was said to be 1,000 years old and was still in use. We hired a guide and went.

Located near the village of Maeva, the trap, shaped something like a giant keyhole, sat in shallow emerald water in a sluggish part of the lagoon. The trap was high-tech, Huahine-style. Based on the islander's knowledge of tides, currents, and piscine behavior, the device had captured a millennium's worth of fish—but had also allowed enough to escape to keep the populations healthy. As we watched, a young man in a canoe scooped up small fish that flashed silver as they tumbled into his sack.

I said to our guide, "His family owns the trap?" Being a Westerner, of course, my first thought was of property.

"No one owns the trap," our guide informed us. "Anyone in the village can gather fish here."

I've lived near water all my life; every place I've been has gotten overfished. "So there must be pretty strict limits about how many fish people can take."

The guide seemed baffled by this notion. "No, people take as many as they like."

"Then why..."

The guide read my mind. "No one is allowed to sell the fish," he said. "Only to trade. So why take too many?"

He gestured toward the young man. "Look, here's how it works. This fellow comes to the trap. Back on shore, he sees an old lady who can no longer fish for herself. She compliments him on his catch. She wouldn't ask for fish—that would be rude. But of course, he gives her some. He asks for nothing in return—that would be rude, too. But she says to him, 'My mangoes are just getting ripe. Come take some from the tree.' That's our economy. It's as simple as that."

I stood there in the tropical sun and wagged my head in wistful admiration. *As simple as that.*

On the sail to Bora Bora, I was reminded of an anecdote about Cézanne. The great painter was once asked if he ever tired of staring at Mont Saint-Victoire, a favorite subject. "My good man," he is said to have replied, "I'd be content to spend my whole life looking at this view, only moving my feet a little left or right."

The dual peaks of Bora Bora—the taller square one is Otemanu, the conical one is Pahia—inspire a similar trancelike devotion. You can gawk at them all day long, taking pleasure from each tiny shift in perspective, every accident of sun and shadow. Green-tinged clouds float over the lagoon; wisps of mist scud past the summits. It really is as gorgeous as you've heard. That said, even before we sailed into Bora Bora's lagoon, we could see that, relative to its neighbors, the island was, well, overdeveloped. Planes flocked in and out; parasailers drifted by; helicopters clattered overhead. We were barely through the pass before we saw the cruise ships and the jet skis. Overwater bungalows intruded on substantial swaths of shoreline.

> The instant our faces hit the water, I understood why people spoke in hushed tones about this spot.

And yet...Bora Bora was magnificent, its lagoon incomparable. Even in its post-Edenic state, it remained a must-see place.

We picked our way through the harbor and headed at once for the Bora Bora Yacht Club—a relic of the time when the island was little visited, except by long-haul sailors passing through. Not a real yacht club but a restaurant, bar, unofficial post office, and provider of sundry cruising services, the place was anything but elegant, and therein lay its charm. Its thatched roof was ragged. Its few dockside tables may have been haphazardly cleared, but the joint was comradely, truly eccentric. The interior was festooned with the ensigns of long-gone visitors—flags from Norway, Argentina, South Africa, Connecticut. In five minutes we'd gotten advice about renting bikes ("Watch the scooters!") and had bummed a ride to the village of Vaitape to shop for groceries. ("Don't pass out at the prices!")

There was only one problem with the Yacht Club—as an early arrival on the scene it had staked out a prime, once-quiet location in what has become a noisy neighborhood. We soon gave up our mooring and headed for the far side of the island.

The East Lagoon is the Grail, the fantasy come to life. Yet not many people go there because the navigation is a little daunting. At various spots the water is very shallow; channel markers are few; the instructions in the cruising guides are less than scientific. ("Keep the five tall palms in front of you until you're around 200 yards from the *motu*...") But nothing more than close attention is required to get you through the shallows, and once inside...wow! With perfect clarity, a silvery sea bottom reflected tints of celadon, jade, turquoise, ultramarine. Huge rays dragged their purple shadows behind them; the barely rippled surface reflected scraps of fleeing cloud.

As was our custom, we sailed as far as we could go—to where coral pinched off the lagoon at the south end of Motu Piti Aau. We dropped anchor, stepped into the dinghy, and headed for Taurere Beach, the jumping-off point for the fabled snorkeling of the Coral Garden.

The beach was a mix of crunching sand and knobs of ancient reef. We walked it for about a third of a mile, then donned masks and flippers to ride back on the current. The instant our faces hit the water, I understood why people spoke in hushed tones about this spot.

The density and variety of the undersea grottoes were amazing; amethyst, butter yellow, terra-cotta—the colors contrasted wildly with the silver-green water. There were fish in iridescent blue, velvety teal, screaming vermilion; fish with stripes, fish with streamers, fish with polka dots. The spectacle wound through twisting coral canyons; we arched and pivoted to follow them. Somehow an hour passed before we got out of the water.

The next day we faced an interesting dilemma.

Over sunrise coffee I asked Marilyn what she felt like doing.

"Exactly what we did yesterday," she said. "Walk the beach, snorkel Coral Garden."

I felt precisely the same. I didn't want to touch the anchor, didn't want to move the boat. That Bali Ha'i thing had kicked in. We were immobilized by splendor, stymied by perfection.

The only problem was that our presence was expected that evening at the social event of the season. By coincidence, the Hotel Bora Bora was celebrating a major anniversary that very night. By further coincidence, it happened to be Marilyn's birthday. We'd decided that it was damn nice of the Hotel Bora Bora to throw a champagne reception and seven-course feast for, say, 150 of her closest friends.

But the hotel was on the other side of the island. The short way to it was blocked by a reef; the long way would waste a large part of this precious day.

"Let's just dinghy in later," I suggested.

"Dinghy in?" said my wife. "We'll be all dressed up."

"Mine's drip-dry. Isn't yours?"

"It's three miles away."

"That's why God made outboards."

"It'll take forever."

"What's the hurry?"

"And dinghy back at midnight?"

"It's almost the full moon."

"You'll have drunk a lot of wine," she predicted.

That was a safe surmise. Then again, our dinghy's top speed

was around three knots. "So just this once," I said, "I'll dinghy while impaired."

Our plan, I confess, was less than fully baked; then again, some of life's most enchanted evenings are the emanations of half-baked plans. We stuck to it. We had our day of marvelous snorkeling. We showered on the transom of the boat, and then, just before sunset, we changed into our last remaining clean, dry clothes and got into the dinghy.

It was eight feet long. Its gunwales were just six inches above the water. Our clothes were soon peppered with spray.

Oh, and have I mentioned that we didn't know exactly where we were going? Even with the dinghy, we couldn't get directly to Hotel Bora Bora from where we were—that much we knew. Our plan was to tie up at the first dock we found, then improvise.

And so we putt-putted along. The sun sank into the sea. Marilyn lifted her shoes from the puddle accumulating on the dinghy floor. Finally we came to a hotel dock. We tied up, smoothed our damp clothes, and walked in like we owned the joint.

It turned out to be Club Med.

By then we'd been living on a sailboat for a week and a half. We were accustomed to a heightened level of peace, quiet, and privacy. Suddenly we were assaulted by strangers in aloha shirts, inquiring as to whether we were having a fabulous time and urging us to sign up for the shark-feeding. It was rather dizzying.

To be fair, the confusion was on both sides. When I approached the desk and asked for a taxi, the desk clerk looked at me strangely. I explained that I was not a guest that I was only tied up at their dock. She stared at me as if I'd arrived not by dinghy but by spaceship. Suddenly I felt a vague discomfort that seemed familiar though I couldn't at first identify it. Then I remembered: It was stress.

Eventually, the taxi arrived, and our travails were washed away by the first glass of Moët, obliterated by the second.

The party was everything Marilyn deserved for her birthday. Candlelit tables on a gorgeous beach. Music moving from traditional Tahitian to cool jazz. The food—from *foie gras* to timbale of lobster and morels to noisettes of lamb with *tapenade* and polenta—was world class.

But the high point of the evening—one of the high points of my life, in fact—was the midnight dinghy ride back to the sailboat.

We had the legendary lagoon of Bora Bora entirely to ourselves. Nothing stirred as we glided through flat water and air the temperature of skin. The moon was bright enough to paint an arrow on the surface, guiding us along. Northern constellations tumbled upside-down and weirdly low in the sky; the Southern Cross, beacon of the Antipodes, reminded us how far from home we were.

When I finally switched off the little outboard, the silence was instantly filled by the muffled roar of monumental surf against the reef. Miraculous, these mid-ocean havens inside their unlikely moats of coral.

A little wobbly and rather damp, we climbed onto the transom and took a last look at the foreign stars.

"Happy birthday," I said to Marilyn.

Laurence Shames, formerly the Ethics columnist for Esquire, *has written articles for* The New York Times, Playboy, Vanity Fair, Saturday Review, *and other national publications. He is the author of many books including:* Not Fade Away: A Short Life Well Lived, The Big Time: Harvard Business School's Most Successful Class and How It Shaped America, Virgin Heat, *and* The Naked Detectives. *He lives in Key West, Florida.*

3

BRUCE NORTHAM

A MARVELOUS TRANCE

Drinking kava and juggling machetes—just another day in Fiji.

Viti Levu, Fiji's largest and most populous island, has its share of sun-and-fun resorts. Inexpensive ferries and flights reach dozens of other beach-rimmed islands that cater to the chic as well as the ten-bucks-a-night-thatched-hut dweller. From Nadi (pronounced NAN-dee), site of the international airport, all roads lead to the capital Suva, where Fijian women with untamed afros mix with sari-clad Hindus. On the outskirts of town, swaths of sugarcane and coconut plantations dominate the landscape. Suva is usually the jumping-off point for adventurous travelers fleeing the insulated resorts that dot the south coast for the smaller islands' quintessential South Pacific scenery.

At a Nadi bar, drinking Fiji Bitter, I was asking the bartender about visiting highland villages when a stocky man named Severo said he had overheard my questions and introduced himself in the soft tones of Fijians. While not a professional guide, he offered to take me to the interior if I covered his expenses. This amounted to about $15 a day. An invitation from a village chief is required to enter most Fijian villages. It is akin to asking to swim in someone's pool and receiving a smiling yes. Severo could get me those invitations, and I hired him. The next day we made our steady ascent on Viti Levu using a medley of buses, taxis, injured pickups, and feet, leaving the sunblock flock on the beaches behind.

We reached the village of Navai, which naps at the base of Fiji's zenith, the 4,341-foot Mount Tomanivi. Long-needle pines and towering palms loom over traditional thatch-domed, wooden *bures*, along with a few proudly maintained boxy corrugated-steel abodes. (Hurricane relief introduced the metal structures and they quickly caught on.) The whole village blooms like a garden, filled with hibiscus, plumerias, and birds of paradise. Flanked by a river and surrounded by misty mountains, Navai is communal peace defined. And, like most Fijian villages, there is no hint of litter.

Every child is taught four essential tenets of "chiefly behavior": respect, deference, attentiveness, and humility.

Two hundred residents live in sixty-five newly electrified homes. Hydroelectric power wired Navai in 1999, eliminating the need for kerosene lamps and batteries. The lone fluorescent bulb and listen-to-rugby-on-the-radio bill runs about a buck a month. People still cook over wood fires.

The universal mountain-dweller maxim emerges: Simplicity breeds familial content. The villagers' delight in family life contrasts the price Western families pay for trudging the rat race. Here in Fiji, everyone seems somehow related and has cousins galore.

Fijian friendliness stems from tribal custom. Family and friends—old and new, often one and the same—are life's greatest gifts. Every child is taught four essential tenets of "chiefly behavior": respect, deference, attentiveness, and humility. A well-rounded person, say Fijians, treats everyone with interest and respect.

After climbing Mount Tomanivi, I headed to the town meeting hall. I pulled off my mud-caked boots (twice their original weight) and the chief and his entourage greeted me for a customary *yaqona* ceremony, which centers around the preparation and drinking of kava.

Now a U.S. drugstore staple in the form of "herbal" pills that are said to promote relaxation, kava has long been a ritualistic beverage throughout the South Pacific. In Fiji, it is the opiate of the masses (well, most of the men anyway). Kava is made from ground *waka*, the long, dried root of a pepper plant. *Waka* granules are put in a large teabag-like pouch that's submerged in room-temperature rainwater. The pouch is wrung and re-dunked until the concoction fogs to brown. Historically, *waka* was masticated then spat out as kava-infused saliva for consumption. Today, kava is made in a *tanoa*, a block of wood with legs that has a depression carved in the middle. Some *tanoa* are lavished with intricate carvings. Others are more utilitarian.

As cool dusk set in, the rite commenced with Severo making a prayer-like presentation to the chief explaining my presence in Navai, and handing over the customary gift of kava. Then came the men-only drinking session—a chief's council bread-breaking.

Villagers sat cross-legged, shoes off. The cocktail, also called grog, was ladled into a *bilo*, half a coconut shell, and systematically distributed around the semicircle of six men. The seating arrangement is determined by tribal seniority (the unofficial drinking age is around sixteen), with everyone imbibing in an unspoken pecking order. The guest, me, sat before the kava mixologist, who was centered behind the bowl. The elderly chief sat to my left. The group ceremoniously clapped once, loudly, with hands cupped, to summon the first person's six-ounce gulp, then acknowledged the quaff by clapping again three times. I took a swig and found the grog tasted faintly bitter, like muddy river water. It slowly numbed my lips and tongue, then everything else, eventually imparting a euphoric grin. Think: earthy codeine smoothie.

My low-key hosts switched between English and Fijian, which reminded me of serene Italian. They remained calm even when discussing a heated, holy subject like rugby.

Each of us consumed a six-ounce bowl every ten minutes—happy hour lasted four hours. *Sevu sevu* was originally a ceremony to settle differences between warring chiefs; the kava got enemies past their anger and in a relaxed mood to discuss the situation. Now it is an archetypal story time, certainly more interactive than barking at *Monday Night Football*. The gathering was a combination of telephone, television, newspaper, and gossip column. It was time to talk.

"You live in New York City?" the chief inquired.

"I do."

"Many people," he nodded.

"Too many," I agreed, then confessed that I often encounter a thousand people in a day, speaking to no one but myself. I think that's when they prayed for me.

During a pee break, I reveled in the cool fog and full moon rising while two grinning children hid behind a tree, encouraging a game of hide-and-seek. To the south, an isolated storm cloud steamed over a mountain, a communion of gray and white flaring the high jungle sky with lightning and trailing drapes of rain.

Kava *talo*—kava again. The kava session waxed pensive, contemplative, then sleepy. Some women and children came and sat on the perimeter of the circle, beaming. They didn't drink kava. One of the women asked me to dance and my smile became transfixed.

After a sound sleep I awoke on the mat-covered floor, without a hint of a hangover, to the smell of lemon tea brewing. Contentedness: what all the ages have struggled for.

I couldn't hover indefinitely above the clouds. The easiest transport option to sea level was by river plunge. Leaving Navai, I ricocheted across Viti Levu's high-altitude backbone in a paint-shaking pickup to the village of Naitauvoli. En route, wild horses and pigs moseyed about the wet, dark-green cloud forest of billowing bamboo clumps and willow-like rain trees in the rugged mountains. Sitiveni, the Fijian cowboy driver, used his wide-splayed bare feet on the pedals as he navigated the savage Monasavu Dam road—I use the term "road" loosely. As we drove, hooting and banging down cliff-edged hairpin turns, I asked, "Ever had a wheel fall off? Trucks ever tumble off cliffs?" After a skidding pivot Sitiveni smiled "yes" twice, leaving big space for imagination.

That night, I found myself at another kava ceremony. I was now on a cupped-hand-clapping kava binge. Several members of the Waiqa (pronounced wine-gah) River Band, who periodically float to the lowlands to play local music festivals, had joined the circle. Their voices enhanced the reflective traditional chant that opened the *sevu sevu*.

No discussions about cloning or euthanasia, but plenty of banter about rain, fruit, and family. The people pause before answering questions. Occasionally, the thoughtful pauses were checked by youngsters naughtily peering in. The children have a don't-speak-unless-spoken-to respect for elders. Experiencing collective pride, respect, politeness, and esteem for elders—in what would be considered a clapboard shanty by the U.S. evening news—would be a valuable lesson for fractured families living on Park Avenue.

After two hours of calm communication, everyone slowly focused on me expectantly. I felt a little uncomfortable with the silence.

"Is it O.K. that I'm here?" I asked. A senior slowly assured me, "You are no stranger here, Bruce." Outside the hut, I stared at the moon lingering next to a pine tree. I introduced myself to an elderly woman sitting on the floor of her home, weaving large floor mats from dried pandanus leaves. I sat down to pet her dog for a few minutes. I lay down on the ground, and the dog and I bonded famously. I asked the animal's name. The woman didn't look up from her weaving as she said, "Brown." I continued wrestling with the dog. Twenty minutes later, still not peering up from her craft, she mused above the silent calm, "Bruce and Brown." Floored on a floor mat.

Back in the hut a few men had nodded off. (Several of the doorways I peered into during my trip revealed groups of men drinking grog seemingly all day and all night. The only common side-effect of long-term grogging appears to be dry skin.) They were roused and we sat on a table-long cloth on the floor to eat the creamed-spinach-like *roro,* finely grated taro leaves that are twice-boiled in coconut milk, along with roasted mutton and lemon tea, which is made from boiled lemon leaves. We ate with our hands, dipping our glistening digits into finger bowls. Women fan the flies while the men eat, then dine second, seemingly eating twice as much as the men.

I've run risky rivers in a mix of wooden, rubber, steel, and plastic inventions, but none produced more hyperventilation than negotiating the Waiqa River after a fat rain on a bamboo *bilibili* raft.

At first, the idea of running rapids on twenty-five-foot bamboo trunks lashed together with twine seemed as logical as bowling with an eggplant. The two gondoliers were Waiqa River Band mates. Elected second in command of one raft, I stepped onto the back end, the senior pilot manning the front. At first I wasn't sure what to do with the ten-foot bamboo pole in my hand.

Balancing precariously on something better suited for a log-rolling contest, he jockeyed this needle through a narrow aqua chasm with a bag of navigating tricks you can't learn in a gym. This energy is not identified with civilization but with the flight from it. Imagine balancing on a long floating ski—we surfed those tippy bamboo toboggans through a whitewater maze flanked by unforgiving vertical canyon walls. The nearly interlocking walls of the gorge were storm-born architecture filled with a misty, wavy spray.

On another boat, Severo and his musician/guide also rode their *bilibili* down what began as a wide, winding river. Then the river suddenly entered a narrow gorge where parallel rock walls pinched it into a rampaging froth. The sun stood noon-high above the walls, which were covered, every now and then, by canopy. We glided onwards, gaining speed.

My pole was only bothering fish, but up front the extreme gondolier pilot maneuvered skillfully to keep my pack and camera upright. They sat tied to the back of a little bamboo throne secured by twine to the center of the raft.

Like running the Colorado River through the Grand Canyon, there is no turning back. But while rubber rafts bounce off rock walls, bamboo splinters. My companions' bewildering level of athleticism included using the guide poles to prevent collisions with suddenly appearing rocks and bending canyon walls. They slashed overhead obstacles, such as low-hanging lianas, with a machete, and faced each other in mid-rapid to casually clarify navigation. In times of peril, the lead men dived from the rafts (leaving me solo and rudderless), swam to shore and sprinted barefoot along the riverbank over fallen trees and mossy boulders to dive in front of the boat and swim-kick-sway it away from unforgiving obstacles protruding just ahead.

It takes one man two days to build a *bilibili*, which is strictly a one-way craft, to be left downriver for anyone heading seaward or needing wood for construction or fire. At the age of ten, highlanders begin undertaking this old trade route—once the primary access to the coast. Until recently, they had to walk back home. Now travelers return by whatever vehicle is going their way.

The trip was routine for my friends until we encountered a massive palm tree that had fallen across the canyon creating an impassable dam. Many miles from a road, the obstacle didn't faze the two captains. They just exchanged a glance that I read as, "Jeez, this one's a doozy."

Their emergency portage solution would impress a knife juggler. The men separated to opposite banks, one took a machete swipe at the base of a forty-foot rubber tree, the high end falling next to the guy on the opposing bank. Upriver, holding the rafts close to a vine, I watched them share the machete to cut long strips of bark by casually hucking the big glinting blade back and forth across the raging, thirty-foot-wide river like playground pals tossing a tennis ball to each other. They systematically cut enough peels of bark to bind into one long piece of twine, used to guide the rafts over the tree.

I knew if their mojo held, we'd prevail. The river continued swinging through the rock and the ages, through sweet air, droopy green gardens, and waterfall drizzles. Sunlight shimmered through mist and lianas.

The meander through the gorge walls diminished into flat open water and plains of palms. No question here about what to do with in-between moments. Words fail. We pulled out at the Waiqa's confluence with the unhurried Monasavu River. True freedom, far from the planet's growing array of widening roads.

I made camp on the coast for a few days. During a long trek the sun was setting when I encountered a man in his sixties in the middle of the path, clutching a machete. He turned out to be

Eroni Tabua, a taro farmer and eldest son of a chief of the nearby village. He asked if I'd like to have lunch, but I realized that I'd never asked for the chief's permission to enter the village, so I was reluctant to accept Eroni's hospitality. I explained that to make it back to camp by dusk I needed to move on. He insisted that I take a five-minute detour from the trail. I followed him into the thicket, slightly paranoid. Eroni stopped in a grove of fruit trees, shook a few trunks and bushes, catching falling objects with one hand. He tossed each fruit into the air a few times, whacking it rapidly with a knife in midair, caught the slices and handed them to me. Instant fresh coconut and papaya variety plate.

His family owned the plantation upon which we stood. There in the heart of it, Eroni's soft-spoken voice carried the kindness as a torch for the world, as pleasant and intelligent as any thoughtful professor of the humanities.

I opened my Fijian phrase book to find another word for thanks. Instead, the farmer took the book, opened it and randomly found a word, *pikiniki*...picnic! Having such a character machete-hack a fruit salad while you discuss taro farming makes you reevaluate the meaning of concepts such as peace. Eroni then contemplated my inevitable return to Fiji and said, "Next time, come to my village straightaway."

Bruce Northam is an adventure author, speaker, and tourism consultant whose books include Globetrotter Dogma: 100 Canons for Escaping the Rat Race and Exploring the World *and* The Frugal Globetrotter: Your Guide to World Adventure Bargains. *He is the travel columnist for* The Improper *and has also written for the* New York Post, Details, New Choices, *and various travel publications. He speaks frequently on freestyle travel at colleges and universities and corporate and travel industry events, and he lives in New York.*

4

AARON PERRY

VIVE LE SURF

The waves of life, surf, and fantasy intersect for a young traveler.

"SO, HOW GOOD DO YOU SURF?" SHE ASKED.

She smiled with Polynesian grace while I fidgeted and tried to answer. She was about twenty, I guessed, and finally I replied, with all the audacity I could muster at age fourteen, "I don't know. I guess I'm pretty good."

From the passenger seat of her temperamental Renault, I glanced at the early morning ocean as she leaned into the next turn. I was vacationing on Moorea with my parents, and she was working at the hotel where we were staying. We had started talking, and she mentioned that her cousin had an extra surfboard and could take me surfing. The car raced around a final turn, where a sign read Haapiti.

"This is my...town," she said in hesitant English. The car turned into an emerald valley, and beyond the hedges lining the pavement I could make out houses shrouded by the fronds of palm trees or in the shade of the hillside.

We crossed a small stream that trailed into an iridescent pool beyond a cluster of houses.

"My cousin live in house there. Oh...do you speak...French?" she asked at the last moment.

We were greeted by a tall, lanky Tahitian, about eighteen years old. I reached up to shake his outstretched hand. He was smiling.

"*Ça va?*" The coffee cup is his right hand suggested that he had just awakened.

"My cousin," interjected the girl, beginning to laugh, "no speak English."

My two years of high school Spanish did little to help. "Uh, *qué tal, amigo*?" I stumbled on every syllable. The girl almost fell over laughing.

He poured me a cup of coffee, and we talked. But as every sentence was channeled through the girl, our chat took on an air of negotiation. Still, I could compare Moorea's "island hospitality" with that at home in Southern California: I couldn't conceive of meeting someone on the beach at La Jolla who'd offer to loan me a board after talking for only five minutes.

As my host disappeared into the hallway to get the board I was to borrow, the girl and I wandered across the back porch, stopping to admire the view of crystalline lagoons and the surrounding outer reefs. She handed me some fruit and a baguette, then she turned to gaze at the distant white water fringing the reef pass.

"Say, three to four, yes?" she said and turned to me smiling. "I surf, too, but not when so big. But my cousin, he pretty good, too, like you."

I'd only been surfing for about a year but, with my mouth full of bread, I told her that three-to-four-foot surf should be O.K., because I'd surfed six-foot waves at home last winter.

"No, no," she said, her lips pursing as her voice became serious. "Three to four *meter.*"

Later, I realized the gravity of my mistake as I paddled out to the reef pass and stared into the eye of ten-foot grinders.

On the horizon I could see Tahiti. Turning toward shore, I could just make out the shape of a car skirting the base of the deep green peaks of Moorea, which were sprinkled with clouds.

Most of the time, I kept my eyes on the reef. Some hundred yards on the other side of the pass, across waters of deep purple depth, a wave would appear from nowhere. The larger waves would hit our side of the pass and transform into flawless cylinders that would crash directly onto coral, then continue moving down the reef. It turned out that where we were surfing was not *that* dangerous, because the reef was relatively deep below the surface and the waves were not gapingly hollow. But, at the time, fear outweighed strength, and my eyes darted about nervously.

I turned to paddle, avoiding a glance over my shoulder that would have looked into the teeth of the beast, as I tried to catch my first wave. When I did, I was content simply to race across the wall of water until it backed off in the deep channel. Sometimes I'd see my host taking off farther outside, in the peak of the wave. His skill would have shone at any break in La Jolla.

Between sets of waves, we would sit together and try to talk: I would begin in excited English, then listen as he would answer in French, and then I would continue again in English. Eventually the conversation deteriorated into hand signals. I would point to the sky and whistle to warn him of an oncoming set, and he would nod in complete understanding.

It was my best day of surfing ever. I never fell, even when compensating for my "pretty good" ability. Paddling back to shore, my friend could not stop describing something: perhaps the idyllic conditions, or how I happened onto Haapiti on one of the best days of the year.

When we reached the inner lagoon, we stopped to watch the surf. He pointed at the horizon, and I looked up to see the biggest set of the day, the spindrift feathering along the barrier reef.

Shouting and laughing we picked up our boards and took a last look at the water before turning back to the road. At that moment, walking back down the hill to his house, I realized that I understood him perfectly.

Aaron Perry wrote this story originally for Islands *magazine.*

5

JAMES C. SIMMONS

DREAMLAND

A giant of Western literature, like so many young sailors, had the time of his life in the South Pacific.

HERMAN MELVILLE HAD BEEN AT SEA FOR EIGHTEEN MONTHS when the Marquesas Islands loomed ahead on the horizon in late June. His imagination had been fired years before by his uncle's stories about his visit to Nuku Hiva. "The Marquesas!" he exclaimed excitedly in *Typee*. "What strange visions of outlandish things does the very name spirit up! Naked houris—cannibal banquets—groves of coconut—coral reefs—tattooed chiefs—and bamboo temples; sunny valleys planted with breadfruit trees—carved canoes dancing on the flashing blue waters—savage woodlands guarded by horrible idols—*heathenish rites and human sacrifices*."

The Marquesas Islands are among the most beautiful in the Pacific. Yet this beauty has little in common with the palm-fringed atolls of popular fantasy. With crumbling volcanoes forming a rough terrain of cloud-shrouded basalt rock peaks and abrupt cliffs interminably battered by the ocean waves, the Marquesas Islands seem to belong to a separate universe.

The *Acushnet* cruised along a rock-bound coast. Sea birds screeched and wheeled overhead. The scents of fruits and flowers wafted over the excited crew crowded against the gunwales. They caught sudden glimpses of lush valleys, deep glens, waterfalls, and waving groves of coconuts. As they passed one particularly impressive valley, a sailor next to Melville suddenly urged, "There—there's Typee. Oh, the bloody cannibals, what a meal they'd make of us if we were to take into our heads to land! But they say they don't like sailor's flesh. It's too salty. I say, matey, how should you like to be shoved ashore there, eh?" Melville shuddered at the thought, little knowing that within a few weeks time he would find himself a captive in that same valley.

The *Acushnet* sailed slowly into Taiohae Bay and dropped anchor. The ship rolled gently in the swells. Silvery waterfalls slipped out of niches high up the jungle-covered walls of lofty peaks, dividing the green, clear to the sea. The sweet smells of tropical blossoms scented the air.

To the astonishment of the men aboard the *Acushnet*, several French naval vessels, led by the sixty-gun frigate *La Reine Blanche*, were already anchored there. Unknown to the Americans or British, the French had laid claim to all the Marquesas Islands as a colony, and they had already put 200 soldiers ashore at Taiohae Bay.

"Our ship was now wholly given up to every species of riot and debauchery," Melville confessed later. "Not the feeblest barrier was interposed between the unholy passions of the crew and their unlimited gratification.

Foreign ships were still a novelty at Nuku Hiva. It had become customary for the island men to paddle out in canoes, while the women stripped naked and swam out to meet the approaching ships. And this was precisely the welcome experienced by the dumbfounded whalers. Melville described it later in *Typee*:

> As they drew nearer, and I watched the rising and sinking of their forms and beheld the uplifted right arm bearing above the water the girdle of tapa and their long dark hair trailing beside them as they swam, I almost fancied they could be nothing else than so many mermaids—and very like mermaids they behaved, too.
>
> We were still some distance from the beach, and under slow headway, when we sailed right into the midst of these swimming nymphs. They boarded us at every quarter; many seizing hold of the chain plates and springing into the chains; others, at the peril of being run over by the vessel in her course, catching at the bobstays, and wreathing their slender forms above the ropes, hung suspended in the air. All of them at length succeeded in getting up the ship's side, where they clung dripping with the brine and glowing from the bath, their jet-black tresses streaming over their shoulders and half enveloping their otherwise naked forms. There they hung, sparkling with savage vivacity, laughing gaily at one another, and chattering away with infinite glee.... Their adornments were completed by passing a few loose folds of white tapa around the waist. Thus arrayed, they no longer hesitated but flung themselves lightly over the bulwarks and were quickly frolicking about the decks.... The [*Acushnet*] was fairly captured. And never I will say was vessel carried before by such a dashing and irresistible party of boarders!

As dusk fell, the sailors hung up lanterns. The Marquesans then put on a display of dancing. Few dances are more sensual and provocative than those of the South Seas in which the arms and hips move in a manner suggestive of physical love. The slow, graceful movements of the hula soon gave way to the crisp, precise undulations of the drum dance chorus, as the dancers fluttered their bodies at impossible rhythmic speeds to the beat of the corps of drummers. The sexual excitement built quickly into a frenzy. Encouraged by their men, the women offered themselves to the sailors. Within a short time a sexual orgy was underway, which the ship's officers made little or no effort to stop.

"Our ship was now wholly given up to every species of riot and debauchery," Melville confessed later. "Not the feeblest barrier was interposed between the unholy passions of the crew and their unlimited gratification. The grossest licentiousness and the most shameful inebriety prevailed, with occasional and but short-lived interruptions, through the whole period of her stay."

The islands of Polynesia, and especially Tahiti, became closely associated in the popular imagination with an unbridled, joyous sexual freedom totally foreign to the experience of Western civilization.

By the late eighteenth century the South Seas loomed large in the popular imaginations of Europeans, less as a specific geographical place and more as a state of mind—what historian Gavin Daws called "a dream of islands." There one could still find, it was commonly believed, people living in a state of primal innocence, an Eden before the Fall, a paradise inhabited by Noble Savages. They were perceived to be both happy and good because they had not yet been corrupted by the unnatural bonds of civilized European society. The islands' natural beauty and fecundity and the inhabitants' striking lack of envy, greed, or hatred seemed to confirm the speculations of Jean-Jacques Rousseau and other philosophers about man's natural goodness.

"We have discovered a large, fertile, and extremely populous island in the South Seas," Captain Samuel Wallis of the H.M.S. *Dolphin* wrote shortly after his discovery of Tahiti on June 18, 1767. "'Tis impossible to describe the beautiful prospects we beheld in this charming spot. The verdure is as fine as that of England, there is plenty of livestock, and it abounds with all the choicest productions of the Earth."

To the European explorers, more accustomed to the Mongoloid Indians of America and the Negroid primitives of Melanesia, the discovery of the Polynesians came as an exciting surprise. For there, living on scattered islands of great beauty, were a people with light skin colors who conformed closely to accepted European standards of beauty.

The islands of Polynesia, and especially Tahiti, became closely associated in the popular imagination with an unbridled, joyous sexual freedom totally foreign to the experience of Western civilization. The appeal was simply overwhelming, and few men were strong enough to resist the temptation. The Englishman John Turnbull, who circled the globe between 1800 and 1804, confessed after his visit to Tahiti and Hawai'i: "Nothing can withstand the seduction and artifices of the southern islanders. Women and a life of indolence are too powerful for the sense of duty in the minds of our seamen. Had we relaxed our efforts for a single moment, our ship would have been deserted."

In 1768, the year after Wallis' discovery, Tahiti was visited by a second European expedition, two French ships, the frigate *Boudeuse* and the store ship *Etoile*, under the command of Captain Louis-Antoine de Bougainville. The welcome received by the Frenchmen was such that Bougainville named the island La Nouvelle-Cythère, the New Cythera, after the Greek island where

Aphrodite, the goddess of love, had been born out of the sea.

The *Boudeuse* and the *Etoile* anchored off the northeastern coast of Tahiti. The next day the chief of the district came on board the *Boudeuse* with many gifts of fowls, pigs, and fresh fruit. Because the welcome had been so cordial, Bougainville ordered a camp built on shore near a stream where the sick might recover their health and the ships might replenish their water casks. The French offered nails in exchange for services, and the islanders were eager to help their visitors gather wood, water, and fruits. Bougainville wandered about the countryside and decided that he had been "transported into the garden of Eden. Everywhere we found hospitality, ease, innocent joy, and every appearance of happiness."

The officers in their cocked hats and powdered wigs, breeches, stockings, and buckled shoes presented an outlandish sight to the dumbfounded Tahitians. The amazed natives gathered around them excitedly. "The boldest among them came to touch us," Bougainville noted. "They even pushed aside our clothes with their hands, in order to see whether we were exactly like them."

As the sailors wandered about the valley, young girls constantly invited them into their houses and offered them food and sex. When the Frenchmen accepted, as they almost always did, and the love-making undertaken, the rooms quickly filled with curious islanders eager to observe what sexual techniques and skills their white-skinned visitors had brought with them.

"Here Venus is the goddess of hospitality," Bougainville concluded approvingly. "Her worship does not admit of any mysteries, and every tribute paid to her is a feast to the whole nation."

But the most sensational discovery made during Bougainville's stay at Tahiti occurred not on the island but rather aboard his very own ship, the *Boudeuse*. Ahutoru, a young Tahitian warrior who had befriended some of the officers, was on board. His new friends had taught him some European manners, given him Western food to sample, and even dressed him in Western clothes. Suddenly, he caught sight of the servant to the expedition's naturalist, Philibert Commerson. "A woman," he shouted in his own language, "you have a woman with you." And so she proved to be. She had successfully kept her sex a secret throughout the voyage, masquerading as a man among several hundred soldiers and sailors until unmasked by an islander who saw through her disguise at a glance. Under questioning by Commerson and others, she confessed to the deception and explained she had been an orphan with no prospects who had gone to sea seeking adventure. And thus Jeanne Bare became the first woman to circumnavigate the world. Commerson never revealed in his writings his feelings about his assistant. But he did name a plant after her, *Baretia*, for its "uncertain sexual characteristics."

Ahutoru, the handsome young Tahitian who had made the discovery, was completely enthralled with European culture and pleaded with Bougainville to take him back to France. The commander was skeptical about the wisdom of separating the Tahitian from his culture but soon relented. He had proven himself quite useful to the officers in procuring them island women and made them promise that when they arrived in Paris, they would do the same for him. Once in France he apparently had no difficulty fulfilling his own sexual fantasies. His appearance in Paris created a sensation in 1769. Ahutoru was presented to the king. He learned to speak French and developed a passion for the opera. He was reputed to have had numerous liaisons with actresses. After eleven months, Bougainville put him on a ship bound for the South Pacific.

Bougainville had one doubt after his ships departed Tahiti. Some of his men developed gonorrhea. He assumed correctly that the disease had come to the island with the arrival of Wallis' ship the year before. This was the first warning that the paradise they had just enjoyed was, in actual fact, quite vulnerable.

The reception such as the Tahitians gave Bougainville became the norm for subsequent ships to call at the island. Unlike the French before him, Captain James Cook was shocked at what he saw on Tahiti and complained: "There is a scale of dissolute sensuality which these people have ascended, wholly unknown to every other nation whose manners have been recorded from the beginning of the world to the present hour, and which no imagination could possibly conceive." Then, as an example of this debauchery, he offered up a performance staged for himself and several of his officers by eager islanders.

> A young man, near six feet high, performed the rites of Venus with a little girl about eleven or twelve years of age before several of our people and a great number of the natives without the least sense of its being improper or indecent, but as appeared, in perfect conformity with the custom of the place. Among the spectators were several women of superior rank, who may be said to have assisted at the ceremony, for they gave instruction to the girl how to perform her part which, young as she was, she did not seem to stand much in need of.

Cook's men obviously did not share their commander's disgust at the open sexuality of their Tahitian hosts. Two of his Marines deserted shortly before the *Endeavour* was supposed to set sail. The islanders advised him that both had run away to the mountains with their girlfriends. Cook was furious. He imprisoned several Tahitian chiefs and threatened to execute them unless his men were returned. They were. He sailed away with his crew intact, but the Tahitians deeply resented his heavyhandedness, which appeared to them to be outrageously misplaced.

As more and more ships called at Tahiti, the islanders evolved an ingenious theory to explain the sexual frenzy of their visitors. Because they never saw any women on the visiting ships, they concluded that the white race consisted entirely of men who had to travel all the way to Tahiti to enjoy the pleasures of heterosexual sex. In their minds there was no other explanation for the eagerness with which the Europeans embraced the island women and the persistence with which they kept returning.

Of course, the European stays at the Polynesian islands were limited to just a few days, a couple of weeks at the longest. Thus, they could not in such a short time learn much of consequence about the island culture. They could not know, for example, that the Polynesians were among history's greatest navigators, able to cross thousands of miles of the Pacific and arrive at a predetermined island. Or that they had highly sophisticated skills at stone carving and masonry that allowed them to create vast temple complexes and enormous statues. They were also excellent farmers. Their neatly cultivated fields, abundance of food, and neatly constructed houses impressed all their early visitors.

Yet for the Europeans, and later the Americans, sex became the only thing that really mattered about Polynesian society, the sailors and whalers sought escape in sexual indulgences, while the later missionaries struggled to abolish such sexual activities. What the visitors failed to understand was that among the islanders promiscuity was largely a teenage privilege. After a certain age they were expected to marry. And in Polynesian society marriage always represented the union of two large families and so had political, as well as emotional, dimensions.

"Tahiti was a small civilization perfectly in balance," British historian David Howarth has observed. "But the balance was pathetically easily upset by intrusion. In spite of their good intentions, Europeans fatally upset it merely by their presence and especially by the introduction of their diseases and two of their ineradicable concepts: the concept of private property and the concept of sin."

Within fifty years of Wallis's discovery of Tahiti, the local culture had gone into a fatal decline under the impact of a corrosive foreign influence. The islanders enjoyed none of the immunities to Western diseases. A people whose isolation had sheltered them from all serious infections suddenly found themselves grappling with such diseases as tuberculosis, smallpox, diphtheria, measles, and pneumonia. Venereal disease became almost universal within the space of just a few months. When Melville arrived in Tahiti after his Marquesan adventure, he cast a disbelieving eye on cultural blight caused by a corrupt and unsought civilization and concluded sadly: "But amidst…tokens of improvement, painful proofs are everywhere making themselves manifest that the natives are doomed to extinction, from the operation of causes more or less connected with the arrival of the white men."

Hand-in-hand, the imperialist and the missionary together shaped the nineteenth century, as they took charge of much of the world. The most destructive of these foreign influences in Polynesia were the missionaries, most of whom came from London to found an empire of God on earth. In their view the state of paradise proclaimed by such early explorers as Bougainville did not exist. The Tahitians lived in a state of sin, and the missionaries had a divine obligation to journey to the Pacific to redeem them.

The missionaries introduced the concept of laws into a society which had never had any legal system in its history. Along with the laws came the entire complicated bureaucracy of judges, lawyers, and clerks. Having created crime, they then quickly established a police force and a jail. Virtually all the traditional entertainments of Tahitian society were declared sinful, hence criminal. Dancing, wrestling, play-acting, singing (except hymns), tattooing, and nudity were prohibited. And, of course, sex outside marriage was strongly condemned and discouraged. Henceforth, the island women were required to go out in the cumbersome dresses and bonnets favored by the missionary wives, cut off their long tresses, and stop wearing garlands of flowers. The goal was to make them as unattractive as possible to the men. The Tahitian love of sex continued, but was now carried on in secret, away from the prying eyes of the missionaries.

So when Melville visited Tahiti in late 1842 the two-fold impact of diseases and the missionaries had already destroyed much of the idyllic society that had prevailed until so recently. The Noble Savages of Polynesia were no more. Instead he found aged Tahitians sadly chanting a song of impending doom:

> The palm tree shall grow,
> The coral shall spread,
> But man shall cease.

James C. Simmons is the author of fourteen books and more than five hundred magazine articles on travel, history, biography, and wildlife. Before becoming a freelance writer, he taught courses on British and American literature at Boston University and San Diego State University. His books include Americans: The View from Abroad, Passionate Pilgrims: English Travelers to the World of the Desert Arabs, *and* Castaway in Paradise: The Incredible Adventures of True-Life Robinson Crusoes, *from which this story was excerpted.*

6 THURSTON CLARKE

LOOKING FOR BALI HA'I

One writer's imagination inspires another's search.

I FIRST MET JAMES MICHENER IN 1991 WHEN WE WERE BOTH in Honolulu for the fiftieth anniversary of the attack on Pearl Harbor. I had just finished reading *Tales of the South Pacific*, his Pulitzer Prize-winning collection of short stories about American servicemen in the Pacific during World War II, and I wanted to ask him to what extent they were based on his own experiences as a naval officer. Had he known anyone like the Tonkinese wheeler-dealer Bloody Mary, or nurse Nellie Forbush, or her French planter, Emile de Becque? And was there an island anywhere like Bali Ha'i, the lush, mountainous "jewel of the vast ocean"?

But Michener so expertly jujitsued our conversation that as we left the bar where we were talking, I realized he had learned plenty about me—but revealed almost nothing about himself or Bali Ha'i.

The following year I read in his autobiography, *The World Is My Home*, that he had been searching for Japanese stragglers on remote Mono Island in the Solomons when he entered a "truly pitiful" village, "with scrawny residents and only one pig." A cardboard sign attached to a tree said "Bali-ha'i." He jotted the name down, he said, "for some purpose I could not then envisage," because it sounded so beautiful and musical.

A half century later Bali Ha'i has become a brand name for paradise, and islands compete for the honor of being the "real" one. An internet search yields dozens of resorts promising "Bali Ha'i suites," "Bali Ha'i views," and "a Bali Ha'i atmosphere." Hawai'i's Kauai argues for the Bali Ha'i mantle on grounds that the movie *South Pacific*, based on the Rodgers and Hammerstein musical adapted from Michener's book, was filmed on its spectacular north coast, where there is now, naturally, a "Bali Ha'i beach."

Or just maybe Bali Ha'i is Upolu in Western Samoa, because some stories say Michener based his Bloody Mary on that island's legendary hotelier Aggie Grey—although she was not Tonkinese and never sold grass skirts to American sailors.

Or is it Bora Bora, because Michener called it, "quite simply...the most beautiful island in the world," although it was too far from Guadalcanal to be Michener's Bali Ha'i?

Tales of the South Pacific places Bali Ha'i near an island Michener called "Vanicoro," which he describes as lying sixteen miles east of a much larger, but unnamed island containing not only Tonkinese laborers and French planters, but a bustling American military base with a couple hundred thousand or so American soldiers.

It seems that only the island of Espiritu Santo in the nation of Vanuatu matches the description of the larger island, and about twenty-five miles east of Santo is Aoba, a volcanic island that, like Michener's Vanicoro, is frequently shrouded in mist.

Bali Ha'i, Michener said, curved itself "like a woman into the rough shadows formed by the volcanoes on the greater island of Vanicoro," meaning that if Bali Ha'i existed it should be just off Aoba.

On the same day that I boarded the first of seven planes that would take me to Espiritu Santo, Michener died in Austin, Texas, at the age of ninety. So few of Santo's residents listen to the radio that when I arrived, three days later, no one had heard of his death. Many people I met there were genuinely saddened. Two men who had met Michener during one of his postwar visits wanted to send sympathy cards to his relatives.

At first glance, Espiritu Santo seemed a good place to search for the ghosts of Bloody Mary and Emile de Becque. Michener had spent many late nights in the Quonset hut on Santo typing *Tales of the South Pacific*. He seems to have set two of these tales, "Fo' Dolla'" and "Our Heroine," on Santo, and their parallel love stories had provided the structure for the musical and movie.

In 1942 this backwater island of practicing cannibals—where all the cars could be counted on two hands—became the largest forward U.S. base in the Pacific, with five airstrips, repair facilities, warehouses, and hospitals, a mess hall feeding a thousand men an hour, a sizable military population, and more services than many American cities, including a telephone system with seven exchanges, an optical laboratory, and forty-three cinemas.

Santo remains haunted by this American occupation. My plane landed on a former American airstrip, and I drove over the Seabees' coral roads into the main town of Luganville, which rested on a mangrove swamp the Seabees had filled with coral rock. Its inhabitants lived in patchwork shanties of corrugated American metal, in bungalows set on former American barrack foundations, or in Quonset huts that had weathered five decades of rust, hurricanes, and earthquakes. Water flowed from my showerhead thanks to the American waterworks, and after driving past copra plantations and ranches using the steep matting from American landing strips for fencing, I had tea with a man who used heavy spoons stamped "U.S. Navy."

Santo has its share of gorgeous white-sand beaches and jungle-fringed swimming holes, but most visitors today are divers attracted by its wartime remains. They dive the *President Coolidge*, a liner converted to a troopship that sank off Luganville, and they dive "Million Dollar Point," where departing U.S. servicemen drove hundreds of American vehicles into the water. Popular souvenirs are American shell casings and heavy, six-ounce Coca-Cola bottles stamped "Oakland 1942."

Everyone agreed a Frenchwoman named Françoise Gardel had been the model for Bloody Mary

Santo's taxi drivers and guides have embroidered their wartime history in a predictable fashion. I was shown "Dorothy Lamour's favorite swimming hole" (though I'm told she never set foot on Santo) and was invited to admire the foundations of a brothel that "could have been patronized" by J.F.K., though he apparently had spent at most one night on Santo before his boat headed to the Solomons.

The tales still swirled around *Tales of the South Pacific*. No one I talked to had read the book, but a video of the 1958 movie was still making the rounds, encouraging speculation as to who had been the basis for Michener's characters.

Everyone agreed a Frenchwoman named Françoise Gardel had been the model for Bloody Mary, although in his autobiography Michener admitted basing her on a Tonkinese plantation worker. Madame Gardel, locals insisted, had been, like Bloody Mary, large and boisterous, "a very tough lady" who ran a bar popular with American forces. She "kept some girls," had a "heart of gold"—and had been a great friend of Michener.

Peter Morris, a British planter who had grown up on Santo, remembered that when Michener returned in 1984, he discovered that Madame Gardel was his only wartime friend to survive. She lived in the same tin bungalow, shaded by the same tree under which Michener had sat writing notes for his stories. According to Morris, the seventy-seven-year-old Michener and the ninety-three-year-old Gardel embraced on the foundations of her former bar and "cried like babies." Afterward Michener paid for her to move to a New Caledonia nursing home, where she died in 1993.

I was also informed that Emile de Becque (Rossano Brazzi in the film), the handsome French planter who courted nurse Nellie Forbush (played by Mitzi Gaynor), had been a composite of several planters. Yvan Charles, who owns the Bougainvillea Resort and grew up on Santo, said, "Everyone who saw the movie told my stepfather that he was De Becque. He may not have fallen in love with an American girl, but he did have a keen eye."

Others insisted De Becque was modeled on a legendary planter named Labord, who enjoyed liaisons with numerous Tonkinese and Polynesian women and, like De Becque, had fathered several Eurasian children.

Everyone I met on Santo, however, believed that Aoba was Bali Ha'i. I accepted a ride with a bank manager from Aoba, who declared, "We know for sure our island is Bali Ha'i because of the movie," although Aoba is even prettier "because it is my home."

I remember reading that Michener had once written to his editor at the *Saturday Evening Post* that his manuscript was a memorial to the bull sessions in the Hotel De Gink in Guadalcanal and that nothing in the stories was entirely fictitious. But after a week on Santo I had found few traces of *South Pacific*. None of the local Bloody Marys or Emile de Becques bore that much resemblance to Michener's characters, and hurricanes had leveled the hospital and the USO stage where Nellie Forbush belted out "Honey Bun."

"But you haven't seen the octagon house yet!" protested Glen Russell, the best of my Espiritu Santo guides. Michener had given his Emile de Becque a unique octagon-shaped house with a spectacular garden and a deep veranda with sweeping views of distant Vanicoro/Aoba. Here, De Becque had asked Nellie Forbush, "Where could I find a lovelier spot than this?"

Thirty minutes from town, Russell showed me an octagonal house even grander than in Michener's tale. It had extensive gardens, a two-story-high ceiling, and twelve-foot Cecil B. DeMille doors opening onto a veranda that overlooked waving palms and waves breaking on a reef. An elderly man introduced himself as the former overseer of the surrounding plantation. He said a French planter named My had built the house in 1936, and it still contained its original fittings. He could remember gay wartime parties, and Madame Gardel, whom he called "Bloody Mary," amusing everyone with her coarse humor.

Michener, too, must have been a guest here, I thought. I imagined him standing on this porch as the breeze filled the house with the scent of frangipani and the setting sun turned Aoba a Technicolor red, making mental notes as navy doctors and nurses in dress whites reclined on this sofa, sipping cocktails and flirting.

Then I noticed mildew spotting the wooden ceiling, saw that Monsieur My's once fine ocean-blue rug was unraveling and worn to the matting, and that the pink palms decorating his cushions had faded to a muddy brown. None of the books I saw on his cluttered shelves dated after 1946. Most of them had "Department of the Navy" stamped inside their covers. Their backs came off in my hands. The edges of their yellowing pages fluttered to the ground like confetti.

I stared at the smoky horizon. Twenty or so miles east, the island that—depending on whom you believed—was Vanicoro or Bali Ha'i was a faint smudge on the horizon, so faint that when I searched for it again as I left, it had vanished.

Bali Ha'i is "Your own special hopes, / Your own special dreams," Oscar Hammerstein's Bloody Mary once sang. I was told that when Michener returned to Espiritu Santo in 1984, a delegation of men from Aoba begged him to visit their island. He refused. It would "ruin the dream," he explained. He was right. As long as Bali Ha'i remains a mystery, you can always hope it might be the next island to appear on the horizon, your own perfect island.

Thurston Clarke is the author of many acclaimed works of fiction and non-fiction, including Searching for Paradise: A Grand Tour of the Word's Unspoiled Islands, California Fault: Searching for the Spirit of the State along the San Andreas, Pearl Harbor Ghosts: The Legacy of December 7, 1941, *and the bestselling* Lost Hero. *His work has also appeared in* Vanity Fair, Glamour, Outside, Travel Holiday, Condé Nast Traveler, The New York Times, The Washington Post, *and other publications. He has been awarded a Guggenheim Fellowship and a Lowell Thomas Award for travel literature. He lives in upstate New York.*

7

TONY PERROTTET

A *FALE* WITH A VIEW

In Samoa, the author enjoys a taste of the old ways.

As usual in Samoa, I'd been woken up by a rooster hopping into my hut at 3 A.M. and crowing two feet from my left ear. I was so addled the next morning that when Kenneky (who was named after President Kennedy) said it was only ten minutes leisurely stroll up to the extinct crater above the village of Lalomanu, I believed him.

"Shoes O.K.?" I asked, pointing at my sandals.

He pointed at his own bare feet and giggled merrily. "O.K., no worries," he chirped. "Ten minutes. Five. Or fifteen."

An hour later, I was plunging up to my waist in virgin rainforest, slipping down branch-filled crevices, clutching onto tree trunks that dissolved into rotten fragments in my hands and cursing the great Samoan vagueness that makes any advice on how to get around this South Pacific hideaway about as useful as consulting a New York subway map.

Kenneky was up ahead with his machete, bounding like a ballerina from one precarious perch to the next and hacking a path along a steep hillside. My own clumsy feet were scratched to ribbons. But there was one thing to give thanks for, as my leg disappeared down another dark vegetation hole: The Independent Republic of Samoa has only one type of snake, a boa, and it's not poisonous.

Finally, Kenneky stopped and looked at me with an eager grin, pointing past some vines. We were on the inside lip of the crater, which was filled to the brim with ancient ferns, and in a tree ten yards away were the giant bats. About a hundred of them hung upside-down from the branches, fighting with each other for space, spreading their wings and gliding into the rippling ocean of foliage down below. The spectacle made me forget my mangled feet, my lost left shoe, even the cloud of mosquitoes that were swan-diving into my rivers of sweat.

"O.K.?" Kenneky asked, cracking the lid off a couple of coconuts he'd picked up en route for a drink, like big hairy eggs.

"No worries, Kenneky," I said, sticking to our vocabulary. "O.K."

Perhaps the strangest thing about my impromptu bush-bash was that none of the villagers in Lalomanu had ever mentioned that the crater existed—I'd only heard about it by accident, from an Australian environmentalist I'd met. As a result, the dozen or so other *palangis*—literally "sky-bursters," or foreigners—who were staying by the beach below, remained in blissful ignorance.

And blissful it certainly was. Samoa feels like the last holdout of the mythic Polynesia: I was staying in my own open-air *fale*—the traditional thatch-roof Samoan hut, which has wooden pillars instead of walls—right on one of the finest beaches in the islands, a stretch of golden sand overshadowed by coconut trees, with the hunched form of Nuutele Island emerging like a green whale across the sky-blue waters. Behind the row of beach huts, villagers lived in their own, larger *fales*, the men with elaborate geometric tattoos and wearing a piece of material wrapped around their waists, known here as a lava-lava, the women in Mother Hubbard gowns, with flowers in their hair.

It was one more scene from what is the most secure Polynesian culture in the South Pacific: the backblocks of the islands, where the *fa'a Samoa*, or "Samoan way," still held sway. You knew it wasn't quite as idyllic as it looked (Samoans, in fact, have the second-highest suicide rate in the world, and have left the islands in droves), but it was certainly laid-back. In fact, as far as one could tell, everyone just lolled about in their *fales* and watched the world go by. You never knew what you might see: Some lunatic might even try to climb a crater.

Sadly, I couldn't sit still in Lalomanu. Next day, after licking my wounds, I headed off in my rented 4WD to explore the island of Upolo—just to see what I could discover about the *fa'a Samoa*, in its early twenty-first-century incarnation. The volcanic south coast is riddled with unmarked turn-offs down steep dirt roads to all-but-unvisited beaches. I picked one at random, named Vavau.

Within a hundred yards, my car was surrounded by a dozen frowning Samoan heavyweights in wet lava-lavas. They were local fishermen, with tiny goggles on their foreheads and black wire spears. Their day's catch of six-inch-long tropical fish hung from their waists like fluorescent Christmas baubles.

"Uh...*talofa*," I tried. "Hello" was the limit of my Samoan.

"*Talofa*," snarled the leader, fingering his spear point (a little unnecessarily, I thought). "Where you going?"

"The rest of the family should be with us soon," Loi apologized for the poor showing of only two dozen relatives.

"Down to the beach."

He considered this for a time. "This is part of our village," he finally said. "Ours."

"Fair enough," I nodded, getting ready to back out. But I obviously wasn't getting it.

"Custom fee. Five tala."

I coughed up the three dollars promptly, and suddenly it was all smiles. In fact, I was their new best friend. "You want to take a photo?" the leader asked. For the next ten minutes I took group shots; finally, they all shook my hand and waved me on down the road.

These custom fees, I found, are a great Samoan tradition going back centuries—and are currently employed to make sure that villagers get some direct benefit from the few sky-bursters who wander their shores. A more recent innovation is a grassroots hospitality system, whereby travelers can stay in remote villages for a fee of about fifteen dollars a night—again, creating an efficient way of channeling money directly to local families, so that they can buy useful things like fresh-water systems, while not saturating the local culture. To see what it all involved, I headed for the last village on the island, Uofato, wedged into a serrated, rainforest-covered valley.

After bouncing across the archipelago's worst (and most spectacular) road and fording a series of streams, I trundled into Uofato after dark and ground to a halt at the last *fale* but one in the village. It was set a few feet back from the gently lapping bay and lit inside with a single lamp: the home of Loi and Sufia, whose names I'd been given as a contact.

My arrival caused an uproar. Loi, who rushed out to shake my hand, was short and unusually frail for a Samoan, with curly black hair that rose in a triangle, like a character from Dick Tracy. Sufia was the grand matriarch of the family, a full-bodied woman in her seventies, with long gray hair; she padded barefooted down to the car, planted a wet kiss on my cheek, then gave me a purple-and-yellow lava-lava that she insisted I wear from then on. Next came the brother-in-law, sister-in-law, nephews, nieces, and assorted cousins, about two dozen urchins who stared at me silently with big round eyes, and one baby that took one look at my pale face and burst into tears.

Obviously, they didn't get *palangis* visiting all that often.

"The rest of the family should be with us soon," Loi apologized for the poor showing of only two dozen relatives.

Half an hour later, I was sitting cross-legged on a woven mat in the *fale*, being served up dinner with Loi and Sulia while one of the saucer-eyed little girls kneeled and fanned us. Plates of roasted breadfruit—which had a consistency a bit like suede—were laid out, along with a gray coconut paste to dip the pieces in. A tiny fried fish and a glutinous salad of salted tinned tuna went with it. Rounding the meal off were bananas roasted till they were dry as chalk.

I thought I was getting the ritual more or less right—at least I wasn't pointing my feet at anyone, which is considered the gravest of insults in the *fa'a Samoa*—until Loi coughed uncomfortably. "Grace, Tony," he whispered. "Don't forget to say grace." He bowed down and said a few words in Samoan.

As we slowly ate, the village bestiary paraded about us. A

half-dozen mangy dogs lay around at our feet, roosters crowed, teams of fat pigs roamed the steps and—strangest of all—dozens of golden baby chicks ran in formation all around. These chirping balls of fluff waltzed right across the dinner plates, making guerrilla strikes at the food. Loi would just brush them away, or lift them up in irritation and toss them across the room, when they'd come charging back in determined little phalanxes.

For the next three days, I hung out in Uofato, trying to pick up what I could about modern Polynesian life. Luckily, the delirium of exhaustion brought on by nights full of crowing roosters, howling dogs, wailing babies, and people saying their prayers aloud at 5:30 A.M. fully prepared me for the pace of the village routine, which was not exactly punishing. There was a flurry of activity from 6 to 8 A.M.—in the coolest hours of the day, everyone went spearfishing, coconut-gathering, cooking, or dyeing pandanus leaves—and then we all kicked back, slug-like, in our *fales*, trying to recover from the effort.

Which is not to say nothing happened. Since I had a 4WD, I drove Loi and a few of his kids up along a cliffside to the family papaya plantation, where they blithely scurried up trees that hung over precipices for ripe fruit. There was a village game of *kirikiti*, a Monty Python version of cricket with a long, three-sided bat (which quite often gets used on the umpire's head, apparently). Then, in the afternoon, Loi took me on a walk along the rocky coastline to the local waterfall. I had a swim in the small rocky pool, surrounded by dripping ferns, while Loi perched placidly on a rock, chain-smoking Rothmans.

Finally, on Sunday morning, Uofato quivered with an unexpected activity. Even at dawn, a cloud of smoke already hung over the village from all the *umus* or stone ovens that were being prepared. Fans of *Babe* would best avoid Sundays. Crawling out of bed, I watched the local choirmaster pluck a piglet from the flock and slaughter it in traditional fashion: He laid a metal rod across the animal's neck and stood on both ends until it expired.

"Do you have your church clothes?" Loi asked eagerly.

"Oh," I slapped my forehead. "How could I have forgotten?"

But there was no escape; after all, this was the event of the social calendar, the be-all and end-all of the Samoan week.

Within an hour, Sulia and the kids had me scrubbed, shaved, and dolled up for the service—in a crimson lava-lava, floral green shirt, and wide blue Air New Zealand tie. As bells pealed along the valley, I joined the whole village meandering into the crumbling church. It was an impressive sight: The congregation was dressed entirely in white, the men in dazzling lava-lavas with ties, the women in round hats crowned with fresh flowers.

Before taking a pew, everyone filed past a table where two pear-shaped officials sat before a big ledger. "Church money," Loi nodded. They were collecting the donation. I gave two tala, a dollar, and the figure was noted down carefully.

Halfway through the service, after the radiant hymns and a fire-and-brimstone sermon, I learned how this "donation" system worked. The pear-shaped officials took the altar and read out how much everyone had given—people nodded at me, when my sum was read out. But one poor woman hadn't coughed up, so she had to stand up and give a blustering apology to the congregation.

To outsiders, the power of the Church is the most exasperating feature of "traditional" Samoan life.

"It's just like the Italian mafia!" one European hotelier I met had fumed; he couldn't understand why his employees were forking over up to 80 percent of their earnings to support the pastor. Today, the Church meshes with the *matai*, or chiefly, system to keep law and order. The downside is a certain dull conformism. "In a small village, things only work if everyone toes the party line," observed Steve Brown, an Australian environmentalist I'd met. "People can't take the initiative—they can't even make a suggestion. The *matai* is law. Non-conformists are simply ostracized."

As I sat there in church—with the doors securely closed behind me, as if they sensed my instinct to bolt—the Samoan kids erupted into a rousing hymn:

Satan is a loser man, loser man, loser man,
Jesus is a winner man—all the time!

It was a good moment, I thought, to move on.

Tony Perrottet studied history at Sydney University and moved to South America after graduation to work as a newspaper correspondent. He covered the Shining Path war in Peru, drug running in Colombia, and military rebellions in Argentina. He now lives in New York and has written for Smithsonian Magazine, Outside, National Geographic Adventure, The New York Times, *the* London Sunday Times, *and other publications. His books include* The Naked Olympics: The True Story of the Ancient Games *and* Pagan Holiday: On the Trail of Ancient Roman Tourists.

8 LYNN FERRIN

FREIGHTER TO THE FABLED ISLES

She island-hops on a unique vessel.

"Aha!" grinned a friend when I told her I'd be sailing through the Marquesas Islands on the freighter *Aranui*. "Those big Polynesian men will carry you through the surf!"

This perk was not in the brochure.

Months later, I stood on the beach at Hane, island of Ua Huka, watching the whaleboat coming ashore from the freighter. Two of the crew jumped out to drag it into the stony shallows. A gaggle of passengers surged forward, scrambling to climb into the wildly rocking boat. I waded toward it, stumbling under my awkward backpack.

Then my moment came, the one that had eluded me for almost two weeks. One of the Marquesan crewmen swept me up into his muscular tattooed arms and carried me through the breakers, as I squealed in ecstasy,

"Yes!...Yes!" The French already sitting in the open boat rolled their eyes. *Quelle horreur!* My hero dumped me over the gunwales like a sack of copra, turned, picked up a rotund German burgher, and dropped him in beside me.

That evening, back on the freighter, it was Polynesian Night beside the swimming pool. The cabin crew had wrapped the railings with palm fronds. Joel, the cross-dressing waiter, had as usual spent most of the afternoon color-coordinating his costuming. Tonight he was a symphony in white: linen skirt and shirt, and a headdress of white frangipani blossoms trailing long straw streamers, accessorized with a double strand of black pearls.

It was also Passenger Talent Night. We Americans had been unable to come up with an act. One wryly suggested "Let's sing 'La Marseillaise,'" but no one knew all the words. Maybe "Home on the Range?" Nah. In the end, the Americans didn't do anything.

But the French! A troupe of French women jumped around in a hilarious send-up of the Marquesan men's Pig Dance, slapping their thighs and grunting with gusto. Two French youths in drag flitted about the deck chirping, parodying the Marquesan women's Bird Dance. We all howled.

Then a young Tahitian couple from the dining room crew stepped out. As the ukulele band struck up a ballad soft as the trade winds, they began to dance, side by side, with sweeping, sensual movements of their arms and legs. The audience grew pensive. I have no idea what the dance meant, but it seemed to evoke lost islands under a wide sky, canoes journeying beneath the stars, love among the flowers. It was so full of longing it caught at my heart.

A passage on the *Aranui* through French Polynesia is one of the world's great ocean voyages. The islanders greeted us with ceremonies of dance and drums and prepared feasts of breadfruit fritters, grilled lobster, and whole pigs roasted in earth-pit ovens. In each port artists—arguably the best in the South Pacific—peddled their carvings and painted tapa for exorbitant sums. Sweating in the fierce heat, passengers followed multilingual guides up rough mountain tracks through fern and orchid to the high ridges, to the crumbling temples with their phallic stone tikis which so outraged the Christian missionaries.

It's the cargo, stupid, I realized when I arrived at the Papeete wharfs, and rolled my baggage through scurrying forklifts and piles of containers.

Captain Taputu Mapuhi, at the helm in flip-flops and shorts, could maneuver this 3,800-ton behemoth into the narrowest of coves. Our sturdy Polynesian crew unloaded truck tires and TVs onto whaleboats and ferried them ashore, and returned with bags of copra and barrels of *noni* fruit. At night, on the stern deck, they played their ukuleles and sang beneath the waxing moon.

Aranui sails every three weeks, year-round, from Papeete, Tahiti, on a sixteen-day journey carrying cargo and passengers northeast to the Marquesas—more than 1,600 miles round trip, plus hundreds more miles meandering among the islands. On my voyage she called at seventeen ports on six of the Marquesas islands—Nuku Hiva, Hiva Oa, Tahuata, Fatu Hiva, Ua Pou, and Ua Huka. Along the way we also stopped at two coral atolls in the Tuamotus, Takapoto and Fakariva, for picnicking and swimming in the pale lagoons, and two full days at sea.

Aranui has been a fixture of French Polynesia since the late 1950s. *Aranui 3*, the latest incarnation launched in early 2003, has space for some 170 passengers in comfortable cabins. The budget bunch hole up in the spartan twenty-four-bunk shared-bath dormitory. Locals traveling a few hours between the islands sleep outside on the lower decks.

On my voyage, *Aranui* carried 127 passengers, mostly French, a few Tahitians, Germans, Italians, and Canadians, and about twenty Americans.

There's an air-conditioned lounge, a small outdoor bar, and a pleasant dining room serving French cuisine. Wines are included at lunch and dinner. But this is no luxury cruiser—no nightclub, spa, beauty salon, or casino. In a tiny conference room, the few Americans gathered for lectures on such subjects as volcanology and Polynesian migrations. The only entertainment was the crew playing their ukuleles.

It's the cargo, stupid, I realized when I arrived at the Papeete wharfs, and rolled my baggage through scurrying forklifts and piles of containers. *That's the back story here.*

My bright compact cabin had ample drawers and closets, a strong shower, and a toilet that bellowed like dragons at the gates of the netherworld. I unpacked and went topside. At the railing I met Rene, from Bainbridge Island, Washington. He told me, "I just got off the cruise ship *Amsterdam* and saw the *Aranui* at the docks. I walked over and asked about it, and signed on for a bunk in the dormitories."

Below us, the foredecks bristled with cranes and nets. Polynesian stevedores—sporting an array of traditional tattoos—lowered an amazing variety of goods into the black maw of the hold: pickup trucks, sewer pipes, outboard motors, outrigger canoes, cartons of groceries. My favorite: an open crate of road signs, warning of bumpy roads ahead.

On top of everything they placed two well-weathered wooden whalers and one small barge, which would carry everything, including us, to and from the shores of fabled isles.

It was mid-morning the next day—twelve hours late—before the task was finished, and we finally slid away from Papeete, through the narrow pass in the reef, and onto the swells of the open Pacific.

As it turned out, I was spellbound by the dark brooding beauty of the Marquesas—high volcanic islands all, with black lava spires rising out of luxuriant forests and swirled with clouds, and great collapsed calderas eroded by wind and rain into steep-walled amphitheaters opening onto the sea. Some of the fluted peaks pile up to 3,000 feet and more. No coral barrier reefs have grown around these islands, so the wild waves smash against the black cliffs, and there are few sandy beaches.

But who's going to get that cherry red Toyota pickup? Or those white plastic patio chairs? Or drink all that Heineken? I was fascinated by the diverse cargo. The islanders love the *Aranui;* she brings them almost all their worldly goods, everything they can't grow, make, or take from tree or sea themselves; everything sold in their tiny general stores.

When the *Aranui* arrived at each port, the splintery whaleboats were lowered and brought alongside. I'd get in line with the other passengers and we'd wobble down the clanging metal stairs, jump in, and motor over to the shore. The islanders were always there, anxious to collect their cargo.

Pascale, our Marquesan guide, led us on hikes up into the valleys to see the *meae* (sacred places) of the ancient Marquesans, who first arrived here around 150 B.C. and went on to discover and settle Hawai'i, Easter Island, and New Zealand. Archaeologists now believe their origins were in Southeast Asia. They were the greatest seafarers of all time.

By the time the first Europeans arrived—the Spanish in 1595—some 100,000 people were thriving in the Marquesas

Islands. Different tribes had evolved in the isolated valleys, warring with their neighbors, building temples, and practicing ritual cannibalism and a daunting system of *tapu* (taboos).

On Nuka Hiva, we drove from the main town of Taiohae—in a sluggish parade of SUVs decorated with palms and hibiscus—over the ridges to Taipivai. I particularly wanted to visit this valley because it was here, back in 1842, that young Herman Melville jumped ship from a whaler and hid with the Taipi people, long before European diseases decimated the population and missionaries destroyed the culture. His novel *Typee*, an embellished memoir of this experience, became a bestseller when it was published in 1846.

When we descended to the hamlet of Taipivai, we found a few cottages amid the bougainvillea, and the locals were chewing on Pringles, not their enemies. Kids were giggling in the bright running stream, and red-tailed tropicbirds cruised overhead. Swatting at *nonos*, the dreaded Marquesan no-see-ums, we followed Pascale up a trail to the *meae*, site of those grisly sacrifices which horrified Melville. Now it was just grassy terraces with moldy old tikis and swiftlets singing in the forest.

The best of the ancient ceremonial sites was Kamuihei, on the north shore of Nuku Hiva, a mile above Hatiheu—a town with a graceful waterfront park beneath thousand-foot-high spears of black basalt cloaked in jungle. Kamuihei, with its shadowy green lawns and mango trees, is known for its enormous banyans, where the skulls of sacrificed warriors were stored. Pascale told us, "There was an oven here for cooking people." Then, warming to his subject: "You could tell when they were done because the hair pulled out easily."

On Hiva Oa, I climbed the hill to visit the grave of Paul Gauguin. The bad-boy artist lived here the last two years of his life, generally making himself unwelcome by insulting the local priest and taking teenagers to his bed. He died in 1903, before he could serve a jail sentence for refusing to pay taxes. Now he rests beneath blocks of red lava with "Paul Gauguin, 1903" hand-scrawled in white paint.

Below, in Atuona, is a small museum with garish replicas of Gauguin's paintings, and a shop displaying items found in his well (assorted bottles and three human teeth). I bought a popsicle in the same general store where Gauguin shopped. When I returned to the ship, the vestibule was redolent with the sweet smell of fresh bread. Dozens of baguettes, from Hiva Oa's *boulangerie*, were piled beside the elevator.

The Marquesans, it seemed to me, are mysteriously affluent for islands so remote and sparsely populated (some 8,000 people in the whole archipelago). Every house has a giant satellite dish in the garden. SUVs and king-cab pickups were everywhere—Cadillac Escalades, Chevy Silverados, Hummers—in a place where there are few roads, gasoline costs more than six dollars per gallon, and the import taxes could bring the tag on a new SUV as high as $100,000.

"Where, please, do they get the scratch for all this?" I asked Pascale. Surely not from raising coconuts for copra or *noni* fruit, the non-FDA-approved health elixir. "Well," he offered, "they get interest-free loans from the government." And ample subsidies. Some fly to Papeete to sell their bone and rosewood carvings to rich tourists. I even heard hints of illicit crops.

With all these ports on so many islands bearing names that sounded like the chants of angry warriors, everything began to blur in the damp heat. Is this Ua Pou or Tahuata? Whatever, the Marquesan villages seemed unimaginably idyllic to me, with their soccer fields and volleyball courts along the waterfronts, and coconut plantations, bristling in the sunshine, filling the valleys beyond.

The most beautiful, I thought, was Hapatoni, on Tahuata, with its nineteenth-century stone road along the shore, lined with big *tamanu* trees and banyans, and a terraced *meae* dating from the fifteenth century. And many scenes are in my memory forever: the old mamas playing bingo behind the Hokatu museum; the Nuku Hiva youth with his intricately tattooed face; the girls of Hane riding their horses bareback along the beach; the pair of manta rays that followed our ship out of Hakahau. Once the *Aranui* passed close to a rock island off Ua Huka, and thousands of fairy terns flew up in squeaking white clouds. On the island of Fatu Hiva, the women wore fresh sachets of *tiare*, ylang-ylang, dill, and mint—and added pineapple eyes dipped in sandalwood powder. At sea in the evenings, we gathered on deck for the papaya-hued sunsets, and later to find the Southern Cross hanging in a black sky prickly with unfamiliar stars.

When there was free time in the ports, some of the passengers made for the post office, presided over by irritable French bureaucrats. Buying a stamp was too tedious a pursuit, but I went for the air-conditioning and internet access. On southern Nuku Hiva, I found a small white sandy beach and went snorkeling alone over coral flickering with blue chromis and Moorish idols. Afterward, I floated on my back and looked up at pastures where slender Marquesan horses—long-legged and silky—grazed under the flame trees.

Often I'd wander back to the dock and watch the cargo scene. On Hiva Oa I saw a man slip into the red Toyota and drive it away. In Hane, the last whaleboat took the plastic patio chairs to shore. No one came to get them. As we sailed away that night, it was all I could see of Hane—those white chairs under the half moon, waves lapping at their legs.

One Sunday, when the *Aranui* called at Vaitahu, on Tahuata, passengers were invited to Mass in the splendid Catholic church. Women in long white lace dresses sat in the pews, singing merrily, strumming ukuleles and guitars. After the service the congregation bid us back to the ship with cheek kisses and more jolly bursts of song.

Occasionally we'd run across a small museum and learn something of Marquesan heritage. One in Hakahau displayed intricately incised bamboo nose flutes and tattoo art. (The word tattoo was derived by whalers and explorers from the Polynesian *tateu.*) On Fatu Hiva, the lushest and youngest island, we perused a collection of wooden stilts (used in what Pascale called "stilt rodeos") and war clubs used to crush an enemy's spine—the skull was spared because warriors carried trophy skulls fitted with boar's teeth—another fine way to terrify the Europeans.

Never mind their bone-smashing, cannibalistic heritage, the Marquesans of today are the gentlest of people. In two weeks I never heard an angry voice. One evening as we stood on the top deck watching the crew unload the cargo, Matthias, a young German economist, remarked, "If these were the docks of Hamburg, they would all be yelling." Below, balancing on beams above the gaping hold, the Polynesian musclemen went about their scary acrobatics—swinging from ropes, hoisting loaded fuel drums into suspended nets, dodging trucks, without saying a word. Each of them just knew what to do, and did it.

When the voyage was over, I dawdled in the fleshpots of Papeete for a few days before flying home. As my flight was approaching the California coast, I could see snowfields shining on the distant San Jacinto Mountains. I had forgotten snow.

I thought back to my last night at sea on the *Aranui.* After packing up in my cabin, I had wandered out to the stern deck. A bright highway of moonlight shimmered away to the horizon where the round clouds piled up like silver balloons. I thought of the ancient Polynesians, afloat on these waters in their great voyaging canoes, not knowing what lay ahead, and how brave they were.

Then, from the crew decks below, came the plink of a ukulele.

Lynn Ferrin worked at Motorland *and* VIA *for thirty-seven years, spending seven of those years as the magazine's editor-in-chief. Her work has also appeared in the* San Francisco Chronicle, Dallas Morning News, Denver Post, Boston Globe Magazine, Islands, *and several anthologies. She is now a freelance writer living in San Francisco.*

9

LAURA FLORAND

THE HEART OF THE DANCE

Who is that old woman in the corner?

"Plus BAS, Laura!" Vanina yells from the front of the class. "Lower!" She shakes her head. "And keep your knees together!"

She pronounces my name Polynesian style, Lo-RA, with the fierce, rolled R of an exasperated Tahitian. Getting yelled at is progress. When I first enrolled at the Conservatoire Artistique Territorial de la Polynésie Française, Vanina would look at me, squinch her eyebrows together, part her lips as if to say something, and then abandon the effort, as if she didn't know where to begin.

The glass-walled Conservatoire has all its doors open to keep the air flowing. At eight in the morning, it is already sticky hot, but we're only a third of a mile from the water, and the sea breeze helps. Tiny, sensual Vanina leads the class, a black pareu wrapped around her waist, a red hibiscus in her black hair. We all wear pareus rolled to emphasize our hips, a concept that drives the Western women in the class nuts at first. Who would want to put a lot of bulk around her hips?

Because Tahiti is part of a French territory and during the colonial period brought in Chinese laborers to work the plantations, our dance classes are a mix of three ethnicities—Tahitian, French, Chinese. The French, Chinese, and my lone American self all like to be skinny. The Tahitians don't seem to care; it's not your size that matters, it's the way you move your hips.

Right now, I'm not doing so good at that last. We are attempting to learn *'ori Tahiti,* the famous sensual Tahitian dance. Its best-known form, the *otea*, features incredibly rapid hip movements, the sound of drums dominating dancers and audience alike, and a *more* or bark skirt flashing around a dancer's legs in a blur of speed. (Yes, bark. Grass is not actually involved in any part of Polynesian dance costumes.)

I've been at this for at least a month now, but my hips feel choppy and frenetic, producing nothing remotely resembling the sensual blur of Vanina's. The drummers push us even faster and several women protest, laughing. The drummers just grin from behind their long, wood *toere* drums.

"Lo-RA!" says another voice, not Vanina's. "Keep your feet together! And *PLUS BAS!*"

I take a deep breath and very carefully do not let my aggravation show. I mean, I like the old grandmother over there in the corner. She's fun, and during breaks she has all kinds of stories to tell. She danced for Tony Bennett in Las Vegas when she was young; she lived in Hawai'i. She's cool. But I wish she had better things to do with her mornings than sit in a corner and kibitz on Vanina's class. I've got enough criticism, thank you. And when I get old may I never get that fussy.

"Mamie," everybody calls her fondly. That means "Grandma,"

so I assume she's Vanina's grandmother, although it's also a term of respect you use for grandmother-aged women who aren't related. Still, there's got to be some reason she's always sitting in the corner of the class while Vanina teaches, one big leg folded up to hold the end of a crown of flowers between her toes as she braids it.

And when I say "big leg," I mean "big leg." She's not only tall (surely at least six feet), she's quite wide, swelling out in all directions past her little plastic chair. Today she wears jasmine woven around the knot of her stringy, white-gray ponytail.

"Lo-RA! Is that how you would blow a kiss to your lover?" Mamie Louise calls from her corner.

I grit my teeth together. *First*, I'm trying to remember the order of the steps. *Then,* I'm trying to do them correctly: low enough, with my feet close enough together, and my hips fast enough, and my heels...I haven't figured the heels out yet, but I keep hearing, "Lo-RA, *tes talons!*" which means there's got to be something I'm doing wrong. On top of that, I'm trying to remember what gestures go with the steps, and now even those gestures are getting criticized? I appreciate the fact that Vanina and Mamie are no longer gazing at me in silent despair, but maybe their expectations are too high.

"That *is* how I blow a kiss to my lover!" I protest over my own gasps, in my heavily accented French.

Mamie gives me a severe look. "As if you are a fish gasping for air?"

O.K., I am never going to blow any man a kiss ever again. Maybe Mamie needs to take up some other hobby. Maybe she could go braid her leis out in the yard and gossip about the neighbors or something.

I concentrate on Vanina, the class teacher, trying to imitate her incredibly beautiful, sensual movements. Now Mamie yells something at *her* and that almost makes me laugh, releasing my sense of frustration. I guess she really is just one of those fussy old ladies who can never be satisfied. Imagine, correcting Vanina, the most beautiful dancer I've ever seen, who has won enough Heiva contests to prove it!

"Yes, Mamie," Vanina says meekly and then cries out in delight: "Coco!"

We all turn. I blink at the short little man carrying a huge cardboard box into the room. Can this be Coco Hotahota, leader of one of the most important Tahitian dance groups in the world? Yes, it is—pictures of him are often in the papers, so I recognize the square face rounded by a bit of extra flesh. Why, he's *famous*. I didn't realize he knew Vanina. Maybe she used to dance in his troupe.

He gives Vanina four *bises* as she flies over to him. Then he sets his box at Mamie's feet.

"Mangoes!" Mamie says with satisfaction, accepting this tribute with no more surprise than a ruler would a tithe from her subjects. I peer in, excited by my deep love of island mangoes, but then frown. They are *green* mangoes. I can get green mangoes in the grocery store back home. What kind of tribute is that?

Why is he offering tribute to Mamie, anyway? Is she his grandmother, too? O.K., he's too old—maybe his mother-in-law?

He sits down across from her on another undersized plastic chair and leans toward her, hands linked between his knees, speaking quietly and respectfully while the dancers all hunt for knives and pass out the hard-as-rock mangoes.

"Wait!" Mamie holds up a regal hand, cutting off Coco and all the chatter and fixing me with a keen eye. "Lo-RA. Do you *like* mangoes?"

"Yes," I say tentatively. I love ripe ones. There is absolutely no give in the flesh of the green one I've been handed, but everyone else seems enthusiastic enough. I'm sure I'll take to it right away.

"Green ones?" she challenges, gaze piercing.

"Yes!" I say defiantly. "Green ones are the best!"

Mamie narrows her eyes at me suspiciously and nudges through the box until she finds one with the faintest suggestion of a blush of yellow-orange on it. She makes a *moué* of dissatisfaction but hands it across to me. "Try this one," she says imperatively. "It's the ripest."

All the other dancers are munching away delightedly by the time I get mine peeled, so I take a big enthusiastic bite, determined to show I'm no wimpy, foreign American. My teeth wedge into something as hard as an unripe apple and tasting somewhat like peas.

I flick a quick glance at Mamie, but she is again honoring one of the most famous figures in Tahitian dance with her attention, leaving me to my own devices. I said I liked green mangoes; now I have to fulfill my boast. I try another bite, wishing I liked peas, wishing mangoes were a little bit smaller.

"Why is Coco here?" I whisper to one of the other dancers, a lovely, long, elegant Tahitian, bronze, black-haired, black-eyed, who always stares at my blue eyes as if afraid I might be a demon. She has also won the Heiva at least once, I understand.

She gives me a blank look. "To see Mamie Louise."

From her tone, I might as well have asked why a monk had come to church. I nod wisely, as if I understand any of this. "He knows her?"

"She's Mamie Louise!" the other dancer says incredulously. "Of course he knows her! The President of the territory knows her, too, and if he's lucky, she'll talk to him."

I hadn't realized she'd still been teaching as she talked about how dance was the center of Tahitian culture, that it held an entire people and its traditions.

I look at Vanina, currently slouched inelegantly in another plastic chair, chomping on a mango, but still slim, beautiful, vibrant, an exquisite dancer. I look at Mamie in her worn XXXL t-shirt with the jasmine in her stringy gray hair. She is laughing at something Coco has said, her black eyes snapping with energy. "Whose class is this?" I ask slowly. Shortly after arriving in Tahiti, I had decided it would be cool to learn a little Tahitian dance and wandered down to the nearest place I could find classes—the Conservatoire. I had signed up in an office, the receptionist had directed me here, and when I walked in Vanina had been teaching, as she had every day since. Naturally, I had assumed…

The other dancer stares at me as if I am yet another foreigner who has stayed out in the sun too long. Either that or blue eyes indicate idiocy, as she's often suspected. "Mamie Louise's," she enunciates carefully, doubtless blaming things on the language barrier.

There is a big part of me that is having trouble getting my head around this. It is the part of me that doesn't want to put something bulky around my hips. It is the part of me that thinks dance is just physical beauty, beauty in motion, and therefore the young and dancing are the most important in the room. And it isn't really a part of me; it is all of me.

But what was it Mamie had said the other day? She'd been talking during our break, chatting with all of us. I hadn't realized she'd still been teaching as she talked about how dance was the center of Tahitian culture, that it held an entire people and its traditions.

I could see, if I really thought about it—which I was doing for the first time—why you wouldn't want to toss an entire people and its traditions on to any young dancer to carry on. Why you would be a fussy old lady sitting in the corner, demanding perfection. And why the fat, old, demanding grandmother in the corner might be the most important person on the island.

"We're really privileged," the other dancer says. "Mamie Louise is the heart and soul of Tahitian dance. It's like she holds our whole culture in her hands."

Vanina abruptly tosses her mango seed into a trashcan and leaps to her feet, whistling for the drummers to come back. My stomach stuffed with the half of the mango I've managed to cram into it, I take my place back on the floor. As the drums fill the room, Mamie Louise glances past Coco to purse her lips. "Lower, Lo-RA. And faster. And keep your feet together."

I have occasion to deeply regret my culinary curiosity as my hips churn my stomach. The drums take over the room and the whole street. Passersby swing their hips to the beat; we can see them through the glass windows. Mamie talks to Coco and watches with an eagle eye.

Somehow or other, by sheer dumb luck, I've wandered into the heart of the drums, the heart of the dance, the heart of Tahiti.

Laura Florand has lived in Tahiti, Spain, and France and traveled to many other places. Her book Blame It on Paris, *a wacky true story of love and family across cultures, will soon be available. Her work has appeared in previous Travelers' Tales anthologies under the name Laura Higgins.*

10 EUGENE BURDICK

THE BLACK AND THE WHITE

Many years ago, this writer discovered that there's a bigger gulf between north and south than most of us imagine.

HIS NAME WAS ZOLA, ZOLA MARTIN. THAT INCREDIBLE NAME signed to an innocent letter was what first called him to my attention. That plus the fact that the letter was postmarked Tahiti and that beneath the politeness of the letter there was a rasplike indication of toughness.

He had written to criticize a sea story which I had published two years before. In that story I had described the fate of a group of survivors adrift in a sailless lifeboat. The story was based on an old incident that had turned up in British Admiralty files.

> My dear sir,
> In your otherwise excellent story you state that your survivors in a lifeboat without sails drifted northeast at the rate of three knots an hour until it

> was thrown up on an atoll of the Society Islands. It appears to me that this is a very unlikely circumstance.

He backed this assertion with a dazzling knowledge of the wind, currents, and waves of the Pacific. He made an intricate calculation which demonstrated that the drifting boat would have missed the most southerly of the Societys by at least one hundred miles and went on to suggest that either the Admiralty report was written by sailors who did not know their true location or, in fact, the lifeboat had been able to put on a bit of sail.

I wrote him and thanked him for his criticism. Also because I was working on a number of other sea stories I asked him some detailed questions about ocean and island life in Polynesia. He responded and we began an exchange of letters that lasted several years. His letters, in English, but written in an elegant copperplate French handwriting were, at first, very distant and factual. Over the years, however, I came to know the following facts about him: Zola was fifty-five years old, he had a steady small income from vineyards in Burgundy, was properly married in church to a Polynesian woman, had five children by her and had sent all of them to European schools.

In one of my letters to Zola I asked him, quite casually, why he had left Paris to live in Polynesia. When his reply arrived two months later, even before I opened the envelope I could tell it had been written in a different mood. The handwriting was still elegant, but somewhat more sprawling; there was a brown smudge on the envelope as if a cigarette ash had burned out on it. When I opened the letter the top half of the first page was smudged and I sensed at once that it had been blurred by spilled alcohol.

> Proust has described life in Paris and its rottenness very accurately [Zola wrote]. There is no need for me to try

and improve upon him. The forced masculinity of the bon vivant made them seem like dandies with the minds of roosters. The simpering of the women, their endless efforts to strike a balance between seductiveness and purity, came to nauseate me. The constant grubbing for money, whether it was done by elegant men at the Bourse for millions of francs or by peddlers, for a mean percentage, pervaded everything. But the basic flaw, the most awful consistency in Paris, was the true inability of anyone to love. It is no accident that Proust was a tortured homosexual. He was well aware that love in Europe is a kind of organized and shrewd torture, a device for skewering people on the twin spikes of eroticism and propriety.

I came to Polynesia, to a tiny island, to escape all this. Do not conclude, my dear sir, that I am one of your Rousseau romantics. I am not. But love in these islands does have simplicity, a spontaneity, a kindness that we Europeans have lost. Here a man can sometime feel some of the bull-like assurance which a man should feel without being bound up in the awful artificial skeins of Western notions of marital love. Nor does he have to become involved in a slippery smart evilness of adultery. Here a man can live the life he is supposed to live: the life of the body, the life of the mind, the life of the heart. Some terrible by-path which we Europeans and you Americans have taken has been avoided here in Polynesia.

And then, quite surprisingly, he invited me to visit him. Something about the burnt paper, the alcoholic sprawl, the urgency of his words made Zola more than an unknown person. I wanted to see him.

Almost by accident I did.

A movie company operating at Papeete had chartered a flying boat to search for shooting locations and were going to make a sweep through the Tuamotus and Marquesas. They offered to drop me off at the Frenchman's isolated atoll and pick me up within five days. We made the flight in a World War II PBY, flown by two English pilots with mustaches, lean handsome faces marred only by slightly bloodshot eyes caused partly by Hinano beer and partly by flying over the glare of open ocean. They both had hard Manchester accents. The plane badly needed paint and inside it was dirty, but the two engines were in magnificent shape. The two pilots tried to give the impression of flying by the seat of the pants, but actually they could both pilot and navigate beautifully. They hit the Frenchman's atoll on the nose and made a long languid sweep of a descent which was both artistic and safe.

The atoll was the shape of a teardrop. At the heavy rounded end the land rose fifteen or twenty feet above the surface and was covered with cultivated coconut palms. The thin point of the tear also was slightly elevated and there were signs of an inhabited native village there. The atoll was four miles long and two miles wide at the widest point. Like most atolls only 5 or 10 percent of the other ring rose high enough above the water to be livable. The pilots needed only the one pass to detect a long streak of green-white water which indicated enough depth to land.

They brought the plane down exquisitely, the first contact with the water so subtle that it felt as if oil had been splashed along the keel. As we came to a standstill they cut one motor, the power of the other propeller turned us in the water and we had stopped precisely in front of the Frenchman's house. One of the pilots came back, tossed a yellow rubber life raft over and handed me a paddle. He tossed my gear down to me without saying a word, but as he pulled the hatch shut I could see that beneath his mustache he was smiling. I was only ten yards from the plane when the prop-wash caught me and pushed me halfway to shore. I knew they had done it deliberately, a final signature of their skill.

As I rowed the rest of the way in I looked at the Frenchman's house. It was the largest Tahitian-type house I had ever seen outside of Papeete. On three sides it had a long overhang of roof which formed a veranda railing which was barbed with dozens of small intricately carved tikis.

"What difference would it have made if you had written? Everything would be the same. Here there is no need to prepare for a pleasure."

Every form of building has its marks of perfection. Thatch roof comes in two qualities: pandanus or coconut thatch. Pandanus is infinitely superior. Another mark of quality is how close the spines of the thatch mats are laid together. The closer together, the more that are used, the thicker the roof, the longer it will resist the attack of the wind, rain, and rats. On Zola's roof the spines of the mats were no more than a quarter inch apart. From the house down to the beach there was a lawn that was neatly clipped. Separating the house from the coconut grove was an artful arrangement of fruit trees very carefully blended for shape and color. A papaya tree by itself can have a slightly obscene look, but here, the papaya trees were scattered among mangoes and frangipani trees so that they looked tall and elegant.

Zola was on the beach to meet me. He walked out into the water up to his thighs and steadied the yellow boat as I climbed out.

"Ah, ah. The literary friend from California," he said, although he must have been guessing for I hadn't any way to tell him of my arrival.

He was a surprise. Somehow I had expected a tall, lean somewhat withdrawn man. Zola looked much more like a rounded bourgeois shopkeeper. His face was rubicund. His manner was cheerful and friendly. He talked very fast. And he gave off the slightest odor of gin. His eyes, however, were those of the man who had written the brilliant letters. They were large, almost beautiful, a deep black. He had a birdlike energy, quick small gestures which seemed ineffectual, but were remarkably efficient. He hustled my gear out of the rubber boat and onto the veranda in a flurry of jerks, steps, tugs, and pulls before I could give him a hand.

"I would have written, but the chance to come was so sudden that I did not have time," I explained.

"And I do not have a radio," Zola said with delight. "It is a pleasure to have you. What difference would it have made if you had written? Everything would be the same. Here there is no need to prepare for a pleasure."

His curious eyes glanced over me, his mouth pulled up into a laugh. Together we pulled the boat up onto the beach.

"You have a beautiful place here," I said, waving my hand to take in the entire atoll.

"Yes, it is beautiful," Zola said quietly. "And all of this with no politics." He burst out laughing.

In our correspondence we had had a long debate on whether or not politics figured large in the life of Polynesia. He insisted that there was no such thing. He was wrong, but that is another matter. He paused and for the first time the smile vanished from his face. "I shall also demonstrate to you that my description of love and the South Pacific is precisely as I said in my letters."

His wife was waiting for us on the veranda. I knew from his letters that her name was Toma and that she was in her early forties. Uniformly when Polynesian women have reached this age they have started to take on weight. The breasts and the thighs begin to thicken. But Toma was different. I guessed from her face that one of her parents must have been Chinese, because her cheekbones were higher and her face was thinner than those of most Polynesian women. She was quite slim. She wore a pareu that had been washed enough so that the glossy cheapness that it had when it came off the looms in France or England had disappeared. Her hair was thick and very black and was drawn up into large loose bun on her neck.

Zola paused for a moment at the bottom of the stairs, his arm around my shoulders, and restrained me. He bounded up the stairs, put his arm around Toma and stood smiling down triumphantly at me.

"A pretty picture, eh?" he shouted. "A picture of the East and the West and a proof that the twain shall meet. Where is your camera? It would tell you more than a thousand words of conversation or a hundred books."

I explained that I had no camera and he roared. Toma came down the steps and shook my hand. She spoke a few words of English, just enough to say hello and to welcome me. After she had shaken hands she went up the steps ahead of me, went over to a large fresh sprig of *tiare* that was in a jar of water, plucked one of the flowers and put it behind my right ear. Zola and I sat down in the rattan chairs to talk. Toma drew off to one side and then did a thing which is very disturbing to Occidentals, but is typically Polynesian. She studied me from head to foot, without any attempt to disguise her interest. She stared at my tennis shoes, my bare legs, my khaki shorts and shirt, my arms, my neck, and my face. Her attention was direct and obvious and she punctuated every few seconds by a nod of approval. She shook her head, however, when she came to my colored glasses as if they were somehow out of character. I knew that within a few hours she would have described my physical appearance in the greatest detail to everyone else that she met on the atoll. I have sometimes heard these descriptions of others by Polynesian women and they are uncanny in their ability to reproduce verbally the physical looks of a person. Every small spot, the length of the hair, the shape of the ears is remembered perfectly.

When Toma had finished her scrutiny she came over and asked us in French if we would like something to drink. She offered us coconut water, lime juice, or fresh pineapple juice. I settled for pineapple juice and she turned and walked down the steps towards the cookshack. At the bottom of the steps she turned and said "With gin?" I nodded and she smiled broadly.

Later Toma served us an excellent Tahitian lunch: raw shrimp in lime juice, small red fish buttered and then broiled whole on hot coals, a plate of *fa-fa*, and a plate of freshly cut pineapple. There was also a large carafe of Algerian red wine. When we had finished this, Toma brought over a large tin coffeepot of very strong coffee and we sat on the veranda sipping.

Zola and I began to talk in English about the matters we had discussed in our letters. Like everyone else in the South Pacific we also exchanged gossip. That incredible gossip about people and events which stretch over an area much vaster than in the United States but in which land and people are so few that events on islands thousands of miles away have a great interest for everyone. We discussed the mystery of the large Japanese tuna boat. It had arrived in the South Seas, spanking new and gleaming, from a shipbuilding yard in Japan and was to be the first effort by the Japanese to fish the tuna-rich water. It had left port on its first cruise, disappeared and was never heard of again. We gossiped about a Chinese gentleman in Nouméa who was reputed to be running opium in the South Pacific by an ingenious device. In Laos his agents mixed raw opium with paper pulp, pressed into ordinary pages, printed up into books, and then mailed to him. The eventual consumer merely had to dissolve the book pages in vinegar and the pulp floated to the top and could be skimmed off. Left in the sun for a few days the mixture became almost pure opium. No one knew if it were true, but it is a good story.

"But what is here is yours," Zola said. "Treat it as your own." Those words were a mistake. If he had not uttered them I would not have discovered his secret life.

Our conversation droned on and eventually Zola said that he wanted to take a nap.

He asked me if I would like to look through his library and led me into a large airy room which had a view of the lagoon. He apologized for the condition of the books and pointed out that the salt air, humidity, and tiny bugs of an atoll were all highly destructive of anything as soft as paper.

"But what is here is yours," Zola said. "Treat it as your own." Those words were a mistake. If he had not uttered them I would not have discovered his secret life.

Zola was right. The books were in very bad shape. Although he had shelved them carefully with blocks of wood between each book to allow circulation of air, the edges of the pages were brittle and came away in tiny crisp fragments as I turned the pages. By the time I had gone through a half dozen books there was a semicircle of broken, powdered paper on the table.

Even so the library was exciting. It contained not only works on Polynesia and all the languages of the world, but it contained typewritten manuscripts of old songs; genealogical tables of Polynesian families; beautiful little sketches, as fragile as the tracery in a butterfly's wings of long-vanished and old-fashioned huts; long verbatim records of stories that were passed on from generation to generation orally; a meticulous file of the signs that appeared on various tikis and *maraes* along with shrewd guesses as to what they meant. It was a magnificent example of practical scholarship done by a single man.

On a small table in the corner of the room there was a box, built very much like a cigar humidor. On the top it had a small brass plate which said "Memoirs." I opened it without a moment's hesitation. It might have been the memoirs of anyone, and, after all, Zola told me that I could look at everything. The humidor was two-thirds full of handwritten manuscripts. I recognized the handwriting as that of Zola. But oddly enough most of the memoirs were written in English instead of French. Later I sensed that he did this so that the manuscript could not be read by the natives, many of whom can read French fluently.

The first entry in the memoirs was twenty-five years old. It was written aboard the ship that carried Zola from Marseilles to Tahiti. It was only ten pages long, but it was remarkable. It was one of the most bitter, lucid, incisive, tragic, instructive commentaries on the European situation I had ever read.

With the strange clarity that is possessed by the very young or the very angry, Zola caught, in acid detail, every affectation, every depravity, every hypocrisy, every flaw of European life. In his letters to me his criticism of Europe had been abstract, here they were personalized. He described the manipulations by which his mother and sister entrapped a wealthy young Parisian who wanted to be an artist into becoming the daughter's groom and a merchant in silk. It is a commonplace occurrence, but in Zola's spare prose, it looked suddenly obscene. There was a description of a business deal in which Zola's father had outmaneuvered his best friend. It was an ordinary business deal, quite legal, but put down without the usual soft words it almost stank of rottenness; devoid of heart or even of meaning. There was a description of a family Christmas reunion, no more than seventy-five words in length, that revealed the avarice and jealousy that hung, like invisible fog, around the Christmas tree, the roasted goose, the presents, the incantations of love. There was a description of the private school Zola attended and it was depicted as an expensive institution for squeezing the life out of children, instilling a feral competition among them, giving them a civilized veneer to hide an inculcated meanness.

It was a remarkable piece of writing and with a bony economy it destroyed individuals, a family, a city, a culture.

Zola had also put down what he had expected to find in the South Seas. He had read the romantic novels of the South Seas, but he had also read the grim anthropological journals and reports of French administrators. He was no romantic. He was prepared for elephantiasis, the neat line of feces along the white sand at low tide, the fact that natural beauty could become boring, the sure knowledge that there would be long periods of loneliness. Zola came to Tahiti as a bitter young man with hard perceptive eyes, a fugitive from the intolerable, expecting no moments of grace, a searcher for himself.

When he arrived in Tahiti he spent only a few days in Papeete and then moved to the tiny village of Tautira on Tahiti Iti. Here his eye was still sharp, his comments clear and unsentimental, but he was entranced. There was almost a mood of delirium, of ravishment, of illumination, in the early pages he wrote on Tautira. The gentleness of the Tahitians, their complete lack of duplicity, the apparent absence of status were precisely what he needed to wipe out the bitter memories during this period. I quickly scribbled down in my notebook:

I return to my hut to find Kaoko rifling my sea chest. He had ignored the bundle of franc notes, but held in his hand an American box camera, and a large Swiss pocketknife with a variety of screwdrivers, blades, and other gadgets sunk in its thick handle. "I was borrowing these," Kaoko said without the slightest embarrassment.

"Would you have brought them back?" I said in anger.

"No, probably not," Kaoko replied. "I intended to borrow them permanently."

Kaoko had not the slightest sense of guilt. I realized suddenly that he had absolutely no notion of theft…just as the children in Europe must be carefully indoctrinated with a notion of property before they can be made to feel guilt about theft. This man had been brought up in an environment in which there was no notion of theft. I told him that I would need both the camera and the knife and he handed them to me without even the hint of a roguish smile. He simply handed them back.

A few days later he wrote in his diary:

Last night I slept like a dead man on the beach. I had gotten drunk on beer and wine and the dancing. I fell asleep with the stars in my eyes…big, explosive, pure white stars lost in the purest blackness. When I closed my eyes, the stars still seemed to glint somewhere in my eyeballs, tiny pleasant dots of light.

During the night I awoke slowly and there was a hand in my lava-lava. It was the hand of a girl who was crouched down beside me, staring into my face and smiling. She was very slim and her breasts were barely large enough to hold up her pareu.

She bent her head close to my ear and whispered into my ear in French. She told me that the dancing had excited her especially because she had never seen a white man dancing. As she spoke her hand wandered over my legs and between them.

> For a moment on that warm beach my European conscience rebelled. I felt I could not do what she wanted. What she wanted to do was technically a crime in every civilized country of the world. She sensed my reluctance and laughed. It was not a nervous or hysterical laugh, it was the curious laughter of an inquisitive child. I took her and it was sheer pleasure. She made love in the style that the natives call *maori*: quick, savage, silent. At the climax her tiny body arched up, she moaned, and then her fingernails scratched down my face. It was over quickly, but it was a very skillful performance and the girl was deeply satisfied. I am not quite sure how I feel today except that I am excited.

I knew then that Zola had not intended for me to read these memoirs. It was the kind of document that is kept only for the eyes of the author. I had always been curious as to why authors would specify that certain of their letters or notes or unpublished writings be destroyed upon their death. It had always struck me as a wanton waste of talent, a reckless and selfish pouring away of creative energy. Now I understood.

I should have stopped reading but I could not. The memoirs went on to describe his meeting with Toma.

Toma came to Tautira from the atoll on which Zola was now living. She had relatives in the village and had been living with them for a year. At Zola's invitation she had moved from her relatives' house into his. They lived together for six months and then Toma told Zola that she was pregnant. Zola insisted upon being married, and being married in a church. Toma was puzzled, but she consented. After the first child was born they went to Toma's native atoll and at once Zola decided that they would live there. After this the entries in the book became very scanty. For five years he wrote no more than a line or two a month, recording the planting of coconut palms, the amount of copra harvested, the birth of children, the arrival of books on the trading schooner. It was as if his days were so satisfying that he no longer needed the solace of the memoirs.

Six years after his arrival on the atoll, however, the entries in the memoirs began to lengthen. One of them said:

> Toma is still as attractive as when I married her. Still as kind. Still as generous. At one point she began to take on weight and I did something for which I am ashamed. I insisted that she diet and stay slim. She argued that weight is a sign of prosperity and of dignity. But she has gone along with me.

A few days later there was another entry:

> There is a blankness about Toma that disturbs me. I have been trying to teach her to read and write French, but she simply does not have the interest. She will spend ten or twelve hours a day gossiping with members of her family on some petty thing such as the name of a new child. But she will not give attention enough to learn to read or write. I am puzzled.

A month later there was a long entry:

> I think I understand Toma and through her, the Polynesian personality. She lives literally in the moment. She loves *tiare* and her eyes will light up when she sees them, but she will not plant them. She has started vegetable gardens five times at my insistence, but each time has allowed the gardens to wither. She loves radishes, but not enough to grow and fertilize and water them. Three times she had agreed to hire workers to build an outdoor privy next to the bathhouse. But each time the money has gone for calico or tobacco. Flowers, radishes, a privy...the future. Polynesians do not know how to calculate future pleasures. I do not know why this should exasperate me but it does.

The entry after this was the last one: "I am bored, bored, bored, bored."

Later that afternoon Zola and I went for a long walk around the island. He was cheerful and talkative and his knowledge about everything about the South Seas was monumental. The habits of fish, the diseases of coconut palms, the old histories of great Polynesian kings, where infanticide was practiced and where it was not, were only a few of the things he discussed in the greatest detail. Now, however, I listened with a new ear. Zola's encyclopedic knowledge of Polynesia no longer seemed to me to be based on a simple fascination with the people, rather I had the impression that he was trying desperately to use the facts and information to fill a great yawning chasm of despair. He threw facts into it as his Polynesian chiefs threw victims over cliffs to satisfy a dimly seen, but terribly feared deity.

We had almost finished our walk when we met a young boy and girl walking in the opposite direction. They said hello to us and then vanished on the path. Zola turned and looked at me.

"They have just finished making love in the bushes," he said. His voice was expressionless.

"How could you tell?" I asked.

"Really it is an exercise in probability," he said. "Quite literally every time a Tahitian girl or boy meet casually it leads to sexual intercourse. The only exceptions are if they are sister and brother, or if one of them is malformed. Then also the boy's face had a few scratches on it. As you probably know Polynesian women at the climax scratch the man's face. The men often do the same thing."

"I knew that, but it still surprises me," I said. "They are so gently in everything else that you would think when they are making love that it would carry over there, too. I have never been able to understand their use of violence in sex."

Zola turned and looked out toward the sea. The tide was just starting to flood, crabs scurried about gradually moving toward the sand like a disorganized army in retreat. The waves boomed solidly against the reef, but aside from the sound, there was only a flat layer of foam to show their force.

"For them sex is not really an act of love," Zola said. "It is a way to break tedium, a way of breaking the monotony of endless beautiful days. It is like a game, but no more than a game."

Zola's face was held in a tight little smile, but his eyes were suddenly deep and black with a strange expression. I sensed that he had looked over the edge of the chasm.

That night after dinner a strange thing happened. We ate on the veranda overlooking the lagoon, watching the water gradually change into an even flawless green. In the center of the table was a flower-and-shell arrangement which Toma had made. It had a startling miniature beauty to it. Tiny shells, stamens of some sort of flowers, the green from the throat of wild orchids and edging of blue petals which had been picked from flowers.

"That is a beautiful arrangement, Toma," I said.

Toma was pleased. Zola looked down at the arrangement and smiled.

"It is a beautiful arrangement," Zola said. He watched it intently for a few moments and the smile went from his face. He bent forward and with his hand gently pushed the tiny arrangement apart. He looked at me as he spoke to Toma.

"Put it back together Toma," he said.

Without a word Toma leaned forward and her fingers flicked over the diminutive shells and flowers and petals. Almost at once it was back in order. Then I realized that it was back in *exactly* the same order, it was an exact duplication of the first arrangement.

I looked up from the arrangement and Zola was watching

me. His lips were turned up in a smile but there was something like a pleading in his eyes.

"Can you do any other arrangements?" Zola asked Toma without looking at her.

"No, this is the only arrangement I make," she said. She smiled. "They taught us this when we were children. Mai-tai, eh."

"Mai-tai," I replied.

"Mai-tai and every girl on the island can do this single arrangement and the girls on the island have been making this arrangement and no other for over four hundred years," Zola said. His voice was empty.

Zola's face was held in a tight little smile, but his eyes were suddenly deep and black with a strange expression. I sensed that he had looked over the edge of the chasm. Between us hung the knowledge that Toma could make only one flower arrangement, could cook *poa* only one way, cook fish only one way, make love in only one way, sing in only one pattern of songs, dance one kind of dance. Anything outside of the simple patterns did not interest her. And years ago Zola had come to know all of them.

Zola and I did not discuss this during the remaining days I was on his atoll. We walked and talked constantly, but he never referred to himself. When the PBY returned I rowed the old rubber boat out to it after saying goodbye to Zola and Toma. The sweat was pouring into my eyes by the time I reached the plane. I was tired. Just as I shipped my oars and looked again at Zola's house the salty drops of sweat fogged my vision. Zola seemed shrunken, small, hunched, almost bleached. He had stopped waving. Toma seemed life-sized and natural.

He was a prisoner not of a dream, but of those faded years in France which had instilled into his nerves and brain and soul an interest in questions beyond himself and beyond the day in which he existed. He had escaped only the real presence of European life; twisted through his mind like a maze of black jets were a set of conditionings and experiences which had burned into his youthful mind. From these he could never escape.

Zola is typical of a whole breed of men, of white men who live in the South Seas. Sensitive to the rawness of their native society, they flee to the apparent tranquility of the South Pacific. But by then the damage has been done.

To every white man in the South Seas this dread knowledge of thinness, sameness, an endless unrolling of identical acts, the haunting absence of distinct personality, must some day be faced. For many it is too much to face. This is one reason why so many of the white men of the Pacific are the most quietly desperate alcoholics in the world. They have burnt all their bridges; there is no path back to Paris or Dubuque or London. They must, because of pride and sometimes sloth and sometimes poverty, stay in the South Seas. But the original vision has been cauterized over with the scars of experience. So they must be sustained by alcohol or gambling or opium or driving economic activity or, as in the case of Zola, by a frantic search for the fullest knowledge of a culture which he did not really value.

There is a lesson. If you want to live in the South Seas start early. Early, very early, our nerves become civilized. It is not easy to then slough off the coatings of civilization; they are more durable and tough than the softer stuff of primitive life.

Eugene Burdick (1918-1965) was a decorated naval officer who attended Stanford University and earned a Ph.D. in psychology from Oxford University. He taught at the Naval War College in Newport, Rhode Island and at the University of California at Berkeley. He is the author of eight books, including The Ugly American, *which he co-authored with William J. Lederer.*

11 KATHRYN J. ABAJIAN

LISTENING TO LULLABIES

She learned more than just a spoken language.

I FOLLOWED FALE TOLU'S SON OBEDIENTLY. WINDING ALONG the edge of the rainforest, nine-year-old Ioane led me confidently to the beach. Though he hadn't spoken a word to me since we'd met, his eyes brightened with pride when his father assigned him to "accompany the *palagi* everywhere in the village." So his brothers stayed home, and we took off for the beach on my first day in Lotofaga Village, on the small Samoan island of Upolu, mere hours since I'd turned in my semester grades.

Passing shiny rubber tree leaves, tall pandanus plants, and opulent red, orange, and pink bougainvillea, we came to an opening in the path that suddenly revealed a palm-tree framed white sand beach—pristine and without anyone else in sight. I walked onto its movie-set magic, amazed at this seemingly untouched treasure, the only sounds the breeze rattling palm branches and the ocean's distant heartbeat crashing on the outlying reef. Half aloud, I said, "Oh, it's beautiful. It's so beautiful." Then I spent the next two hours floating in a warm turquoise South Pacific sea. Ioane sat on the sand the entire time, his arms wrapped around his sarong-covered knees, and watched me silently.

The next day we repeated our short trek, again without a word, Ioane once more in the lead along the path to paradise, his brown body bare except for a faded lava-lava tied at his waist. The path widened a bit and yet again revealed the empty beach. I stopped to listen and absorb while Ioane abruptly strode toward the water, flung his arms out to his sides and in a high-pitched voice instantly quite fluent chanted, "Bee-you-tee-ful! Oooh, soo bee-you-tee-ful!" Then, taking further control of our conversation, he grabbed a stick, ran down to the wet sand and wrote his favorite English word in foot-high letters: R-A-M-B-O.

And so we began our summer afternoons. We spoke in his version of English and I learned to do nothing every afternoon. When Ioane would tire of climbing the coconut trees to get my lunch, finding the perfect shell for my spoon, or running to the village store to get a large, deeply-scratched bottle of Coca-Cola to share, he would join me in the water where I'd occasionally agree to karate-chopping, action-figure play, despite a nearly forty-year difference in our ages.

I'd come to Samoa for the summer as a volunteer English teacher hoping to learn more about this culture that had intrigued me on my first week-long visit the previous summer. And this time, I really wanted to learn some of the language. But both were harder lessons than I had expected. I had to be taught, after breaking it, the rule for sitting properly on the *fale* floor: Unless I was sitting cross-legged, I needed to point my feet away from anyone else. I learned not to walk in front of a chief in his home, and I was careful to wrap a lava-lava over my shorts in a village. And I learned that if I asked to see a fine mat unrolled, the owner felt compelled to give it to me.

But it was the language that truly confounded me. Before I came I'd naively thought I would learn it easily, that I might even become fluent during that first month. Even after I arrived I hoped I might just pick it up naturally, possibly even absorb it, merely by being surrounded by it—the same way the heavy moisture, day and night, had already begun to seep into my pores. Of course it didn't happen. I spent those first weeks completely lost in the language—everywhere except with Ioane and his friends on Lotofaga beach and in the teachers' room at lunch.

During our frequent breaks, I had my primary language lessons. Over cups of hot tea, the Samoan teachers amused me with stories about the differences in British and American English. We laughed over our different pronunciations of "water." The Samoans' British English sounded lilting—*wahtah*; my California dispatch sounded harsh—*waader.* They told me about the English words Samoans often use to name their children. The school's principal had two houseboys, twins named Gin and Tonic. Another family had twins they called Horizontal and Vertical. I met a young man, Telefoni, named after the telephone his mother used to announce his birth from a New Zealand hospital. And I learned of more than one boy born in the 1960s named Kenneti, after J.F.K.

Most memorable was Greta, a blonde Norwegian teacher whose husband was Nigerian. She told about the time her husband brought his Samoan co-worker, Lanu, home for dinner.

"If we leave work early, we may get there in time to watch Greta make *fufu*," Gilbert assured his buddy.

Lanu's eye's bulged as he coughed a burst of disbelief.

"What is wrong?" Gilbert asked. That's when he learned that the Samoan term for self-indulgence, for pleasuring oneself, is (you guessed it) *fufu*.

> We were each handed one wordlessly, an impromptu cocktail of coconut milk minutes fresh from the tree. The young men's tranquil kindness stirred us all, welcoming us beyond language.

That certainly perked up my ears. I'd have to listen carefully to avoid my own gaffes. One of the first expressions most visitors learn is the commonly used, *fa'a Samoa*. They'll tell you it means "in the Samoan way," but it has its nuances as well. It's the islanders' palms-up expression for our "whatever," that wry acceptance of life as it is. If someone's late to an appointment? Well, that's *fa'a Samoa*. If the bus doesn't come for hours? Ah, it's *fa'a Samoa*. If Sisilia's husband spends most evenings dancing in a bar? Yes, that's *fa'a Samoa* as well—an omnipresent Samoan lack of urgency, a studied conservation of concern. *Popole fua*? Not to worry. *Faifailemu?* Take it easy. Two miles to the next village? We'll sit beside the road awhile and wait for a "picky-up" to come by.

To understand *fa'a Samoa* is to understand much about the culture, but at that point I was mostly catching on to the variant uses of the expression. I still hadn't caught on to it in practice; I still wasn't living "in the Samoan way," totally relaxed and without worry about most things. And I still couldn't form an original Samoan sentence.

Then, after living on the island for three weeks, I began to care less for mastery of the language as I realized I was actually picking up an important part of the islanders' dialogue that seemed to sift into and between the lines of my thoughts. Of course I couldn't understand more than a few actual words—little of the vocabulary and none of the syntax—but I gradually grasped a particular decorum and courtesy in its tone.

One Saturday afternoon, my friend Vita invited me to a meeting of his *aiga*, his large extended family, held in a village near town. That's where I started to comprehend the language as I sat on a bench, outside the family group, entirely captivated with the dynamics of Samoan patriarchy. The Talking Chief, a man chosen for his oratorical abilities and his talent to garner respect with his voice and words, sat cross-legged on the *fale* floor, the other men making up a semicircle around him. He spoke first, with eloquence and adept—I later learned—in the most formal level of the Samoan language. He properly wandered around his topic, approaching it from all sides, skimming its circumference and spiraling through its interior. Next, each man spoke in turn, some with wives sitting directly behind them quietly nudging their husbands' opinions.

No one interrupted, no one talked over anyone else's sentiment, and no one raised a voice in contention. In fact, it seemed as though a delegate from each family was giving a sort of speech, saying his piece in a measured and methodical manner. Vita told me later they were discussing thorny land rights issues and everyone needed to hear and be heard. Despite misgivings I had about island patriarchic power, I heard cultivated civility and mutual respect that afternoon.

A few weeks before I was to leave, I was invited, along with some friends from the U.S., to a traditional Samoan meal with a family in an outlying village near Fagaloa Bay. Soon after we arrived, as we stood talking beside our jeeps, I watched three robust young men walking up the road toward us, two shouldering huge palm branches, the other carrying coconut-filled palm baskets suspended from both ends of a pole. They stopped in front of us, put down their loads and silently began to hack holes in the tops of the coconuts with their bush knives. We were each handed one wordlessly, an impromptu cocktail of coconut milk minutes fresh from the tree. The young men's tranquil kindness stirred us all, welcoming us beyond language.

Within minutes we sat in a semi-circle on mats on the *fale* floor, ready to eat the artfully arranged food: fish poached in coconut milk and *palusami* made of onions and coconut cream wrapped in baby taro leaves—all set before us on palm frond placemats. Before we ate, and as my friend Larry sat beside me whispering a translation, the chief spoke to us according to his protocol, explaining in Samoan how honored he was that we were his guests. Next, the most venerated in our group communicated for us in Samoan, explaining what an honor it was for all of us to be in the chief's presence. Then each man prayed aloud in turn, both apparently assuring God of his place in the hierarchy of esteem.

While we ate, Foi—a tall Samoan man openly pleased with our company—silently attended to us, replenishing our plates and cups. Foi didn't speak English, yet he clearly communicated his admiration for the feminine qualities of two women in our group. He spent his time between refills sitting right before them, stroking his gold lamé shirt, noticeably envying their womanly charms. His pleasure glistened; Foi was sweet and luscious in his movements and in his yearning attention to them.

It was my first direct experience with a *fa'afafine,* a man "like a woman," and completely unexpected. Yet, Foi seemed innate to the moment, a part of the enchantment of Polynesia, part of the palpably sensuous and promising air.

After our meal, the family held a *fiafia* for us, an hour of music and dancing—mostly Samoan earnestness and American music. At the end of the evening, Foi danced alone in the middle of the *fale* floor, swaying, flowing, and liquid to the guitar strums of a Samoan farewell song. Just as the Samoan language is made up of mostly vowels, Foi was vowel personified, his entire body sinuously mellifluous.

In complete harmony with the island's essence, Foi danced languidly, in touch with more than the music. Then the entire family began singing to us. They were joined by about twenty village children who, I realized only then, had been standing in the dark watching from outside the *fale*: "*Tofa* my *feline*...Goodbye my friend. I won't ever forget you." Then, heady with the music, I followed my friends around the perimeter of the *fale* floor, saying individual good-byes as each family member touched my hand or kissed my cheek. The youngest reached up and circled my neck with a freshly made *frangipani* lei.

So that's how it happened to me. That was the moment I completely bonded with the island and its islanders as both spoke to me through music that night. And I finally realized that to speak Samoan, to give voice to the culture, I first had to slow down to listen, an effortless lesson after all in a place where the air, so heavy with fragrance, relaxes both breath and thought.

Finally, at the very end of my summer there, I realized I'd learned a new language after all. I'd become fluent in a kind of poetry whose rhythms had gradually become a part of me. I'd learned to savor sensations I could easily absorb while everyone around me spoke lullabies.

Whenever she's not listening to the breeze rattle palm branches, Kathryn Abajian can be found teaching writing and literature in the San Francisco Bay Area. She is the author of memoir and travel essays and arts reviews. Her first book, First Sight of the Desert: Discovering the Art of Ella Peacock, *traces her relationship with a woman who painted the "land she loved."*

12 RICK CARROLL

LAST OLD BOYS' CLUB IN THE PACIFIC

Others may surrender to trends, but down in the South Seas where men are still men, some things remain sacred.

THE LAST TIME I WAS IN TONGA, I DROPPED INTO THE Nuku'alofa Club for a Foster's Lager. My shadow had barely darkened the threshold when every man, sea captain, and senator alike, spun on his bar stool to glimpse the intruder. Eyes narrowed against tropical sunlight, they stared hard at me. I found no familiar face at first.

"Brother Carroll!" came a friendly salutation at last.

Although I had just traveled more than 10,000 miles from home, I was immediately at home, down in the South Seas at the Nuku'alofa Club. You see, I am a dues-paying, non-resident member. A brother, if you will, of Tonga.

Seldom, if ever, have I wanted to belong to an organization that would have me as a member but a few years ago, on assignment down in the South Seas, I found myself quite alone, although not for long, in the Kingdom of Tonga.

The great navigator Captain James Cook himself, called Tonga "the friendly isles" and little has changed in that regard since he "discovered" these wonderful islands in 1773—as I soon discovered myself.

In short order I was invited to the Nuku'alofa Club, introduced about, and after a few good yarns over several rounds, was nominated by the Honorable Senator John LeMoto, and seconded by the president of this august body. Having no pressing affairs in the kingdom, I accepted.

"We are the oldest club of this sort in the South Pacific," said Carl Riechelmann, a fourth-generation Tonga resident, then in his tenth year as president, who welcomed me to the fold—after I paid my dues and bought a round for the house.

Now, Tonga's a long way to go for camaraderie, but I always find an inexplicable sense of well-being in this tin-roofed British clubhouse founded in 1914.

In a world where men of a certain age are hard put to find comfort in—dare we say?—an all-men's club, the existence of the Nuku'alofa Club will come as welcome news to aging boys everywhere.

Neat as a pin and cozy as a treehouse, the Nuku'alofa Club smells like pool-cue chalk, old tobacco smoke, and that thin musty scent common to all male retreats from church sacristy to college frat house. Voices are deep and the mood is cheery. A framed portrait of the Queen of England watches over the gentlemen like an ancient fraternity mother.

The club is divided into three parts: A billiards room complete with dartboards and a slate table imported from Great Britain. An honest library full of first-edition leather volumes and newspapers of the day, albeit several months late from Lon-

Conversation is of adventure, real and enhanced; deals pending and closed; royal gossip, rugby standings, liaisons.... Manly conversation, in short. I like to take my pleasure here when torrential rains beat a tattoo on the tin roof.

don, Sydney, and Hong Kong. A well-stocked bar attended by a white-jacketed steward who calls members, "Sah," and keeps all well served.

No money changes hands except on private wagers. Sign your chit, pay at month's end. Laggards are posted. Bar opens at eight o'clock sharp every morning—a godsend for topers—and closes when the last man leaves—another civilized practice. No missionary inroads here.

Often the last man is The Crown Prince of Tonga, life-long bachelor, who calls himself "HRH" (short for His Royal Highness) and likes to watch videos on the club's VCR, sole concession to the great world beyond.

Conversation is of adventure, real and enhanced; deals pending and closed; royal gossip about what the king did or didn't do; rugby standings locally and overseas; and the inevitable reflection on liaisons, past, present, and future. Manly conversation, in short. I like to take my pleasure here when torrential rains beat a tattoo on the tin roof. Jack London would have, too.

All is not perfect in the last Polynesian kingdom. Rumors swirl that the clubhouse may come down, victim of redevelopment. Progress stalks this island as elsewhere.

"We certainly would resist any change that threatens our existence," says Riechelmann, bristling at the very idea.

And then there are the termites, ever chewing away the foundation, but wood is cheap and carpenters handy and repairs accomplished although the clubhouse looked in dire need of fresh paint.

The Nuku'alofa Club sits, like a lost command headquarters out of a Spielberg film about WWII British aviators, in the heart of Tonga's capital, midway between the coral-block church and the termite-bitten Royal Palace of His Majesty King Tau'aufaha Tupou IV. His Majesty is naturally, by birth and gender, a member-in-good-standing and thus, a royal brethren.

Since its founding on May 15, 1914, the Nuku'alofa Club has withstood earthquakes, hurricanes, World War II, and women's lib—although that is due largely in part to the club's location—450 miles south of Pago Pago and a good fifteen hours by jet from Los Angeles.

Over three-quarters of a century the male sanctity of the Nuku'alofa Club has been breached only once, and then only by accident. It happened when an American naval officer of the opposite gender gained the mahogany and ordered a Pink Gin, perfectly acceptable under club by-laws which then permitted officers of foreign navies as guests.

"We never guessed the United States Navy would accept women as officers aboard ships," Riechelmann told me, "but here she was sitting on a stool at *our* bar."

"Whatever did you do?" I asked.

"Well," he said, "she was permitted to finish her gin and after she left, we revised our by-laws. You have to keep on top of these things, you know," he said, winking.

On one prior occasion—in 1956—the old boys relaxed the by-laws to invite a feminine visitor, the late, beloved Queen Salote but then only for a brief cheerio on her fiftieth birthday.

Except for those rare and royal incursions, and an annual event called "Family Day," when wives and daughters are welcome for a few hours in the afternoon, this male oasis remains inviolate. No women allowed. Oh, women may call on the phone but deeper inquiries stop at the front door. High heels trot not across the glossy checkerboard floor. Only the sweet perfume of frangipani permeates this relic sanctum.

Others may surrender to folly and trend, but down here in the South Seas where some men are still men, some things remain sacrosanct. One of them is the right to gather in fraternal order.

In a world that won't hold still, the days dwindle for all masculine outposts. Whenever I order a Foster's Lager, I lift a toast to an endangered species—my 175 dues-paying brothers of the Nuku'alofa Club. Here's to us, the last gentlemen in the South Pacific. Carry on, old chaps. Stiff upper lip, and all that.

A former daily journalist at the San Francisco Chronicle, *Rick Carroll has written award-winning articles about Hawai'i and the Pacific for the* Honolulu Advertiser *and* United Press International. *He is a contributing editor for* Hawai'i Magazine *and is the series creator and editor of* Hawai'i's Best Spooky Tales. *He is also the author of* The Unofficial Guide to Maui, The Unofficial Guide to Hawai'i, *and* Huahine: Island of the Lost Canoe, *and co-editor, with his wife Marcie, of* Travelers' Tales Hawai'i. *He and Marcie live in a nearly-300-year-old seaport on the Outer Banks of North Carolina and in Ka'a'a'wa, O'ahu, ancestral landing site of early Polynesian voyagers.*

13 BOB PAYNE

MARKED BY THE MARQUESAS

These islands carved his spirit.

On the Marquesan island of Nuku Hiva, where the novelist Herman Melville lost his heart—almost literally—to a cannibal princess, a local artist assures me the geometric design tattooed in a band around my right ankle is definitely Marquesan. No matter that I'd had it done years ago in a different part of French Polynesia, near Tahiti. He assures me, too, that he knows exactly what the design means: "It says your ancestor is a turtle."

I could be happy with that. In Polynesian mythology the turtle is a figure of respect. A god, in fact. But the trouble is that this artist is one of a number of supposedly knowledgeable locals, who, during my visit to the Marquesas, will explain to me the meaning of my tattoo—each with a different interpretation.

"You are a dangerous man, a warrior," one will say, obviously unaware of my dismal record at any kind of physical confrontation.

"Where crowds gather, you go," will say another, who, I have to think with some cynicism, already knows I am a journalist.

"Hmmm," yet another will consider, "I think the man who makes this does not finish."

The reason for these various interpretations is understandable, and disheartening. The Marquesas—a dozen major islands, all dramatically high and green, about eight hundred miles northeast of Tahiti—are considered by many people to be among the most beautiful in the world. But they also have one of the most tragic histories.

During a few decades in the 1800s, the population, once estimated at as much as eighty thousand, plummeted to a couple thousand, largely as a result of diseases introduced by Westerners. And for the few Marquesans who survived, their culture, their history, their arts, and their language were so nearly eradicated by missionaries and other Western influences that, seemingly, almost all their collective memory has been lost. Sadly, no one would be able to tell me the meaning of symbols as pervasive in Marquesan society as the cross is in Western culture, because no one really knew.

Yet despite the Marquesas' tale of tragedy, I would discover, as I traveled through the islands, a story of hope. A story of people who are not only rediscovering their past—often with so little historical evidence to guide them that what they are actually doing is reinventing themselves—but who are also leading a cultural revival that is spreading throughout French Polynesia.

"They know they must live in the future," Patrick Chastel, a French schoolteacher on the island of Hiva Oa, told me. "But they have also learned, because of the big hole in their history, that if they are not to lose their self, then they must have a past, too."

In fact, as any number of Marquesans wanted to make sure I knew, they have a past perhaps eight hundred years older than that of the Tahitians, who often dismiss them as country-bumpkin cousins, but who happen to be descendants of the Marquesan voyagers who probably first populated Tahiti.

"Tahiti people are Marquesas people, except they don't respect so much the old ways," a Marquesan on Ua Pou told me as he bought alkaline batteries for his Walkman.

The Marquesas themselves were settled from Tonga or Samoa at least by A.D. 500, about one thousand years before they were chanced upon by the first Europeans—Spanish explorers who were sailing from Peru in search of a great continent rumored to lie at the bottom of the world.

The islands were known to their inhabitants as Te Henua Enana, Land of Men. But in 1595 the Spaniards' leader, Alvaro de Mendaña, named them Las Marquesas, in honor of his sponsor, the Marquis de Cañete, viceroy of Peru.

The first Western contact did not immediately prompt a wave of tourism: The next Europeans, who sailed with Captain James Cook, did not arrive for another 200 years. Many other ships soon followed Cook's, however, and introduced all manner of novelties to the Marquesans, including smallpox, which wiped out much of the population. The missionaries arrived, too—the Catholics ultimately proving to be the most successful in converting the few Marquesans who had not succumbed to disease. In the process, they nearly destroyed all the old "superstitions"—communicated largely through song and dance and the art of tattooing—that served as a repository for the Marquesan culture.

Yet while Western contact with the Marquesas proved devastating (even today its population is only about eight thousand, and many once-crowded valleys remain hauntingly empty), it also helped create the vision of the South Seas as paradise. Novelist Melville contributed to the myth with his highly successful book *Typee*, based on his brief stay among the Marquesans after he, as a young sailor, deserted his ship. Another contributor was painter Paul Gauguin, a master at capturing tropical color and light, who is buried on Hiva Oa, where he died in 1903, after a famously scandalous life there.

Intrigued by their descriptions, and by the accounts of lesser-known visitors, my own interest in the Marquesas had been nearly lifelong. In 1983 I'd even attempted to sail there from the United States aboard a yacht on which I was crewing. But thwarted by uncooperative winds, I instead ended up in the more southerly Tuamotus and, eventually, Tahiti. What finally drew me to the Marquesas this time was my desire to discover the meaning of my tattoo.

"You don't give a tattoo to a pig, a cat, or a dog that walks by," he told me. "Why give one to a tourist?"

The tattoo, which I got not because I was less than sober, but because the South Pacific has always been a special place for me, had been done by a Marquesan living on Moorea. But he was unable, or (it belatedly occurred to me) unwilling, to explain the significance of the design. Knowing the meaning became important to me, if only to reassure myself that the artist, belonging to a people known for their love of a good practical joke, had not permanently marked me with a message that said something like, "This moron can be talked into anything."

How much a sense of humor the Marquesans have, and how distinct it is from that of the Western world, was made dramatically clear to me during my flight from Tahiti to Nuku Hiva, largest of the Marquesas, aboard a prop-driven plane in which the cockpit was visible from the passenger cabin. We were just finishing our meal, which had come in a clear plastic bag, when a big, roundish young Marquesan, who was sitting in the front row, blew up his bag and popped it with a loud bang just behind the pilot's head.

The rest of the passengers aboard the full flight (all Marquesans) seemed to think this was enormously funny. The pilot, a Frenchman, however, did not. He lurched forward, putting the plane into a nose dive.

Oh my God, I thought, as we plunged toward the deep blue ocean, it really is possible to die laughing. The pilot recovered in time to avoid disaster, and a short time later, with my heart rate almost back to normal, we descended more reasonably toward Nuku Hiva.

Like the other geologically young Marquesas, Nuku Hiva seemed to be all sharp-edged volcanic peaks, with few reefs, no tranquil lagoons, and—of more immediate concern to me—not much flat land on which to build a runway. The precipitous topography, in fact, dictated the airport's location on the opposite side of the island from the biggest town, Taiohae, population 1,600, where I had reservations at an inn.

I didn't give much thought to what that might mean, until I called the lodging's owner, Rose Corser, an American who was the only longtime English-speaking resident of the islands I would meet during my journey, to ask how I was supposed to get to her place.

"There's a road, but we've had rain for about three months, so you'll want to take a helicopter," said Corser, a recent widow who, with her late husband, had arrived in the Marquesas by sailboat some twenty years earlier. To cover a distance of eleven miles, the seventy-dollar one-way helicopter ride seemed like an extravagance. But I followed Corser's advice and—with my heart rate accelerated once more—got a seven-minute education in why the Marquesas have remained so undeveloped, and why some of the old ways have been able to survive, if only barely.

Rising nosily from the airstrip and dodging a rain squall, we rode up and over one of the greenest, most rugged landscapes imaginable. Spine-backed ridges and deep-cut valleys, awash with full streams and waterfalls, made it likely that for most of history, neighboring communities were accessible only by sea, if at all. It seemed a landscape that—smallpox and religion aside—did not easily yield to intrusion, a landscape that could hold onto things. Including, it occurred to me, as we just cleared jagged Mount Tekao, crashed helicopters.

Descending toward Taiohae Bay, where the seas rolled in with enough force to make the handful of yachts riding at anchor look very uncomfortable, we clattered down to a landing pad on the water's edge. While I waited for Rose Corser to pick me up, I came upon the first of many Marquesans whose full-body canvas of tattoos would leave me feeling...unfinished.

Tattooing, one of the few Pacific island arts to have much of an impact on the world, was first observed by Europeans when the Spaniard Mendaña and his crew stopped in the Marquesas. Originally limited to high-ranking persons, it later became a way not only of identifying where a person was from but also of commemorating significant events in one's life. Yet when I first visited Tahiti some twenty years ago, tattooing had been so nearly eliminated by church disapproval that the few examples I saw were mostly of the American "jailhouse" variety—eagles, snakes, hearts.

More recently though, all that had changed in French Polynesia. Suddenly, tattoos were much more in evidence, on both men and women, and they were much more traditional—seemingly abstract designs that upon closer look might be recognized as human or animal figures, faces, or eyes. Just as with the best wood and stone carvings, the best designs, I was told, were from the Marquesas.

"The work being done there is almost of museum quality," a painter and gallery owner on Moorea had said, while trying to sell me an exquisitely carved stone figure for a price that made a black pearl seem not such an expensive gift after all.

That Marquesan at the helicopter pad was a work of art, too. Although, as I would discover, not a particularly rare one. Not only were his arms, legs, and shirtless chest and back covered in myriad designs, so were parts of his neck and face. He didn't understand English. (Few Marquesans do; generally they first speak their own language, which is distinct from Tahitian, then French, which they learn in school.) But this islander apparently took my interest in his tattoos as an indication that I wanted to add to my own—which, compared to his, seemed an almost paint-by-numbers effort.

I definitely did not want any more, though, feeling that back in the States a tattooed forehead, say, would have been looked upon unapprovingly. So I was relieved when Rose Corser arrived.

"Oh, sure, a lot of visitors get tattoos," she told me as we bounced along toward her waterside bungalows at the western edge of the village. "And some Marquesans think that's fine. They think it shows you appreciate Marquesan culture."

However, a guide I met named Jean-Pierre did not think it was fine at all. Quiet but not afraid to speak his mind, Jean-Pierre, who had grown up in a remote valley where Melville had once stayed, believed that tattoos should have a special meaning, but that too often now they had no other purpose than decoration. It was particularly wrong, he thought, for visitors to get them.

"You don't give a tattoo to a pig, a cat, or a dog that walks by," he told me. "Why give one to a tourist?"

A good question—and one I hoped to find an answer for on a neighboring island.

Ua Pou, youngest of the Marquesas, was even more precipitous than Nuku Hiva, with a craggy profile that would remind me of Bora Bora, and an airstrip built on very little flat land. (Well, in fact, it was built on a slope and hooked at one end, which must be a delight for anyone who thinks conventional landings are much too mundane.)

The six-mile ride to the town, Hakahau, was easy enough though, and I found myself the only guest (in fact, I was the only guest everywhere I stayed) at a four-room pension that sat on the side of a hill overlooking a tiny harbor.

The little pension was owned by Hélène Kautai and her husband, known to one and all as "Doudou" (Sweetie). Although she herself was Marquesan, Hélène was appalled at my mangling of the French language.

At meals she would often refuse to pass me a dish until she was satisfied with my pronunciation of it. In my own defense, it is not often one gets to practice "More goat, please." She did, however, help arrange my meeting, on her veranda, with a schoolteacher named Toti Teikiehuupoko, who was president of the Motu Haka association.

The group, Teikiehuupoko told me, had been formed in 1978 to see that the Marquesan language was taught in the schools, which up until then had held all classes in French. And preserving the language is still the main mission.

"We believe the language is the bank, the reserve, of the Marquesan culture," Teikiehuupoko said. "We believe as long as the language is alive, the culture will follow."

In the beginning, the Church, still a powerful force in the Marquesas, was opposed to any efforts at cultural revival. The idea that Marquesans could respect God and respect Marquesan traditions, too, was one it had tried to discourage since its very arrival. But the instrument of change, the instrument without which a Marquesan cultural revival might never have happened, sprang, ironically enough, Teikiehuupoko said, from within the Church itself.

It came in the form of an enlightened Catholic priest, Monsignor Le Cleach'h. Teikiehuupoko told me about the now-retired cleric, who for many years lived on Ua Pou and whose many accomplishments included a translation of the Bible into Marquesan. He was able to convince others that the islanders could praise God through traditional songs, dances, and other cultural expressions. It was the priest's support of Motu Haka that allowed it—and a cultural renaissance that reverberated throughout French Polynesia—to flower.

Today the association is involved in promoting and preserving not only the Marquesan language but all aspects of Marquesan culture. So it did not surprise me, when I started asking him about the issue of tattoos, that Teikiehuupoko, a well-preserved middle-aged man, with a professional demeanor, slipped off his shirt quite unself-consciously to show me his own substantial array.

"It is important to be of the world," he said, pointing out various sections of what was a lifelong work in progress, "but it is important first to be of the Marquesas."

As for visitors getting tattoos, he said, he saw nothing wrong with that, as long as they thought carefully before choosing a design, and knew the significance of it. Mine, he said, either represented the tail of a fish or meant that, before I was a person, I was a mountain.

Mountains, a spine of them running down the middle, form a spectacular part of Hiva Oa, of which Robert Louis Stevenson once said, "I thought it the loveliest, and by far the most ominous spot on earth."

Ominous because of the thousands of *pae pae*, stone platforms once used for house foundations, that still lie abandoned among the lush tropical underbrush. Ominous, too, because the isle has a reputation for being less friendly toward outsiders than Nuku Hiva or Ua Pou. (At least that's what the residents of those islands told me.) Hiva Oa, for me, turned out to be a pleasant experience, nevertheless.

Much of that was due to the hosts of my pension, Gabriel and Félicienne Heitaa, with whom I spent evenings critiquing the American soap opera *The Bold and the Beautiful* (its title rendered in French as *Love, Glory, and Beauty*). And to Patrick Chastel, who invited me to visit his classroom, where his teenage scholars—after a stirring, if somewhat abbreviated, lecture on the geography, history, and future outlook of the island of America—wanted only to know how old I was, if I were married, and if I were personally acquainted with Leonardo DiCaprio.

Frustratingly for me, I could not convince the Heitaas that the soaps (which portrayed an America in which nobody worked and everybody had a lot of money, a beautiful house, and a big car) were not a true picture. They, it turned out, had been to America—to Los Angeles, where they had visited Disneyland, toured Universal Studios, and spent as much time as possible at what much of the rest of the world apparently considers this country's greatest cultural achievement—the malls. As a result, they had seen with their own eyes that the soaps have gotten it exactly right.

"It is finished, the Marquesas Islands alone in the Pacific," Chastel explained to me as a kind of defense of the Heitaas' point of view. "But you must remember that although in Europe there were 2,000 years between the beginning of history and now, in the Marquesas there are only 200 years between the Stone Age and *Love, Glory, and Beauty*."

How short the distance is between the past and the present was made clear to me one day when I heard that a German tourist from a small cruise ship had disappeared during a day excursion to Fatu Hiva, least developed of the major islands, and that the ship had finally sailed away without finding any trace of him.

A widespread explanation was that the German had been eaten by an eel living in a river near where he had last been seen. Apparently, some generations back a fisherman had wrongfully killed the river's original eel, and the feeling was that one of its offspring was just settling an old score. The most hotly debated point was not whether the story was true. Few seemed to doubt that it was. The big question was whether this was a good or bad use of tourists.

That was a question on which I did not take sides. But how short the bridge is between past and present, and how perilous negotiating the distance can be, is something I thought about every time I considered my tattoo. Of course, I told myself, I didn't believe in Marquesan "superstitions." But if I did, what would a background check of my ancestry turn up? A turtle, a fish, or a mountain?

Or, perhaps, the uncertainty meant I could choose whichever interpretation I wanted. Or that, in some weird way, the tattoo artist and the men who interpreted his work understood, as I did not, that I was supposed to choose them all. I have always been drawn to the sea and to high places, so what more appropriate links to the past for me than a turtle, a fish, and a mountain? And who is a more dangerous man, after all, than a writer? Are not journalists warriors? I know all my journalist friends think so.

And it occurred to me, finally, that perhaps the most telling interpretation was that the man who made my tattoo had not finished it. Because are not we all, Marquesans included, works in progress?

Bob Payne is a contributing editor for Condé Nast Traveler *and a frequent contributor to* Outside *and* Islands.

14 LINDA HAGEN MILLER

PETTICOAT JUNCTURE

Ah beauty, with feet of clay.

"I HAD A POSTER OF THIS TAHITIAN GIRL HANGING OVER my bed all through college," Drew said. He described her in detail: She's coming out of the ocean, topless, of course, wearing a bright sarong wrapped lazy and low around her hips. Her gold-brown skin glistens with coconut oil and drops of water drizzle down her arms, her chest, her belly. A red hibiscus is tucked in her ebony hair. She's smiling—at Drew—and she's walking right toward him. How he ever fell asleep at night is beyond me.

We were straight-off-the-plane Peace Corps volunteers, leaning on the gunnels of a rusted World War II landing craft, chugging across the Truk Lagoon and wondering what sort of parallel universe we were about to enter. Most of the volunteers were freshly minted college graduates, many were newly married, and about a dozen were single guys and girls.

Drew wasn't the only one suffering from island fever, lusting and fantasizing, hoping to get lucky. All the single guys, and no doubt many of the married men, had the same high-definition Technicolor scene running through their heads.

Drew wanted to be sucked into the Tahitians' world, enveloped in green and turquoise. But mostly he fantasized about falling in love with an island beauty—for two years or forever, whichever came first. When he sent in his Peace Corps application and was asked where he'd like to serve, he checked every island group on the roster: Samoa, Fiji, the Philippines, and Micronesia. Tahiti wasn't on the menu, but in Drew's mind, the requisite brown-skinned beauty could be found, waiting, on any South Pacific island.

> The Chuuk Lagoon is so big that the Japanese anchored their fleet of destroyers and troopships and aircraft carriers here during World War II.

Truth be told, before we got our posting, few of us knew where Micronesia was, let alone Truk (now called Chuuk). To find it, I dusted off my atlas, found Hawai'i then traced the longitude lines south to Tahiti where I thought I'd find Micronesia. It wasn't there. The Pacific became a very large body of water as my fingers ran west across the blue. There it was, just above the equator, nearly in the Philippines. No wonder my Mom was so freaked out.

"Micronesia" means "tiny islands" and over two thousand of them stretch across a swath of the Pacific Ocean the size of the continental United States. Six districts, each with its own language, dance, and customs. Nearly five different landscapes as well—the flat, sand spit Marshalls; rain-drenched high islands of Ponape; Chuuk with its forty-mile-wide lagoon dotted with a smattering of densely jungled islands; Yap, most traditional of all where the men wore loincloths and the women were topless; the Northern Marianas, which our fathers knew as the launching pad for the *Enola Gay*; and Palau, so beautiful it would eventually become the centerpiece of a reality television show.

The Chuuk Lagoon is so big that from the center you can't see its fringing reef. It's so big the Japanese anchored their fleet of destroyers and troopships and aircraft carriers here during World War II. It's so big it could swallow a Peace Corps volunteer whole. And it has.

In the late 1960s, with an eye toward the future when Micronesia, then the Trust Territory of the Pacific Islands, would gain independence, the United States sent a secret weapon to Micronesia: Peace Corps volunteers. Our overt mission was to live among the islanders, teach them English, work in the hospitals and government offices, put in water systems, and improve sanitation. In the process, our government hoped we'd spread good will and win a few hearts and minds.

But it was the end of the '60s and Uncle Sam was nearly as naïve as we were. They hadn't bargained on the fact that they were sending a whole contingent of draft-dodging, rebel-rousing, pot-smoking idealists who would just as quickly damn their country as praise it. But that's another story. This is Drew's tale.

He was from Connecticut and had just graduated from an Ivy League college with a degree in history. His father wanted him to go to law school—step into the family practice—and was appalled at this two-year detour. I detected blue blood. Drew's Peace Corps job would be teaching English as a second language and as a single man, he would be sent to one of the remote outer islands. His optimism was infectious, and even though the rolling landing craft was making me queasy and the sun was beginning to blister my shoulders, I was just as prickly with excitement.

One of the Chuukese interpreters pointed ahead. “That island’s Fefan, it means woman in Chuukese. Can you see her?” A robust figure reclined dead ahead, a Rubenesque giant clothed in green. Drew was sure he’d found nirvana.

But it was only Fefan, where we’d live with local families for a month, learn the Chuukese language, and get daily reality lessons. Some of us would be “deselected,” deemed too unstable or immature or otherwise wacky to be trusted as an emissary to a foreign country. And some of us would opt-out on our own after a few weeks of bathing in a bucket, peeing in an outhouse on stilts over the ocean, scratching mosquito bites till they bled, squishing tablespoon-sized cockroaches, and surviving on a diet of breadfruit, rice, and Spam.

None of this deterred Drew. He took to the new language effortlessly, learned how to spearfish, and got a solid tan. He spent hours sitting with the Chuukese men and flirted outrageously with the girls. George, Clark, and Ed, volunteers who were finishing up their two-year Peace Corps assignments and were spending the summer as our mentors and teachers, told stories of volunteers who “married” Chuukese girls for the duration of their stay. “They love Americans,” Clark said. “Yeah, they hope you’ll really marry them and take them back to the States, but if you don’t, and as long as you stay on the dad’s good side, it’s O.K. to take a Chuukese wife. Really.”

When training was over, Drew packed his duffle bag and headed solo to an outer island with a population of less than one hundred. The island had no electricity, drinking water was scooped from rain catchments, and his contact with the Peace Corps office would be a monthly grocery list he’d call in on the single-side-band radio. When, and if, he needed to hang out with other volunteers, he'd ride all day long in an open motorboat across the lagoon to the district center, Moen.

It took about six months before Drew needed a cold beer and a collegial atmosphere. "Well, did you find your island princess?" I teased. He led into his answer by talking about, of all things, petticoats. Thanks, or no thanks, to a strong missionary influence decades earlier, Chuukese girls were a lot more modest than Drew's topless Tahitian. They wore Puritan-inspired cotton dresses with square necks, puffed sleeves, full skirts, and fitted waists. The missionary mold broke wide open in the fabric choices though; riotous floral prints in hothouse colors. Under these graceful but modest confections they wore white cotton petticoats that were always two or three inches longer than the skirts, edged in bright rows of crocheted yarn.

"I had my eye on this really pretty girl from day one," he said. He told me she would walk down the beach past his hut every evening, giggling with her sister, teasing him with a mixture of shy and bold. All the signals were there. He was sure his fantasy was about to become reality.

On the evening Drew planned to make his move, he sat on a coconut log wondering what sort of pick-up line could possibly work in paradise. She walked toward him and, seeming to read his mind, smiled in that universal language that says "yes." Drew's stomach fluttered, he smiled back. Just then she reached down, took hold of the edge of her petticoat and lifted it to her face. With a most unfeminine snort, she enthusiastically blew her nose.

Linda Hagen Miller lived in Micronesia and Guam for nearly twenty years and credits her Peace Corps stint with kindling a passion for travel that has never left her. She now lives, writes, and travels from Spokane, Washington.

15 CELESTE BRASH

MAMA ROSE'S COCONUT BREAD

Her spirits rose with the dough.

MAMA ROSE IMPALED THE COCONUT ONTO THE WOODEN spike making a tear in the husk. Self-rolled cigarette hanging out the corner of her mouth, she continued with ease, lifting, turning, and thrusting the coconut on the spike till the husk fell away. Inside was a newborn, white nut with brown hairs. Picking up a cleaver she motioned for me to come look. She sat on a coconut wood stool, placed a large bowl between her ankles and then pointed at the three eyes at the top of the coconut. She drew an imaginary line with the cleaver across the three eyes. She lifted the cleaver, lowered it gently to position, raised it again then clack! With one whack the coconut split in half, the water falling into the bowl.

In the Tuamotu atolls of French Polynesia everything is done from scratch. If you want dinner you have to go fishing; even for a glass of water, rain is collected since there are no mountains, rivers, valleys, or potable groundwater in the arid atolls. This day we were baking coconut bread and, in a land of some of the most capable people on Earth, I was learning from the master.

What we couldn't learn about each other through words became irrelevant as the time we passed together, always working towards the same goal, created a bond like I had never experienced in Western society.

I had been living on Ahe atoll in French Polynesia for nearly two months. I had come in hopes of learning some lessons about hard work and self-sufficiency, to live with my boyfriend Josh who was helping his father start a black pearl farm. Ahe was an isolated place: it was a two-day boat trip from Tahiti, had no roads, no phones, and only one store in the village. Our farm was on an islet that was a wet and bumpy half-hour boat ride from the village, which we rarely went to, and I was the only woman living among six work-obsessed men. Lacking the physical strength of a man, I had been unable to feel useful in the workplace, diving and hauling oysters. I had felt that my femininity was a hindrance to myself and to my coworkers. Although I had always considered myself a strong, capable person, the vastness of the lagoon, the starkness of the land, and the lack of female counterparts on the farm made me feel frail and lonely. Mama Rose, who sold oysters to Josh's father, seemed to sense my unease and had started inviting Josh and me to spend weekends with her at her house on an idyllic islet about ten minutes by boat from our farm. Slowly, she began teaching me how to survive in a predominantly male environment that, before I met her, had seemed devoid of softness.

So it was that I visited her on a Saturday morning after she promised to teach me to bake coconut bread. Rose met me on her dock while her husband, my boyfriend, and a few workers from our farm went back out onto the lagoon to go fishing. She was dressed in a faded purple pareu that was rolled at the waist so that the hem touched slightly above her coffee colored knees. In a gesture of misunderstood religious prudishness, she wore a sexy black lace bra, at least one size too small, to cover her matronly breasts. Naked or in a nun's habit she would have maintained the same self-assured, natural manner in movement and attitude.

We walked along her white beach to her house: the bedroom, kitchen, and bathroom were constructed separately into three small, wooden structures with tin roofs. It was there that my lesson about coconuts began, culminating in the pitiless husking procedure.

Once we had husked and cracked several more coconuts (I managed to fumble through one), Mama Rose brought us to two coconut stools positioned at the blue lagoon's edge in the shade of a large leafy tree. A contraption that looked like a wooden cutting board with a round, serrated metal disk at the end was on each stool. She straddled hers.

"You, there," she said pointing at the other stool.

She spoke French, Tahitian, the local Paumotu dialect, and a little English. I spoke limited French. What we couldn't learn about each other through words became irrelevant as the time we passed together, always working towards the same goal, created a bond like I had never experienced in Western society. Our time and labor were being thrown in a bowl creating an unusual recipe for friendship that I was finding delicious.

As if, with the coconut carnage over, we could relax a little, she rolled another cigarette and smiled at me, exposing her perfect white teeth. They glinted in a sun ray and made me think that she blended perfectly into the sand and shimmering lagoon. I wondered how old she was; she could have been anywhere from thirty-five to fifty.

"Coco many work," she said.

"Yes," I said remembering that it had taken some time just to collect the coconuts along her palm-planted white sand beach. They needed to have fallen to the ground but not be rotted or sprouted. We had tested them by shaking them; if they were filled with water they were still fresh.

With another smile that made me feel like I had actually been helpful, Mama Rose picked up half a coconut and slowly, to show me, began to grate it against the serrated disk. Once I had more or less figured out the circular, two-handed grating technique, Rose picked up speed, eventually grating eight or more halves in the time it took me to grate two.

"Now my kitchen," she said lifting her bowl full of grated coconut while I picked up my nearly empty one.

Her kitchen was a small, square, plywood structure painted turquoise. The wood windows were propped open from the bottom letting in a slight breeze and a view of the lagoon. We put our bowls on the plastic table and Rose pulled out two gauzy dishrags and a smaller bowl. She put a large handful of grated coconut into one of the rags and squeezed it tight so the milk strained out into the small bowl. I tried mine, not getting out nearly as much milk but feeling a deep satisfaction of actually having produced coconut milk. It was almost like having learned how to turn water into wine.

Rose pulled out two boxes of "Paradise" brand flour, a sack of instant yeast, some sugar, salt, and a bottle of oil. Making the rest of the morning's work look like a slow-motion scene in an action flick, she threw together these ingredients along with the coconut milk, some coconut water, and a few handfuls of unsqueezed grated coconut, making sure I could see how much of each she used.

She then turned the dough out onto a large coconut wood cutting board and began to knead. The billowing dough mimicked the soft fullness of Mama Rose's belly, arms, and breasts while its sallow cream color contrasted with her healthy bronze skin. She moved rhythmically in an ellipse, forward and down, back and up, her movements graceful and strong. After a few minutes she stepped aside offering me a try. I imagined myself as I had seen her, confidently pushing the dough, but instead it was sticky on my hands and I felt like I was out of time with the silent music that she had been dancing to. Still, I continued, closing my eyes and listening to the breeze and gentle waves on the nearby shore. When I opened my eyes, Mama Rose was looking at me with her brilliant smile.

"You make good cooking you," she said as if I had discovered some secret.

We finished kneading and let the dough rise in a bowl covered with a dishrag.

While waiting for the dough to rise, Rose made us some coffee and we tidied up her kitchen then put some rice and water in a pot to prepare for lunch. She was in constant movement; there was always work to be done but it never felt rushed or unpleasant, just natural. It was as if we should feel lucky to have such pleasant work at our disposal.

We shaped the dough into five loaves and set them aside for a second rise.

Rose handed me a rake and we raked the leaves around her kitchen. Then we went and took her laundry down from the line and folded it.

The bread had risen high and firm above the edge of the bread pans. We put them into her heated oven and then sat down to drink some water while Rose lit another cigarette. The perfume of sweet coconut and fresh bread filled the kitchen and made me feel hungry. From the window I could see the men coming in from the lagoon from fishing.

As the men approached the kitchen, the bread was just coming out of the oven. We had no idea how long they would be gone, but somehow Mama Rose had it timed perfectly.

The look of delight on the shivering men's faces at the warm scent of the bread made Rose glow. It was then that I realized how important this "women's work" was, not just for the men but for the sanity of us all. Our bread was a jewel in the crown, the pillow under the head, the pleasure of life that was needed to keep the balance and make life on the island go on. Together with the men, we fried up the fish and set the table, starting our meal with the warm, soft, sweet bread.

Originally from the San Francisco Bay Area, Celeste Brash lived and worked as a cook on Kamoka Pearl Farm on Ahe atoll for five years. She currently lives on the island of Tahiti with Josh—now her husband—and their two children. She works as a Lonely Planet author and freelance writer and still bakes bread whenever she can find the time.

16

LAWRENCE MILLMAN

YAP MAGIC

Far from everywhere lies everything that matters.

It couldn't be anywhere else in the wide Pacific but Yap.

Behind me is a village meeting house whose thatched gable soars dramatically skyward. Arrayed around me like tutelary gods are giant, moss-flecked aragonite disks—the time-honored local currency that resembles the fossilized tires of an eighteen-wheeler. A young woman swishes by in a voluminous grass skirt that looks instantly combustible. Directly in front of me is a stone path worn smooth by centuries of bare feet and stained a picturesque crimson by betel-juice expectorations.

Traveling here from Guam, Micronesia's most Westernized island (the Kmart of the Pacific, a waggish friend calls it), can feel a bit like traveling to a faraway planet, although the distance is only 515 miles, a relatively short hop in this ocean.

But this faraway planet seems rather uninspiring at first.

None of Yap's four closely bunched islands—Map, Gagil-Tomil, Rumung, or Yap itself—is particularly scenic, at least not in the standard palm-clad, beach-grit, tropically seductive manner. There's dry pandanus scrub everywhere, the architecturally jumbled capital, Colonia, looks as if it had been modeled on an industrial park, and whole villages seem to be constructed out of aluminum siding, their architectural model a Greyhound bus.

But look more closely. In that admittedly drab pandanus you might see a medicine man or woman gathering plants for a magic elixir. One of those aluminum houses might boast a rope strung with stingray stingers, the ultimate in local home beautification. In fact, that same house may be resting on a stone dais that predates the invention of aluminum by hundreds of years.

Even Colonia has surprises. One day in a grocery store I saw a bare-breasted woman (in Yap, a bikini is licentious, bare breasts are not) who'd strapped a brassiere around her waist and was using its "pockets" to carry betel nuts.

The betel nut, in fact, is a perfect emblem for Yap. The green "nut," the seed of the betel palm, is as unassuming as an acorn on the outside. But when it's bitten open, mixed with powdered lime, and wrapped in betel pepper leaf, it produces a pleasurable high, along with a mouth condition that resembles terminal gingivitis.

So, too, Yap's true character lurks beneath the surface. There'll be a sudden storm, typical enough for the tropics, but then your guide will say, "Oh, such-and-such a *mach-mach* (shaman) called it up in a fit of pique."

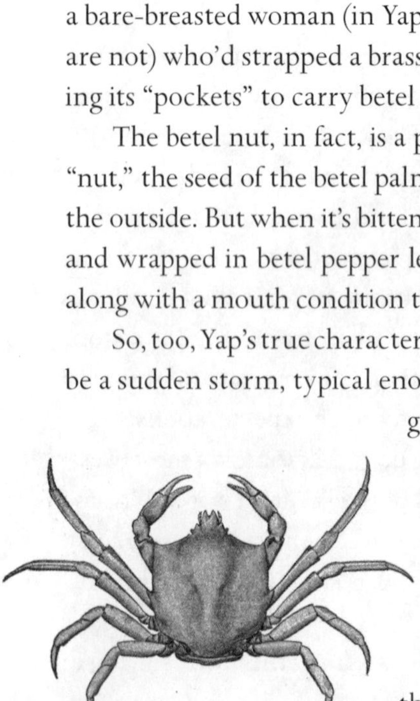

Or you'll notice someone gently ushering a small crab across a path—a kindhearted gesture to a lesser creature, you think. But you'll be told that some of these perambulating crustaceans are ancestral spirits, and to step on one would be disrespectful.

Or you'll see a man wearing a cap that advertises the Santa Monica Yacht Club, only to learn that he's a paramount chief and you must bow low in his presence.

In such a setting time loses all its compulsion. Early in my visit I got a bad scrape on some coral, so I went to the local hospital and asked the receptionist how soon I could see a doctor.

"Right away," she told me.

Two hours later I was still waiting…and fuming.

"You said it would be right away," I complained.

"Yes," she replied, "but when we say right away on Yap, we don't mean right away."

"Well, what *do* you mean, then?" I sputtered.

"Oh, four, five hours. Maybe tomorrow," she said blithely.

An hour later a man showed up with a fish spear stuck in his thigh. Extensive tattooing, varnished to bring out its blue tracery of bird and flower, gave his upper body the look of fretwork, and he was wearing a *thu*, a loincloth so spartan that it would have put a missionary to headlong rout. Right then and there I reckoned my wait within the context of centuries, not hours. Whereupon it did not seem long at all.

From my vantage point in the Yap village there was a glimpse of the wind-ruffled sea through the feathered tops of palm trees, the sound of tiny lizards clattering in the bush, and the more distant tap-tapping of an adze working a breadfruit log into a canoe.

Squatting down next to me was an old *mach-mach*, a man seemingly bequeathed from the Stone Age to the present age. Among his skills he numbered the ability to calm a typhoon, cast a spell on an unpleasant neighbor, and cure a toothache.

Right now, however, he was performing *pwue*, a palm leaf divination, in order to "read" my future.

Slipping four palm leaf strips between his fingers, he began tying random knots into each strip, all the while chanting softly to himself. When he was finished, he counted the knots—each represented a spirit helper who would provide him with some clue as to my future prospects.

The man now fixed me with his ancient gaze and said, in effect, "I'd watch out if I were you."

An islander, upon hearing this sort of warning, might take to his sleeping mat; a *mach-mach's* admonition is a serious matter.

But I wasn't from Yap. And, besides, I was less worried about my bleak future than the fact that I'd brought the old man the wrong kind of cigarettes—Winston instead of Benson & Hedges. I made partial amends for my mistake by offering him a handful of brightly colored balloons. What I really wanted to find out was whether he planned on being buried with his head above the ground, as high-ranking *mach-machs* once did, so they could keep a posthumous eye on things. But I figured it would be impolite to ask.

That same day I began hiking to a place called Qaloog. Located deep in the bush, Qaloog is a ghost town. Literally, a ghost town. The Yapese, many of whom refuse to go there refer to it as the Valley of the Kan, or ghosts, a testimony to its weird numen. According to my guide, Fawgomon, there was a stream in Qaloog that flowed uphill and eels that possessed an inordinate number of heads. And, of course, a profusion of *kan*.

Our path meandered through clumps of taro planted in splashy hollows before surrendering to the inevitable pandanus. We stepped carefully around the triply fluted, sword-like blades, each of which was edged with rows of fine spines. Fawgomon pointed out some *changad* trees, urging me to avoid them, too. He mentioned a friend who'd had a run-in with one that resulted in pieces of his skin falling off.

Now, the *changad* is a tall, respectable-looking hardwood whose bark sweats an acrid white sap that makes poison ivy seem as innocuous as a baby's bottom. So virulent is this sap that you only need to stand near a *changad* tree and shout the name of an enemy, and wherever that person is, he'll come down with the *changad* rash. Or so say the Yapese.

I was careful to give every *changad* I saw a wide berth.

After bushwhacking for a mile or so, and crossing a stream, Fawgomon announced that we were lost. He blamed this on the *kan*, who did not appreciate our thrashing through their territory. I blamed it on the absence of a compass and a topo map.

But at last we reached Qaloog. The village belonged to the jungle; its crumbling stone walls and derelict house foundations squinted at us from the dense vegetation. Only the elevated dais on which the local *mach-mach's* house had rested seemed to be intact. Leaning against this platform, half-buried in the ground, was Qaloog's stone money, or most of it—one piece had been stolen in 1996, Fawgomon said, whereupon a devastating typhoon had struck. (Stone money equals security.)

All of a sudden the silence was broken by a bird call—*oo-oo-oo-AW, oo-oo-oo-AW, oo-oo-oo-OH*. What was this bird? Could it be a Yap monarch, an indigenous bird I hadn't seen or heard yet?

Fawgomon frowned. "That's no bird," he said. He also told me that I was standing in a *taliw*, a taboo place, and to get out of it immediately. Only a *mach-mach* could venture into a *taliw* without fear of retaliation from the *kan* who lived there.

Fawgomon was obviously spooked. I was getting a little spooked myself, so I suggested we head back. Easier said than done. We slashed away at the vegetation, thrust aside cables of creeping vines, crossed and recrossed the stream, and succeeded only in getting lost again. We ended up in a clinging, crepuscular thicket, out of which I half expected a jabbering Ben Gunn to emerge.

In this situation, Fawgomon then did what any Yapese would have done—he stopped for a chew.

"There's wisdom in betel nut," he told me, citing a local adage. And sure enough, he noticed a familiar boulder nearby. It had once been a *kan* who'd made a specialty of harassing children, he said. So now he knew exactly where we were.

Our return hike couldn't have been easier. Soon we found a path that wound through the taro patch. Then minutes later we were driving back to the welcome jumble of Colonia.

All's well that ends well, or so I thought…

Yap is more culturally intact than its Micronesian neighbors, and for good reason—its contact with so-called civilization, at least in the eighteenth and nineteenth centuries, was minimal. The islanders attribute this to magic: Their *mach-machs*, they say, created ill winds that blew foreign ships away.

But since Yap was not as big a commercial entrepôt as Guam or Palau, most foreign ships did not come close enough to be blown away. Thus it seldom encountered the usual agents of cultural change in the Pacific—strait-laced missionaries, hard-living whalers, soft-living remittance men, and emissaries of rival powers. Even after Spain proclaimed its sovereignty over the islands in 1874, Yap did not suffer much change, for Spanish rule was characterized primarily by an absence of rule.

And although during this century Germany (1899-1914), Japan (1914-1945), and the United States (1945-1978) have all taken it under their improving wings, Yap has remained splendidly unimproved, resisting outside influences or making them uniquely its own. There are Yapese who'll proudly tell you that Adam and Eve came from Yap; there are also Yapese who insist

Back in my hotel room I began smearing myself with the herbal potion, which smelled like a jungly version of pesto. I smeared it on religiously, morning, noon, and night, per the medicine woman's instructions.

that the Christian God is really their trickster deity Iolofath in disguise.

And then, of course, there's the *rai*, or stone money. More than anything else, these Herculean disks proclaim Yap's allegiance to its own past.

"Long ago German people come, say only German money good," one Yapese man told me. "Then Japanese come, tell us German money bad and only Japanese yen good. Then Americans come. No more yen, take all away, only dollars good. Then we join FSM—Federated States of Micronesia—still use dollars. Someday maybe dollars no good!"

There are so many of these *rai* on Yap that they nearly qualify as a geographical feature. I saw them next to private houses, village meeting houses, men's houses, and elementary schools, bestowing whatever they rested against (even, in one instance, a sewage treatment plant) with prestige.

And after a while I began to think of them as almost human. I'd be so comforted by their hoary, grandfatherly presence that I'd feel no harm would come to me as long as they were in the vicinity. *There!* I was adopting the mind-set of the Yapese, who use their *rai* not only as collateral for loans but also apparently as hedges against calamity and misfortune.

Aragonite is not native to Yap, so the disks had to be quarried on Palau, 250 miles to the southwest, and brought back via sailing canoe or bamboo raft. The riskier the journey, the more valuable the disk: A typhoon or canoe capsized would create financial windfall. On Tomil there's a piece of stone money called "Without Tears," because no one died in its quarrying or on the voyage back to Yap; it has comparatively little value.

One day at Leang I saw a disk that looked rough-hewn, even unfinished. It was one piece of stone money that I definitely did not feel protected by, and I was curious about its story.

Long ago, the coin's owner told me, there was a very lazy fellow named Marrad. He went to Palau on a quarrying trip, but when he got back to Yap, Marrad tried to make a *rai*, and this specimen was the result.

"I guess it doesn't have much value," I said.

"Oh no," the man replied. "Very valuable. No one expects Marrad to do any work ever. He makes this *rai*. He makes it bad, yes, but at least he makes it. Very, very valuable *rai*.

I may have been wrong about the stone money keeping me out of harm's way. A day or so after my hike to Qaloog, what seemed to be a mass of itching bites appeared up and down my legs. Yet Yap's insects are generally so mild-mannered I couldn't imagine any of them making me itch so incessantly. I even itched underwater, snorkeling among manta rays in Miil Channel; and when I saw one of those slow-moving giants repeatedly scratch a pectoral fin against some coral, I felt a rush of fraternal sympathy for it.

Eventually, each of these so-called bites became fluorescent, then vividly pustular. I was not a pretty sight.

One night I showed my legs to a local at O'Keefe's Kanteen, a popular Colonia watering hole, and he immediately identified the source of my problem: It was *changad*. If you walk in a stream into which *changad* sap has dripped, he told me, the effect will be more or less like wrapping your legs around the actual tree. And

I had walked back and forth in Qaloog's stream many times—a stream that would have been brimming with *changad* sap.

What to do? I wasn't too keen on approaching the old *mach-mach* for help, since I figured he would wonder why I'd ignored his warning. And I'd already spent too much time at the Yap hospital, with little more than a philosophical attitude to show for it. So when I heard about a medicine woman who had a practice near Qokaaw village, I decided to visit her.

The woman studied my legs, studied me, and then said: "You are possessed by a *kan*."

"Possibly," I replied, "but my main concern is this blasted itching. Maybe you can give me a salve to ease it."

She spat out some betel juice and went on to explain that a female *kan* had attached herself to me. I'd probably picked up my *kan* in Qaloog when I wandered into the *taliw*. And as long as she was with me, I'd have bad luck. Not just bad luck—increasingly bad luck. My *changad*-related malaise was positively cheery compared to what would happen to me later on.

A sobering diagnosis. But my condition was not incurable, the woman said, and especially not incurable if I gave her a few packs of Marlboros. (Addiction to cigarettes would seem to be part of the stock-in-trade of a Yapese medicine person.)

Mercifully, her cure did not include a broth of bones, lizard skins, or fruit bat hair. Instead she gave me an herbal potion and instructed me in its application: I was to smear it on my body three times a day, always pushing outward, in order to push away the *kan*.

It was necessary that I perform this action an even number of times. An odd number, and I might be stuck with my *kan* forever.

"Will this potion make my itching go away, too?" I asked. "The itching comes from the *kan*," she replied.

She put a fresh quid of betel nut in her mouth, chewed for a moment, then looked me straight in the eye. The message was clear: Taboo places aren't amusement parks; don't go near one again.

Considerably chastened, I told her that I'd learned my lesson. As, indeed, I had. On Yap, one must respect the rules or else, my own else being the acquisition of a supernatural form of contact dermatitis.

Back in my hotel room I began smearing myself with the herbal potion, which smelled like a jungly version of pesto. I smeared it on religiously, morning, noon, and night, per the medicine woman's instructions. And on the fourth day my ghostly hitchhiker departed. At least I think she departed, because I was now hardly itching at all. Even my *changad* sores, previously so fierce-looking, had turned into vague pink splotches.

Yap's magic, it seemed, had worked wonders on my behalf.

My luck picked up as well. For days I'd been trying to get to Fais, one of Yap's outer islands and reputedly among the most traditional places in the western Pacific. Fais's only communication with the rest of the world was a not-very-reliable radio-telephone—the next best thing, I thought, to no communication at all.

Then I got a call from Peter Reichert, the pilot for Pacific Missionary Aviation. He was flying to Woleai Atoll tomorrow, he said, and could drop me off on Fais en route.

I was elated. I promptly dashed down to the governor's office in Colonia and got a permission form to visit Fais. (You need official clearance for any sort of travel to Yap's outer islands.)

The flight took only an hour and a half. Yet when I stepped out of Peter's nine-passenger plane, I entered a century that was distinctly not familiar. There were no automotive vehicles on Fais, except for one decrepit pickup with a shattered windshield. No one—man, woman, or child—was wearing Western clothes; not even the torn, permanently smudged t-shirts other Pacific islanders seem to consider the height of fashion. Nor did I see a single item of furniture anywhere, unless a pandanus mat counts as furniture.

At one point I began smoking my pipe, thus making myself a figure of intense scrutiny for half the island's children. They'd never seen a pipe before, so I passed around this strange smoke-belching object for their inspection. There were "ohs" and "ahs" of amazement, and one little girl tried to eat it.

Fais' heat was crushing, and after a few hours I began searching around for some sort of shelter. At last I found an official-looking structure with a thatched roof and small, low windows, ideal, I thought, for my purposes. I walked right in and upon hearing a chorus of nervous female giggles, rapidly walked right back out again.

Stupid me! I'd unwittingly blundered into the local menstrual hut. Another taboo violated, and doubtless another medicine person to visit, I told myself ruefully.

As I started looking for a less gender-specific refuge, I heard these words spoken in a pronounced southern accent: "Thank your lucky stars you're not a local, friend. If you were, you would have been fined heavily—probably your entire taro harvest—for that little boo-boo."

I met a shark fisherman and asked him what his tackle was. "I stick coconut in shark's mouth," he replied.

The speaker was a gnarled, bearded figure who looked like the proverbial South Seas beachcomber. In fact, Olney Cleveland Grover ("Just call me O.C.") was a beachcomber of sorts, a

Georgian who'd been a Peace Corps agricultural adviser on Fais and had long since gone native.

O.C. talked up a veritable storm, not, I realized, because he was lonely (although he did admit that he hadn't seen a fellow American in years), but because he couldn't say enough about this single square mile of raised limestone. Where else in the world was there an actual taboo on working during the summer? Where else could you find such a sweet-spirited people? Where else such utter tranquility? He was living in paradise, he said.

Paradise or not, Fais seemed to me like a happy mingling of the old Pacific with Monty Python's Flying Circus. The only book I saw on the island, a Bible, was being used for cigarette paper. I met a shark fisherman and asked him what his tackle was.

"I stick coconut in shark's mouth," he replied.

Then there was the man who pointed to a particular tree and solemnly informed me that its resident spirit was the cause of gonorrhea.

And presently I found myself paying my respects to the local chief, a venerable, elaborately tattooed man whose dignified posture while seated on his mat reminded me of a joss house idol. I joined him on a neighboring mat, making sure to hunch over so that my head was no higher than his.

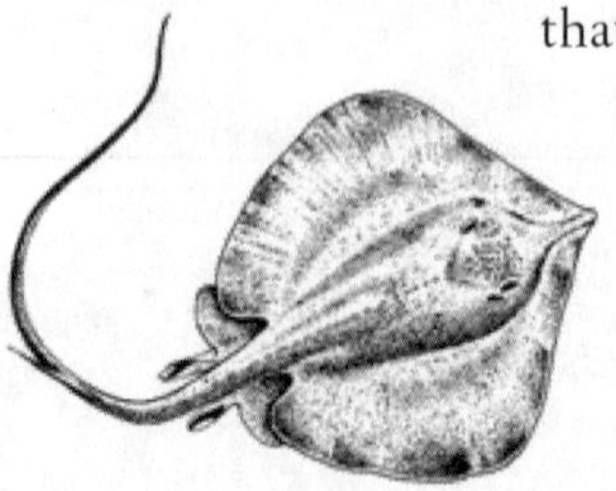

Through his grandson, who spoke some English, he asked me how I liked Fais. When I said that I liked it very much, although it was a bit difficult for a *wassola*, a foreigner like me, to get accustomed to topless women, the old man looked quite appalled.

"But all our women have heads," he declared.

As they glide almost imperceptibly through the water, slowly waving their massive wings, manta rays exhibit a Zenlike calm, compared to which other marine creatures look manic.

So it is with the Yapese themselves: All their motions seem governed by a stately languor, a hoarding of energy for some future time when flailings and wrenchings of bodily parts might be necessary. And yet there's often a reason for this apparent languor.

Consider the men who always seem to be lounging around a *faluw*, a men's house. Their inactivity is actually a survival tactic. For according to Yapese belief, the sea is a woman—and a very jealous one at that. Any male who incurs her wrath "won't see home again" (as one of my guides succinctly put it). Thus men submit to a lengthy period of celibacy in a *faluw* before they go fishing, a gesture designed to throw the sea off the scent of other, less aqueous women.

Although not a fisherman, I often hung out in a *faluw*, too. The mood of transcendent ease made me feel as blissful as a lotus-eater, as though I were experiencing a slow afternoon in eternity.

And one evening I had a dinner in Bugol village that gave me an excellent foretaste of what dinner will be like in eternity. The fruit bat hors d'oeuvre took several hours to cook, and then a neighbor dropped by, attracted by the bat's musky odor, and wanted one, too. Then my host's brother-in-law decided to go out and catch some land crabs, and that took a while. And then there was a betel nut break, and my host told a story about how the god Iolofath generously provided sharks with teeth, and that took a while, too. And then I ate gray matter that turned out to be taro root boiled into submission. (It tasted like carpenter's glue.)

This wasn't all. A sea turtle was still baking over the fire, and there was also a story my host wanted to tell me—now something of an authority on ghosts—about Yap's legendary female *kan*, Leebirang. But on a timeless island there's no reason why the experience of dining shouldn't be timeless, too.

Just before the turtle course, I went for a stroll to stretch my legs. The night was so quiet that my breathing sounded as blustery as a typhoon. I took care not to whistle; the Yapese say that if you whistle at night, you'll have very bad dreams.

At one point I looked up, and there was the Southern Cross sprinkled across the sky like a flourish of sequins. The Little Dipper seemed so close that I felt I could reach up and drink from it. There were stars twinkling and brilliant, stars that the Yapese use as navigational aids, and stars so indistinct that only someone with a powerful telescope could ever navigate by them.

And it seemed to me that all these stars, great and small, bright and demure, were beaming down a special benediction on a certain magical group of islands in the Far Pacific.

Paradise: Perhaps an ideal geography, unattainable in this world and maybe even unattainable in the next. Yet my dictionary also defines the word less fancifully as "a state of delight."

Toward the end of my trip, I was walking along an old stone path when I met a tattooed man wearing a red *thu* and carrying a clump of taro.

He stopped. I stopped.

"Where you from?" he asked

"America," I said.

"Oh," he exclaimed, "I from Yap," and continued walking down the path. A perfectly self-evident statement; yet somehow it left me with a feeling of delight that I retain months later, as I sit at my desk and write these words.

Lawrence Millman is the author of several books, including An Evening Among Headhunters: and Other Reports from Roads Less Traveled, Lost in the Arctic: Explorations on the Edge, Our Like Will Not Be There Again: Notes from the West of Ireland, *and* Last Places: A Journey in the North. *His work has also appeared in* Smithsonian, National Geographic, The Atlantic Monthly, Islands, *and other publications. He holds a Ph.D. in literature from Rutgers University, but considers having a mountain named after him (in East Greenland) one of his greatest accomplishments. He is a Fellow of the Explorers Club and has made twenty-five trips to the Arctic. When he is not traveling, he lives in Cambridge, Massachusetts.*

17 TONY PERROTTET

CROSS-DRESSING IN PARADISE

In Apia, the tropical languor is interrupted by Cindy's weekly transvestite show—where Polynesian tradition meets Madonna.

Apia, the capital of the Independent State of Samoa, is one of the last South Pacific ports that can still be described as "Maugham-esque." At dusk, fishermen in lava-lavas cast their lines from the decaying waterfront. Hymns waft dreamily from the choir practices in the churches; pairs of policemen wearing white pith helmets, like South Pacific bobbies, look chronically underemployed (in Samoa, the few prisoners even get to go home on weekends). Every eyelid is half-drooped, every face has a sleepy, contented smirk, as if all Apia is digesting a huge meal. It looks like nothing could rouse this town from its Polynesian paralysis.

But when I arrived on a Thursday night, things were going to be different—at least according to Tusi, the towering clerk at Ah Kam's Fullmoon Inn, who had intricate tattoos running from his knees to the middle of his back.

"You will go to see Cindy," he told me somberly. "We all go to see Cindy's show."

One by one, the Western stereotypes were pillaged: Cindy threw in a little fire-walking, plus a mock human sacrifice, with muscle-bound Samoan "warriors" grinding their pelvises to rap.

The attraction? Tusi was amazed I hadn't heard: Apia's weekly drag review—the climax of the social calender.

As elsewhere in the Pacific, cross-dressing has long been a part of cultural life in Samoa, mostly for adolescent boys. But in recent years, there has been a huge increase in the number of male transvestites, who take on female roles permanently. *Fa'afafine* (literally, "in the way of women") are now a fixture all over this tiny nation's two islands: Men who grow their hair long, wear floral dresses and vivid make-up can be met in every palm-fringed village.

Even so, Cindy's review sounded like a quantum leap for Samoan entertainment. So, like half of Apia, I made a beeline for Magrey Ta's Beer Garden, where the islands' most celebrated *fa'afafine* puts on her spectacular beneath the stars.

The place was packed. In front of an elaborate stage with an artificial waterfall, crowds of mountainous Samoans and curious *palangi* had gathered in the open air to knock back Vailima beer by the gallonful. Under the lurid green lights, truly monolithic bouncers were ready to crash-tackle anyone in the audience who flailed too wildly.

At the crack of 9 P.M., the lights dimmed, and an ear-splitting roar went up from the crowd as the lissome Cindy and her team of Rubenesque divas sashayed on stage in sequined nightgowns, then lip-synched their way through "Like a Virgin." It was a professional turn that would have impressed the best in New York's Greenwich Village, and no opportunity for innuendo went untouched. Soon Cindy came back with a solo, a Whitney Houston classic, followed by more Madonna, all the while tossing in flirtatious exchanges with the audience.

At first, the show just seemed like a fun, kitschy import from the West—*Priscilla* with a tropical twist—but soon events proved to be uniquely Samoan. To a throbbing disco beat, the dancers came back in grass skirts, with frangipani in their hair. It was a spoof on the chintzy "Polynesian nights," called *fia-fias*, which had been brought wholesale from Hawai'i in the 1970s, to tourist hotels across the islands. One by one, the Western stereotypes were pillaged: Cindy threw in a little fire-walking, plus a mock human sacrifice, with muscle-bound Samoan "warriors" grinding their pelvises to rap.

All in all, it was the last thing I'd come to expect from sleepy, buttoned-down, church-going little Apia.

"So this sort of thing goes on a lot here?" I asked a couple of Samoan women in the next chairs, who had been squealing approval.

"Oh, yes. *Fa'afafine* have been a part of the culture in Samoa for thousands of years."

"Thousands?"

"Hundreds, maybe," she shrugged. "But we adore Cindy."

Back at the bar, the men were no less into the show. The tattooed Tusi was bellowing compliments I later learned included *faipopolo* ("hanging balls") and *ga'au tele* ("big tube").

"Isn't she beautiful?" Tusi grinned. His girlfriend, hanging from his shoulder, cried: "I want my son to grow up like Cindy!"

Samoans may seem a little vague on the history of *fa'afafine*, but Western anthropologists have taken an avid interest—after all, ever since doyenne Margaret Mead first wrote her tome *Coming of Age in Samoa* in the 1920s, studies of the islands' sexual habits have been an academic cottage industry. It seems that Cindy and friends are tapping into a key island tradition, taking over a role once played by women in the pre-Christian era.

Before the arrival of missionaries in the 1830s, jokes about sex were a part of daily life in Samoa. Young Samoan women used to perform nighttime shows in the villages, full of raucous games, teasing, and crude references (observed one appalled missionary: The flower-garlanded girls behaved "like a lot of demons let loose from below.") These village shows allowed for erotic contact between the sexes, and helped educate young Samoan men about the mysteries of the flesh.

But once the Puritanical portcullis of Christianity fell on Samoa, women were expected to be demure and virginal in public. Banter died out. The elaborate courtliness of Samoan society was extended to cover sexual matters: Anyone who made an obscene joke in the presence of a man's sister, for example, could now only expect a crack over the head. (In private, sexual mores were rather less strict than the pastor preached—although hardly the orgiastic free-for-all Mead imagined.)

Enter, in a roundabout way, the *fa'afafine*. Since the 1970s—as urbanization and Western culture have increasingly hit the islands—transvestites have resurrected the exhibitionism of pre-Christian women. They can pass on obscene jokes between the sexes without offending anyone's honor. And spectacles like Cindy's might be seen as a modern revamp of the old village shows, where sexual matters are back out in the open. Only these days, the *fa'afafine* often take on the sexually expressive "feminine personae" of the Madonnas of the world—using Western images brought in by TV, video, radio, and bikini-clad tourists, which are theoretically too risqué for Samoan women.

"It's an ironic social commentary on modernity," observes Jeanette Mageo, an anthropologist at the Washington State University. "Western cultural images obviously have their attraction, but they are also potentially threatening. Samoans are playing with what they see—accepting a part of one image, rejecting another. It's not really a return to the past, but a historical process: Cultures are always going someplace new."

And having a good time on the way, she adds.

Sitting there beneath the stars, watching Cindy's "gals" bump and grind in golden tutus, all the heady social theorizing did seem a bit remote.

In between sets, I dropped back to meet the star herself. Cindy had a sculpted figure, almond eyes, and the throaty voice of a Polynesian Tallulah Bankhead. Like many in this peripatetic island nation, she was brought up in New Zealand, where she had been able to participate in more high-tech cross-dressing shows than Samoans could then dream of. Soon, she decided to bring the bright lights and sounds to Apia, "because I thought it would be fun," and was delighted that she has become an institution so quickly. "They do adore me," she said, batting her long lashes. "And why not? Aren't I fabulous?"

With that, the star put on a leonine wig, stormed back on stage as "Mr. Tina Turner" and broke into a climactic performance of "What's Love Got to Do With It?," bringing the Samoans to their feet and stomping so hard that it felt like the concrete floor was about to crack.

Whatever else, you had to think, Apia's energy level had certainly found a boost.

Tony Perrottet also contributed "A Fale *with a View" on page 55.*

18

JEFF HULL

PADDLING A CHAIN OF PEARLS

The old ways of the sea are kept alive for all of us.

FARE, THE MAIN VILLAGE ON THE ISLAND OF HUAHINE, IS usually a first-gear sort of town: one empty tree-shaded lane running between a line of shops and restaurants and the quay. But on this evening, Fare is aswirl with people. *Roulottes*—trucks with kitchens built on the back—line the quay, doing brisk trade in *poisson cru* (raw fish blanched in coconut milk and lime juice), baguettes, and pastries. Old women at folding tables sell vanilla, taro, mangoes, papayas, and foot-long green beans.

On the wharf, a band is playing, and a woman in a long green pareu sings in Tahitian and French. She seems to be serenading a huge striped marlin hanging from a lift, shining in the setting sun like a silver ingot—the winning entry in a fishing tournament. The lagoon is tranquil, and the wind is cool off the sea, ruffling t-shirts and blouses.

On any other day, this twenty-eight-square-mile island (actually two islands connected by a bridge and surrounded by *motu*) would be a sleepy place. Though it is a short forty-minute flight from Tahiti, Huahine—with a few shops, enough restaurants to cater to either romance or indulgence, and only a couple of resorts—is considered to be one of Polynesia's best-kept secrets and a place where the ancient culture lives on.

This Tuesday in October, on the eve of Hawaiki Nui Va'a, the world's longest and most grueling ocean canoe race, the streets are crowded with squads of young men with flowing black hair, skin filigreed with Tahitian tattoos, and muscles so clearly defined that they resemble walking anatomical sketches. They are the paddlers. Tomorrow, more than seventy slender outrigger canoes will launch from Huahine on a three-day, eighty-three-mile open-ocean slog through wind, swells, and merciless sun in the race from Huahine to Raiatea and Tahaa, ending in Bora Bora.

Tonight, however, there is song, dance, and feasting. I pull up a chair at Chez Guynette, the social hub located on the main street, and watch women in colorful pareus and flower tiaras and burly men, with scrolls of tattoos, drink cold Hinano beer and laugh.

For many, the Hawaiki Nui Va'a is a social event, an excuse to see relatives and friends from other islands they may see only once a year. It's a chance to brag about how the local canoe teams did last season and speculate about their chances this year. In French Polynesia, canoe racing is what soccer is to Europeans, hockey to Canadians. Straight through the culture of Huahine and the Tahitian islands—from the chain's earliest human visitation more than a thousand years ago to the carnival atmosphere quayside the night before the Hawaiki Nui Va'a—glides the canoe.

Many things have disappeared from Tahitian culture—tattoos, dance, tikis—and most have returned. Canoes never left. Huahine is where the oldest voyaging canoe ever found in the South Pacific was discovered, a canoe dated between A.D. 850 to A.D. 1100. It turned up when bulldozers were excavating reflecting pools for Hotel Bali Ha'i (now defunct) near Fare. The discovery of the Bali Ha'i canoe—and the excavation of that site in the 1970s by Dr. Yosihiko Sinoto of Honolulu's Bishop Museum—expanded on existing information of the origins of Polynesian culture.

What has also been found on Huahine is the most extensive collection of ancient ceremonial sites in Polynesian culture. Not far from Fare, in the village of Maeva, stands a great stone platform, a restored *marae*, where high priests interacted with their gods. Other *marae* are scattered behind it, on Mata'ive'a Hill, part of sacred mountain Mou'a Tapu. In ancient times, Maeva was the bustling hub of Huahine and all friendly visitors arrived by canoe. "If you come in a canoe, everybody sees you," explains Mark Eddowes, a British archaeologist from New Zealand. "You're coming in an honest way. You're vulnerable. If you come through the forest, people think you're sneaking over to steal women or pigs."

Canoes are still the main means of transportation, and as a boy growing up in a house built on a sandbar in a lagoon, Manutea Owen used his canoe to paddle back and forth to the schoolbus stop every day. Now twenty-three, Manu is the *peperu*, or man in the stern, on Huahine's own Fare Ara team and a star in the Society Islands. The day before the race begins, I wait for Manu at the launch site for the Fare Ara paddling club, across the harbor from Fare.

Here, along a patch of grassy shore lined with canoes, the Huahine paddlers gather, discussing the grueling nature of the race. They will paddle as hard as they can for four hours from Huahine to Raiatea tomorrow, two hours around the Raiatea lagoon, and to Tahaa the next day, and then they will finish with a five-hour gut check from Tahaa to Bora Bora the final day.

"Most of the pain," says Claude Chong, who has been paddling for twenty years, "is in the head." Morale, he says, is the hardest thing to keep up. "It is important to the island that we win."

When Manu arrives, he bumps fists with his teammates. He is tall and sleek, thinner than most paddlers. Manu's maternal grandfather, a native of Tahiti's Tuamotu Archipelago, was a world-champion spearfisherman. Manu's mother, Ghislaine, runs the island's pearl farm with Manu's father, Peter Owen, an American.

"Being on Fare Ara is a big dream of kids growing up here," Manu says. As a boy, Manu could never pack enough muscle onto his lithe frame to compete, so he stuck to surfing. Still, his canoe was his primary way of getting around. "When I wanted to go see someone, I had to take my canoe," Manu says. "My friend Toto, where he lives, there is no road."

It was Toto, he says, who made Manu the racer he is today. "Toto is a champion. He said, 'Train with me for a month, and we'll race in the one-man championships in Huahine.' He taught me technique and helped me build my strength. I came in second in front of most of the guys on Fare Ara. So I earned a place on the team."

Ironically, his years of not being strong enough to canoe on the team allowed Manu to develop a skill: Surfing taught him how to maximize the speed of waves, critical in open ocean racing. Soon he was the stern man for Fare Ara, steering the team to victory after victory.

In the morning, he would lead his boat against entries from all across the South Pacific—Tahiti, Hawai'i, New Caledonia—trying to defend their title, last year's Hawaiki Nui Va'a crown.

Wednesday morning, race day, I am at the quay in Fare by 8 A.M. A crowd fills every inch of waterfront. When the Hawaiki Nui Va'a race begins—out of sight, in the next bay of Fitii, eventually to paddle across Fare's harbor—I am standing beside Oscar Temaru, the president of French Polynesia. (Due to nasty political upheaval, President Temaru would be voted out of office in two days, and then, after an occupation of government buildings by his supporters, re-elected five months later.) President Temaru stands on a pier amid thousands of race fans, wearing a loose white shirt, two leis of white flowers, and a tall straw hat, its cannon wrapped in black beads. His downslanted eyes are fixed on the line of canoes—dashes of color—that slowly come into view across the bay. I ask if he has paddled.

"Oh, we all have paddled," President Temaru says, lifting a hand to include the crowd. "We had to paddle to go fishing. There were no engines. We have been practicing paddling for years. It used to be our means to cruise the ocean, since the Stone Age. Now, these people..." again a gesture to include the Polynesians shouting over the lagoon, cheering the oncoming canoes, "they come from Bora Bora, Raiatea, Tahaa, Tahiti. They are all here supporting their clubs. It's good to see our boys and girls doing sports instead of drinking alcohol, taking drugs and all that. We are here to support them."

The canoes leap from the horizon, a cluster of evenly stroking paddlers. I can imagine a warring tribe, invaders from another island, approaching Huahine like this: silent, swift, metronomical, inevitable. The crowd begins rumbling, then crying encouragement. Shell Va'a and Ra'i, both formidable teams from Tahiti, vie for the lead as they round the buoy and head through the pass to the open sea. Fare Ara struggles in fifth. Then the canoes are past, the lagoon empty. Motorboats are sucked from the harbor as they follow the race to Raiatea. On land a slow exodus drains

An eagle ray cruises by. I drift through a blizzard of small neon blue-and-white fish that looks like confetti falling up.

Fare. President Temaru ambles off the dock and lowers himself into a waiting Renault for the drive to the airport and his return to the capital.

The racers departed, Huahine is back to its quiet self. Near the southern tip of the smaller of the two islands that comprise Huahine sits a lovely collection of bungalows and guest houses called Pension Mauarii. About three-quarters of a mile west of Mauarii, at the south end of the island the road has a small pullout. I park there, strap on my snorkel and fins, and head for the line dividing the lagoon into pale aquamarine and deep ultramarine. Soon I am soaring over towers and turrets of coral. Fish flit about: a pair here, a squad there, the motion of color always surprising. An eagle ray cruises by. I drift through a blizzard of small neon blue-and-white fish that looks like confetti falling up.

Later, at the Mauarii's open-air dining room, where tables are slabs of tree trunks, I order *varo*, which resembles a cross between a lobster and a praying mantis with sling-blade arms. The meat is delicious—the consistency of lobster, only a bit less sweet and rich. The weather closes fast and soon rain pours into the sea in a long tearing sound.

By the time I reach Fare and order a beer at Chez Guynette, the results of the first leg of the race are in: Fare Ara has finished third, five minutes off the lead. On TV, in the post-race interview, Manutea Owen looks disappointed but stalwart. His teammates, he says, gave their all. There are two more days of paddling. But it's obvious that Fare Ara has a tough row to hoe.

On Thursday, as the teams paddle to Tahaa, I drive the island's east coast toward the place Manu grew up. I stop along a rushing stream, where eels as long and thick as my leg ripple in the current, their pale blue eyes just visible beneath the surface.

Just up the road from the eel stream in Faie, I find the boat launch for the Huahine Pearl Farm. The boat takes me a few hundred yards away, to the farm on a coral head in the middle of the lagoon, where Manu's parents, Ghislaine and Peter, cultivate and sell black pearls. They also produce pottery, vivid pieces that seem to have been fired beneath the sea; in fact, Peter colors his glazes with clay from the lagoon floor. The creations feature Polynesian motifs, many of which have been designed by Manu. Today, Peter and Ghislaine are out, watching the race and rooting for their son's team.

Pearls and pottery in hand, back on the main island, I stroll along the sea to the place where, hundreds of years ago, the princess Hotu Hiva washed ashore in a wooden drum, according to local legend. The story is that she gave birth to all eight of Huahine's royal lineages. Nearby is a *marae.* I walk between its stone walls, trying to imagine the platform lined with the fetishes that would have stood here centuries ago, god images made of ironwood wrapped with tapa cloth, oyster shells, feathers, and human bone and hair of the deified ancestors. I remember that Eddowes said that the *marae* and the area around it would have been more shaded, jungled. A *marae* was a doorway to the heavens of the ancestors, he had said. For the ancestors to be comfortable, they needed a dark place. Even in the sunshine, it chills me to realize that humans were occasionally sacrificed on this platform, in that shady world.

Walking back to my car, I see a man who is stacking equipment in a pickup truck, his radio blaring excited French diatribe, which

I realize is either coverage of Hawaiki Nui's second leg, or Gaston Flosse, defending his ousting of former President Temaru.

"Paddling or president?" I ask.

"Paddling," he says. "They are ninth."

While Manu and his Fare Ara teammates paddle the five-hour slog between Tahaa and Bora Bora on Friday, I explore the culture's ancient past. The thatch-and-*mara* waterfront Fare Pote'e, or gathering house, near the many Maeva *marae* is the loveliest building on Huahine. It houses artifacts and interpretive displays, illuminating the lives of the ancestors, called Maohi, whose canoe was found at Bali Ha'i.

On a two-mile hike up Mata'ire'a Hill, I think about what Etienne Faaeva, who was born on Huahine and owns a pension and campground on the island, told me earlier.

The canoe, Etienne had said, is inseparable from traditional life. "On the *marae* there's a canoe shelter. This tells you the canoe's importance." Like many Tahitians of his generation, Etienne has made an effort to understand the Polynesian customs and traditions once banished by English missionaries and French colonials. We also talked of the race. Etienne mentioned Fare Ara always finishes in the top four.

Fare Ara battles valiantly in the final leg, pulling into a fourth-place finish. Ra'i wins the 2004 Hawaiki Nui. Another year of practice and of big races in Tahiti and Hawai'i loom before Huahine will have another chance to challenge for the paddling world's top spot. Still, what better place to spend a year paddling?

On Saturday, Fare returns to itself. A man walks down the street dangling a purse of reef fish from a palm frond stringer. A woman with beautiful white hair breezes by on a bike, wearing an orange-and-white flowered pareu. Locals buy mangoes, yellow watermelon, and chocolate cake from street vendors, and kids run from the pier and leap into the bay. In the harbor, a canoe heads east while two others glide west.

Late afternoon, I take the launch back to Te Tiare Beach Resort on a small bay on the west coast of the island, unreachable by road. As we cross the lagoon, I watch as the sun peers around clouds to gleam on two sailboats. Sacred mountains tower overhead, into the slopes of which were carved, so long ago, the temples of a thriving culture. These ancient people had the same view of the sea as I have now: a man in a canoe lifting the paddle clear of the water, stained by golden light, his torso twisting with each stroke. The paddler is no racer or star, just a man off on a visit or perhaps returning home. This, I see, is exactly how life goes on here, and always has.

Jeff Hull's work has appeared in numerous publications, including The Atlantic Monthly, Outside, Audubon, Men's Journal, Travel & Leisure, National Geographic Adventure, National Geographic Traveler, *and* Islands. *He lives in Montana.*

19 BOB PAYNE

FACES OF THE PAST

Mysteries abound on Easter Island.

FOUR YEARS AGO, THIRTY-FOUR-YEAR-OLD JOSEFINA MULLOY was living in San Francisco, about a decade into a successful career with the Bank of America. Now she is a tour guide on Easter Island, where, when she was married last year, the wedding gifts included three cows and box upon box of frozen chickens to help feed the 600 guests.

"Yes, it's a long way from San Francisco, not just geographically, but in my mind," she told me one afternoon as we sat on the porch of the little house where she and her husband, Ramon Edmunds Pakomio, live with her eighty-one-year-old grandmother.

I had met Josefina through Ramon, himself a guide, whom, ostensibly, I had hired to show me the giant stone statues, known locally as *moai*, that have become an almost universal symbol for all that is mysterious about man's relationship with the planet. But I was as curious about what the island is like now as I was about its enigmatic past, so I had hired Ramon also to begin learning about how local people work, think, and live.

I had already found out much about this forty-six-square-mile triangle of hilly volcanic terrain, most of it covered by short grass that shades from green to gold with the rains and the dry spells. Administered by Chile, which lies more than two thousand miles to the east, Easter Island is home to some three thousand six hundred people, most of whom speak Spanish but are ethnically Polynesian. Its nearest populated neighbor, tiny Pitcairn Island, is 1,200 miles to the west, making Te Pito o Te Henua, or The Navel of the World, as the locals sometimes call it, one of the most geographically isolated points of human habitation on earth. Yet it is so easy to reach that during my twenty-three hours and forty-five minutes of travel from New York via Santiago, Chile, the only real stress (other than having to watch the same movie three times) was that the customs officials in Santiago insisted on hearing more than once why I was carrying packages of flower seeds, all of which they confiscated.

The seeds were for the couple in whose home I would be staying, in one of the three rooms they rent out to visitors. When I was making arrangements with them via e-mail, I asked if there was anything I could bring from the States. The husband said his wife would be delighted, if it wasn't too much trouble, with some flower seeds for the garden in their front yard.

It was a garden, he said, that she was very proud of, and deservedly so. Unbeknownst to me, however, Chile prohibits the importation of certain agricultural products, including flower seeds. The Easter Islanders, or Rapa Nui, as the locals of Polynesian descent call themselves and their island, are not overly concerned with prohibitions imposed on them by mainland Chile, or "El Conti," with which they have a sometimes contentious relationship.

Where did they come from? What brought them? Why and how did they carve the giant statues and move them, even though some weighed more than eighty tons, all over the island?

I had learned from Ramon that in recent years there had been an explosion of taxis on the island, mostly brought over and operated by Chileans newly arrived from El Conti. (There was a derogatory term meaning "weeds," that was often used for the newcomers.) It takes only about seven minutes to walk from one end to the other of Hanga Roa, the town where almost all the island's residents live, but most people, including locals, now pay a dollar to ride.

"We have become used to the comfort," Ramon said.

I also learned from him that in the high tourist season, between November and February, he and Josefina each earned $700 to $1,000 a month—a reasonable income on the island. Because they own their home and, like all Easter Islanders, pay no income taxes, they are able to put more money in the bank now than Ramon did during the years he lived in California. Their only real expenses are food, water, gas, and what I have discovered is considered a necessity around the world, "Internet connection charges."

But what I learned about Josefina fascinated me the most. In a surprising way, she was a link not only between Easter Island and the wider world, but also between the Easter Island of today and the Easter Island of those shadowy times that gave rise to such as yet unanswered questions as: Who were the island's first inhabitants? Where did they come from? What brought them? Why and how did they carve the giant statues and move them, even though some weighed more than eighty tons, all over the island? And why did the carvers suddenly—possibly in a single day—lay down their carving tools forever, leaving hundreds of statues unfinished?

Until four years ago Josefina would have been indistinguishable from many other young California career women.

"But then I realized work was all I seemed to be doing," she told me as we sat on the porch, shaded by a tree that, like every other tree in the yard, had been planted by some family member for whom it had great sentimental value, and thus could not even be trimmed without a family conference. "And I couldn't imagine how my married friends, who were working as hard as I was, could have a family and children. How do you spend fourteen hours a day at a job and then go home and have quality time with your kids? So I decided to take some time off and see what I really wanted to do."

After considering all her options, she chose one not likely available to her peers at the Bank of America: She decided to go "home" to Easter Island.

On her mother's side, Josefina Nahoe Mulloy is the granddaughter of the late William Mulloy, an American said to have been the only professional archaeologist on Thor Heyerdahl's 1955-56 expedition to the island. Through her father, Guillermo Nahoe Pate, she traces her ancestry back to Easter Island's first inhabitants. According to local legend, they arrived aboard canoes with the first king, Hotu Matua, around the fifth century A.D., from a place that has been lost in time but which most Rapa Nui believe was probably one of the Polynesian island groups thousands of miles to the west.

"I was born in the U.S., but I have always considered myself American Rapa Nui," Josefina said. "And after my first visit eleven years ago, I knew that someday I would be back here to live."

Now, with Ramon, whom she met years ago and became reacquainted with on her return, she is adjusting to island life.

"I've changed quite a bit since I came back," she said. "One of the most difficult things for me at first was to accept that to do nothing was O.K. It was like, 'What am I if I am not doing something?' But now I have learned to be happy doing simple things, like spending time with my family or doing nothing at all."

In fact, Josefina and Ramon are often doing one thing in particular: sharing what they know about their island and their ancestry with visitors from the outside.

It was mostly Ramon who shared the ancient side of the island with me. In my rented, bright red Suzuki, we visited some of the sites tourists come to see and talked about the questions they most often ask. (Actually, we didn't talk about the two I heard most often, which were: "Is there an ATM on the island?" No. "Is there an Internet café?" Yes, but its hours are erratic.)

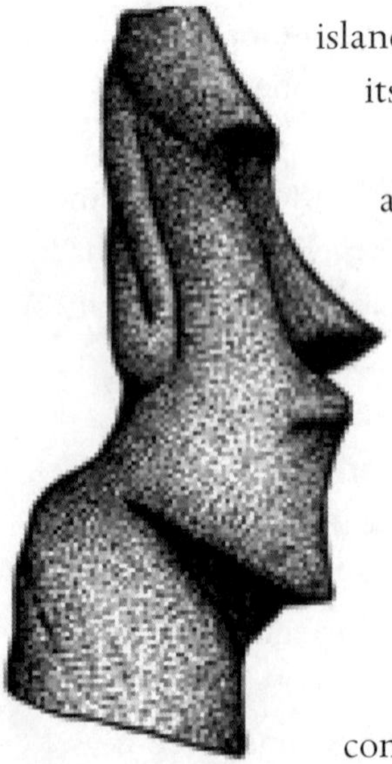

The *moai*, humanlike figures almost always shown from the hips up, number close to nine hundred, according to a survey conducted a few years ago by archaeologist Jo Anne Van Tilburg. The smallest are about four feet tall; the largest (one enormous uncompleted figure) is just under seventy-two feet tall. The *moai* are scattered all around the island—often as if tossed about haphazardly or abandoned during transport—but are concentrated along the coast. They are often tumbled over next to stone platforms, called *ahu*, on which they once stood. Less frequently, they stand on the platforms, where they have been re-erected in modern times.

There are other curiosities, including petroglyphs of animal and human figures; stone dwellings shaped like overturned boats; the ancient ceremonial village of Orongo, associated with a cult of birdmen; and copies of wooden tablets, called *rongo-rongo*, covered with writing whose meaning has long been lost.

We couldn't visit everything, so we concentrated on the sites of most interest to me, beginning with Anakena, a little cove with a pretty crescent of white-sand beach on the far side of the island. I remembered it vividly from Thor Heyerdahl's 1958 book, *Aku-Aku*, because of an accident that occurred while his ship was anchored there, resulting in the drowning of two island children, including the mayor's daughter.

At Anakena, Ramon related to me the legend that Hotu Matua and the first canoe had landed on the beach (there would have been few other alternatives along the island's rock-bound coast). I told him my theory that Heyerdahl had been right in suggesting that the stone culture was created by ancient Incas; that the Polynesians, who were far superior sailors, had gone over to South America and fetched the Incas back—perhaps unwillingly, which could be why every one of the *moai* seems to be pouting.

Despite that long-ago accident involving Heyerdahl's expedition, the beach at Anakena is a popular swimming spot. But most of the time we were there the only other people we saw were a Rapa Nui man who was an artist and the German woman who lived with him in a stone hut, near a point where waves broke with great authority onto the rocks. Among the woman's own theories on Easter Island culture, which she shared with us while we drank coffee out of tin cups at an outdoor dining table fashioned from gray driftwood, was that the red stone topknots that originally crowned many of the statues were not hair or hats, as people often supposed.

"It is plain to see," she said, "that the *moai* is the abstraction of a penis. So why would an erect penis have a hat?"

It was apparently a rhetorical question, because before I could answer—and I could think of several scenarios involving a penis in which a hat might be useful—she answered for me, in a tone you could only call triumphant: "Because it is not a hat; it is a female sexual organ on top."

At Ahu Tongariki, near the southeastern tip of the island, fifteen *moai* were re-erected in the early 1990s by a Japanese company, which used a crane for the job. Because of concerns about stability they replaced only one topknot, which, I have to admit, I studied with more intensity than I might have before talking with the woman at Anakena.

One of the fascinating things about those particular *moai* was that in 1960 an earthquake that killed thousands in Chile, more than two thousand miles away, created a tsunami that roared onto the shore and scattered the *moai* across the lava field behind them like so many multi-ton bowling pins. Moving the *moai*, even with modern man-made devices, has not proven easy, as the Japanese discovered while adding to the unresolved debate about how the ancients did it.

As we crouched at the base of the platform and sifted through rubble that contained everything from seashells to human teeth, Ramon told me that at least a dozen transport theories had been put forward. There's the traditional one—that some kind of supernatural power gave the *moai* a mana that allowed them to walk upright (which may explain why no *moai* was ever moved until it was completely carved, down to the eye sockets, though that would seem to increase dramatically the possibility of damage during transport). And there are variations involving pulling or prying using sizable timbers, which today, at least, the island notably lacks. Theorist Erich von Däniken even proposed that the statues were created and transported by stranded alien astronauts, who used them as some kind of rescue beacon. Considering all the broken *moai* lying around, one would think that if it had been space aliens, such technologically superior beings would have found a way to be a little neater.

But there was something more intriguing to me than how the *moai* were moved, how they were made to stand upright, or how the topknots, which were carved separately from a different type of volcanic rock, were put on top. What most fascinated me was an aspect of ancient Easter Island culture made apparent by a visit to the most famous site of all, the dormant volcano known as Rano Raraku, or "the nursery," where almost all the *moai* on the island were quarried and carved.

Although radiocarbon dating seems to indicate that Easter Island's first residents had arrived by the fifth century, at about the time the Roman Empire was coming to an end, the culture didn't really blossom until the seventh or eighth century. Again on the evidence of radiocarbon dating, most of the statues were probably carved over a period of a few hundred years, the last of them just 150 years before the first confirmed sighting of the island by a European, Dutchman Jacob Rogge-veen, on Easter Sunday in 1722.

Considering the way the statues of Easter Island have taken hold of the world's imagination as one of the ancient, almost ageless, mysteries, I was amazed by the brevity of the period during which they were created. After an afternoon of crawling around on Rano Raraku, I was even more amazed by the evidence of how abruptly the statue carving had come to an end.

The outer face of the volcano is a steep slope—in some places almost a vertical wall—of grayish volcanic tuff, up which wanders a switchback path that Ramon and I took late in the afternoon to avoid the midday heat and the minibuses of other visitors. On its outer slope, at its base, and, to a lesser degree, on the inner slope of the crater, there were, by Van Tilburg's count, 397 *moai*, or 45 percent of all the statues that exist. Some, including a few photographed so often that they form most people's image of Easter Island, stand buried up to their chins at the base of the outer slope. But the majority, including the seventy-two-foot giant, lie on their backs, in various stages of completion. I saw none of the *toki*, or stone tools, used to carve them, but it has been noted that until as recently as Heyerdahl's time they were lying around everywhere, as if the carvers had simply dropped them one day and walked off the job.

From our vantage point high on the slope we could see other evidence of an abrupt end. To the north, strung out across a grassy volcanic plain, was a line of completed statues, all lying face up, where they had been left literally by the side of an ancient road. Van Tilburg has said that those *moai* abandoned in transit account for another 10 percent of the total. All of which has prompted many people to ask, "What could have gone so catastrophically wrong, so suddenly?"

Nobody really knows, but one theory, Ramon told me, is that an obsession with creating the statues depleted the island's resources to the point of collapse, bringing on ecological disaster, tribal war, and, eventually, the near destruction of the society. In the end, during Easter Island's version of the Dark Ages, famine spread across the island, cannibalism arose, and the statues were toppled. Some people have said, Ramon told me, that what happened on that isolated spot in the middle of the Pacific ought to be a lesson to the world at large. Easter Island is not just a cultural treasure, they have said, but a warning to the planet.

So you can imagine my distress when, over the next few days, while driving around with Ramon, or off on my own at one of the island's ten restaurants (where fresh grilled tuna was my preference at almost every meal), I heard a theme repeated often. In the words of Mayor Petero Edmunds, it was, "The world is losing Easter Island."

Despite its isolation, the mayor told me, Easter Island is a community like any other, with many of the problems communities everywhere face.

"This year there is more garbage than last, more cars on the road, more problems with sewage and electricity," he said, adding that because the island has little money to do anything about it, "we are in more danger, with each day that passes, of losing this world patrimony."

The problem is not so much related to increased tourism, which began in earnest with the opening of Mataveri Airport to commercial jet traffic in 1967, but to the island's unique relationship with Chile. By law, any Chilean can settle in any part of the country, and some of those having a hard time making it on the continent have found their way to the island, where the living is easier. The resulting recent population explosion has put an enormous strain on community infrastructure.

Compounding the problem is the fact that by special dispensation Easter Island residents pay no income taxes, so that the local government has no way to raise revenue, making it, according to the mayor, the poorest municipality in all of Chile in terms of resources: "We don't have any."

Also at issue is land ownership, including a dispute over Rapa Nui National Park, which occupies a third of the island. Established in 1935, it has undoubtedly been a force for preservation. But some locals feel that the land was taken illegally, and that UNESCO's recent designation of the park as a World Heritage Site, done without consulting the community, is simply one more example of outside imposition. Some Rapa Nui have occupied parkland and even built homes on it—illegally or legally, depending on one's point of view.

I heard many solutions offered for those problems, ranging from treating the island as an open-air museum with an entrance fee of twenty dollars or so attached to every plane ticket (the money to be divided among various family councils that would manage the ancient sites and the land), to trying to get the aliens back—a task that ought to be considerably easier now that the airport runway has been lengthened (with financial assistance from the United States government) so that it can serve as an emergency landing strip for the space shuttle.

Mostly what I heard and saw, though, was an island where, despite inevitable change brought about by increasingly easy contact with the outside world, life still moved at a pace immensely appealing to anyone used to fourteen-hour workdays.

My most vivid memory of the idyllic pace is of one evening when the couple I was staying with invited me to a barbecue they were having with a few friends on the far side of the island. The barbecue was timed, they assured me, so that we could watch the full moon rise over Rano Raraku. Most of a pig sizzled on the fire throughout the evening, and bottles of Chilean wine were passed around freely. But my hosts had gotten the time wrong by several hours, and we never did see the moon come up. Nobody seemed in the least concerned.

That night of waiting for the moon, I told Josefina and Ramon as we sat one last time on their shady porch, just before I departed on the long flight back to Santiago and New York, was a once-in-a lifetime experience.

"Maybe not," Josefina said.

The first time she visited Rapa Nui, she told me, it still

seemed so far removed from the rest of the world that returning to the States after discovering the huge, loving family she had on the island was one of the hardest things she had ever had to do.

"It used to be that when people left, it was like they were dying, because they never came back," she said. "It was always a very emotional event. But today it is not like that at all. Even when tourists leave you expect to see them again sometime."

So maybe next visit, she said, I'd get the timing right on the moon.

Bob Payne also contributed "Marked by the Marquesas" on page 116.

20 J. MAARTEN TROOST

HEAVEN IS NOT WHAT YOU THINK

The author seeks wisdom on the ways of Tarawa.

When I was a youngster, I often found myself in conversations that began with, *If you were stuck on a deserted island, what then....* And then we would spend hours listing the absolutely essential can't-live-without-them top ten records, or books, or, as we discovered the delusions of adolescence, girls we needed to make our stay on a deserted island an enjoyable one. As the years went by, the lists changed. Iron Maiden was no longer essential listening, but The Smiths were, until they too were tossed off in favor of Fugazi, which was soon discarded to make room for Massive Attack. After crossing off Elizabeth and Carla and Becky, I settled on the woman I wanted to live with on a deserted island, and so this just left books and CDs. As I packed, I was acutely aware of the importance of bringing just the right combination to ensure that no matter what my musical or literary desire, I would have just what I needed, right here on my deserted island. True, Tarawa wasn't actually deserted. In fact, it was overpopulated. But there were no bookstores or record stores, and so I packed as if I were departing for Pluto. For books, it was a mixture of authors we were both likely to enjoy (Philip Roth), combined with a few books we were unlikely to ever read unless stuck on a deserted island (*Ulysses*), as well as a couple of compromise authors (the novelist Ann Tyler for her, the Polish journalist Ryszard Kapuscinski for me). As CDs are lighter, I packed thirty-odd discs that I felt could comprehensively meet any likely musical desire. Did I feel funky? Well, we could go to Sly Stone or The Beastie Boys. Did I want to kick back and chill? Mazzy Star was there to help me. Did I wish I was in Paris, walking on a rain-slicked cobblestone alley on a drizzling October evening? Miles Davis would take me there. Was I up for a bout of brooding? Hello Chopin's *Nocturnes*. Was I feeling a little romantic, a little melancholic? Cesaria Evora would tell me to pull up a chair and have a cigarette.

I was thinking about these CDs a few months later, when once again I was being driven to the brink of insanity by an ear-shattering, 120-beats-a-minute rendition of "La Macarena," the only song ever played on Tarawa. It was everywhere. If I was in a mini-bus, overburdened as always with twenty-some people and a dozen fish, hurtling down the road at a heart-stopping speed, the driver was inevitably blasting a beat-enhanced version of "La Macarena" that looped over and over again. If I was drinking with a few of the soccer players who kindly let me demonstrate my mediocrity on the soccer field with them, our piss-up in one of the seedy dives in Betio would occur to the skull-wracking jangle of "La Macarena." If I happened to come across some teenage boys who had gotten their hands on an old Japanese boombox, they were undoubtedly loitering to a faint and tinny "La Macarena."

What finally brought me to the brink was the recent acquisition of a boombox by the family that lived across the road. One of their members, a seaman, had just returned from two years at sea, and, as is the custom, every penny he earned that was not spent on debauchery in a distant port-of-call was used

In a fit of despair, I went to the Angirota Store and bought *Wayne Newton's Greatest Hits* and *Melanesian Love Songs.* When I put in the Wayne Newton tape, the stereo emitted a primal groan and ate the tape. It was trying to tell me something.

for expensive gifts for his family. Typically this took the form of televisions, VCRs, and stereos, all unavailable in Kiribati. A few shops had begun renting pirated movies sent up from Fiji. These movies were typically recorded by a video camera in a movie theater, with the result that the actors' faces appeared strangely dull and elongated, as if the movie had been filmed by El Greco. Audience members could be seen stretching and heard coughing. If renting a movie, one made sure to avoid comedies since you could hardly hear a word over the laughter and chatter of those fortunate enough to see the movie in a theater. "Could you keep it down," you find yourself telling the screen. But while you could locate copies of *Titanic* and *Forest Gump* on Tarawa, there was little music available beyond "La Macarena." I know because I looked. I looked everywhere. I looked everywhere because I forgot our CDs in my mother's garage in Washington, thousands and thousands of miles away.

It is difficult to convey the magnitude of this catastrophe. I would have been very pleased if I had forgotten my sweaters, which were already rotting in a closet, or my shoes, which, within a month, had turned green with mold. Each day I stared forlornly at our stereo, which we had purchased for an outrageous sum of money from Kate, who had bought it from her predecessor. "If you don't want it," Kate said, "there are plenty of others here who do." No doubt this was true, and we forked over a large amount of bills. Every day at noon, I turned the stereo on to listen to the broadcast from Radio Australia, which Radio Kiribati carried for ten minutes, while they searched for yet another version of "La Macarena" to play for the remainder of the day. Radio Australia claimed to deliver the international news, but you wouldn't know it from listening. Presumably, the world was as tumultuous as ever, but inevitably the lead story on Radio Australia would involve a kangaroo and a dingo in Wagga Wagga, followed by a nine-minute, play-by-play summary of the Australian cricket team's triumph over England. And then it was back to "La Macarena."

I had sent a fax to my mother, asking her to mail the box of CDs. *They're right beside the ski boots*, I wrote. A few days later, we received a fax from her. The CDs were in the mail, she assured us. They were sent by super-duper express mail and would arrive any day. The months ticked by.

In a fit of despair, I went to the Angirota Store and bought *Wayne Newton's Greatest Hits* and *Melanesian Love Songs*. When I put in the Wayne Newton tape, the stereo emitted a primal groan and ate the tape. It was trying to tell me something, I felt. The stereo was more amenable to *Melanesian Love Songs*. With the moon shimmering over the ocean, Sylvia and I listened to Melanesian love ballads—*You cost me two pigs, woman / I expect you to work / While I spend my days / drinking kava under the Banyan Tree.*

With musical selections reduced to Melanesian love songs and "La Macarena," I began to yearn for power failures. When these occurred the techno thump of "La Macarena" would cease, and soon the air would be filled with the soft cadences of ancient songs sweetly delivered by honeyed voices. The I-Kiribati are a remarkably musical people. Everyone sings. There is something arresting about seeing a tough-looking teenage boy suddenly put a flower behind his ear and begin to croon. Everyone sings well, too, so it was a mystery to me why their taste in recorded music was so awful.

Sadly, on many days the power remained on, sometimes for hours at a time, and I would be reduced to an imbecilic state by the endless playing of "La Macarena." It was hot. My novel—and this is a small understatement—was not going very well. My disposition was not enhanced by "La Macarena." I wondered if I could simply walk across the road and kindly ask the neighbors to shut the fucking music off.

Small matters tend to be complex matters in Kiribati. Fortunately, I had Tiabo, our housekeeper, to turn to for guidance. I had been wrong about Tiabo. While it is true she did not direct any come-hither glances my way, she did undulate. She moved with the languorous hip sway of a large woman in the tropics. Two mornings a week, she arrived to clean the house. I felt deeply uncomfortable about this at first, but after some long rationalizations, I convinced myself that there was nothing intrinsically exploitive about the arrangement. She was a single mother, without connections or education. She needed a job. We had a job for her. She was paid well. She conducted herself with dignity. I treated her with respect, and with time we became friends. On her other days, she worked at the FSP office, where Sylvia soon promoted her from cleaning lady to managing the seed distribution program. As it was considered scandalous for a woman to be in a house alone with a man, particularly an *I-Matang* man, who were well-known for groping their housegirls, Tiabo often arrived with her sister Reibo. It was after one little incident that it occurred to me that I needed to watch what I said in Kiribati.

"Reibo," I said. "Have you by chance seen a twenty-dollar bill lying around? I thought I had left it in the basket."

"No," she said. Reibo spoke very little English. Each month, I acquired a little more I-Kiribati, but when my language ability failed, which was often, I usually spoke in English, Reibo replied in I-Kiribati, and we understood each other perfectly. Or so I thought.

Later that afternoon, Ruiti, the FSP accountant, stopped by the house. "Tiabo and Reibo are very upset," she said. This worried me. Had I done something obscene or disrespectful? I was sure I hadn't. Nevertheless, misunderstandings do occur, and I began to worry about being besieged by the male members of their family, demanding some particularly gruesome form of island justice. But I was certain I had done nothing wrong or untoward. I had no idea why Tiabo and Reibo might be upset.

"They say you accused Reibo of stealing twenty dollars. They are crying. They are very ashamed."

Oh, dear.

Stealing, I was told, was a major offense in I-Kiribati culture. I could see why. There is absolutely no good reason for stealing in Kiribati. This is because of the *bubuti* system. In the *bubuti* system, someone can walk up to you and say *I bubuti you for your flip-flops*, and without a peep of complaint you are obliged to hand over your flip-flops. The following day, you can go up to the guy who is now wearing your flip-flops, and say *I bubuti you for your fishing net*, and suddenly you have a new fishing net. In such a way, Kiribati remains profoundly egalitarian.

I-Matangs can choose to play along. I know one volunteer, determined to go native, as they say, who lost her shoes, her bicycle, her hat, most of her clothing, and a good deal of her monthly stipend to the *bubuti*. She was a little dim, however, and it never occurred to her to *bubuti* others, and so she spent her days walking barefoot, with a sunburned scalp, dressed in rags, wondering how on earth she was going to afford her daily fish.

One day, a man, a complete stranger to me, walked up to the door and politely said: "I *bubuti* you for bus fare." Warily, still attuned to big-city panhandlers, I gave it to him. As the *bubutis* rolled in, however, I felt no obligation to comply. Pocket change, sure. The FSP pick-up truck, no. It was my ability, or rather the *I-Matang's* ability, to say no to a *bubuti*, that made foreigners useful on Tarawa. Because of the *bubuti* system, the I-Kiribati tend to avoid seeking positions of power. This was made clear to me when I met Airan, a young Australian-educated employee of the Bank of Kiribati. He was one of a dozen or so Young Turks on Tarawa, benefactors of Australian scholarships and groomed by the Western aid industry to be a future leader. He was, however, miserable. He had just been promoted to assistant manager.

"This is very bad," he said.

"Why?" I asked. "That's excellent news."

"No. People will come to me with *bubuti*. They will *bubuti* me for money. They will *bubuti* me for jobs. It is very difficult."

Jobs are fleeting. Cultural demands are not. Airan begged not to be promoted, and so the management of the Bank of Kiribati remained in *I-Matang* hands. The *bubuti* system was why FSP always had an *I-Matang* director. Sylvia's presence ensured that the organization would not crumble under the demands of the *bubuti* system, which is exactly what occurred when the only other international non-governmental organization to work in Kiribati decided to localize. Its project funds were soon gobbled up in a flurry of *bubutis* and the organization dissolved. Within the *bubuti* system, outright stealing is regarded as a perfidious offense, though this didn't stop someone from stealing my running shoes.

Tiabo and Reibo arrived again in the evening. They were still sobbing.

"Reibo said she did not steal twenty dollars," Tiabo explained. "But if you think she did, you must fire us."

"No, no, no," I said. "Really, I was just wondering where it was. I found it later in my pocket."

Tiabo explained this to Reibo, who began to beam. I did not actually ever find the errant twenty dollars, but I crumble when confronted by tears.

As I continued to be flailed by "La Macarena," I took small comfort in the fact that at least no one on Tarawa had ever seen the video, and I was therefore spared the sight of an entire nation spending their days line dancing. Still, the song grated, and I asked Tiabo if she thought it was permissible for me to ask the neighbors to turn the music down. I did not care if I was polite or not, but I did want to avoid antagonizing the household's youth. They were not in school. They did not work. The traditional rigors of subsistence living did not fully occupy them on Tarawa. And like elsewhere in the world, idle youth have a way of being immensely irritating.

"In Kiribati, we don't do that," Tiabo said.

"Why not?" I asked. "I would think that loud noise would bother people."

"This is true. But we don't ask people to be quiet."

I found this perplexing. Kiribati is a fairly complex society with all sorts of unspoken rules that seek to minimize any potential sources of conflict. Who has the right to harvest a particular coconut tree, for instance, involves an elaborate scheme in which the oldest son has that right for the first year, and then relinquishes it to the next eldest, and so on, until it loops around again, and then it's the turn of the first son of the eldest brother, and on and on, with the result that no one feels slighted or deprived. Then it occurred to me that the repeated playing of a dreadful song like "La Macarena" at provocatively loud levels is an entirely new problem for Kiribati. In the U.S., we have more than seventy years of experience in dealing with noisy neighbors. After much experimentation, we now resort to a friendly "*Turn it down, asshole.*" This is greeted with a polite "*Fuck you,*" which is followed by a call to the police, who arrive to issue a citation, and once again peace and tranquility are restored. Noise pollution in Kiribati, however, hasn't been around long enough for the I-Kiribati to develop such a sophisticated form of conflict resolution. It was like many of the problems on Tarawa. They were new and imported, yet the culture remained old and unvarying.

This thought occurred to me again when I began to notice, with no small amount of disgust, the sudden appearance of a large number of soiled diapers scattered around the house. They had been thoughtfully deposited there by dogs, who had picked them up from the reef, and happily emptied them of their contents. I will not hear another word about the alleged intelligence of dogs. A soiled diaper is like catnip for dogs. They are ravenous for them, and what the dogs didn't ingest, they left in disturbing little piles around the house.

Disposable diapers should have been banned on Tarawa, as they are on a number of other islands in the Pacific. Their availability on the island was a new and disagreeable development. Tarawa lacked a waste management system. There was no need for one until a few years ago, when goods began to arrive packaged in luminous and indestructible material. Before, bags were made of pandanus leaves, food was encased in fish scales, and a drink was held inside a coconut. When you were done, you simply dropped its remains where you stood, and Nature took care of the rest. Now however, bags were increasingly made of plastic, food was found in tins, drinks sloshed inside cans, and sadly, poop resided in diapers, but unlike the continental world, there is no place to put the resulting trash. There is no room on an atoll for a landfill, and even if one did bury mounds of garbage, it would soon pollute the groundwater, which on Tarawa was already contaminated by interesting forms of life. Waste disposal on an overcrowded island like Tarawa was an enormous problem, and while elsewhere in the world, governments could be expected to do something about it, the government of Kiribati carries on as it always does, blithely passing the time in between drinking binges.

"Tiabo," I said. "I don't understand how burning diapers will lead to a scorched baby bum."

Actually, that's not fair. They did do something about it. Once upon a time there was a can-recycling program. Kids gathered all the beer cans that were strewn about the island, and there were many, and carried them to a privately-owned recycling center, which had a can crusher that molded the cans into exportable cubes. The kids were paid. The beer cans were recycled in Australia. Excellent program, one would think. Income was generated. Trash was disposed of in a pleasantly green sort of manner. But then the government, displaying the brain power of a learning-impaired anemone, decided to institute an export tax. Never mind that the product being exported was the rubbish that was fouling the island, the government, as a minister explained to me, "deserved its cut." He sounded like a Staten Island capo. The tax put the can-recycling program out of business. The island remains awash in beer cans.

Beer cans, however, are merely unsightly, whereas soiled diapers are repulsive, particularly for those who are unrelated to the soiler. I grabbed a stick and collected the diapers, placing them in the rusty oil drum we used as a burn bin. We burned everything—plastic, styrofoam, paper, even the expired medicine we found in the cabinet, a tangible catalogue of the ailments that bedeviled Sylvia's predecessors. In case anyone was wondering what they should do with an old asthma inhaler, I can state with some authority that throwing it into a fire is not a good idea, unless you are prepared to spend the rest of the day deaf and bewildered from the subsequent explosion. As I doused the diapers with a generous amount of kerosene, Tiabo came by to see what I was up to.

"You are going to burn the nappies?" she asked.

"Yes," I said.

"You cannot do that."

"I am fairly certain that I can burn the nappies."

"You must not burn the nappies."

"Why?"

"Because you will burn the baby's bum."

This gave me pause. As I stood with match in hand, I did a quick mental inventory to see if I missed something. I checked the tattered remains of the diapers a little more thoroughly. There were, as far as I could see, no babies in the diapers. I pointed this out to Tiabo.

"It does not matter," she said. "If you burn the diapers you will burn the baby's bum."

Tiabo scooped out the diapers and returned them to the reef. I was baffled. I am very fond of babies, and under no circumstances would I ever wish for any harm to come to a baby's bottom, but I was mystified here. Somewhere between cause and effect I was lost.

"Tiabo," I said. "I don't understand how burning diapers will lead to a scorched baby bum."

"In Kiribati," Tiabo explained, "we believe that if you burn someone's...um, how do you say it?"

"Shit," I offered.

"Yes," she giggled. "If you burn someone's shit, it is like burning a person's bum."

To readers, I wish to apologize for the frequent references to all things scatological, but such is life on Tarawa. I tried resorting to cold, heartless, Western logic.

"Tiabo," I said. "I can prove to you that burning diapers will not harm the babies. We can do an experiment. I will burn the diapers, and you listen for the wail of babies."

Tiabo was aghast. "No!"

"I swear. No babies will be harmed."

"Yes they will. You are a bad *I-Matang*."

I did not want to be a bad *I-Matang*. I thought of myself as a good *I-Matang*, a good *I-Matang* who happened to be at wit's end. "But Tiabo, something has to be done. It's not healthy to live surrounded by dirty diapers."

She pondered this for a moment. Then she came up with an idea. "I will make a sign," she said.

On a piece of cardboard, she wrote something in I-Kiribati. The only words I understood were *tabu* and *I-Matang*. "What does it say?" I asked.

"It is forbidden to throw diapers on the reef here. All diapers found will be burned by the *I-Matang*."

"That's good. Will it work?"

"I think so."

We posted the sign on a coconut tree near the reef. The real test came on a Sunday. Due to their expense, diapers are used sparingly, and it was only on Sundays when mothers resorted to their use. The churches in Kiribati are, without exception, shamelessly coercive. It mattered not whether it was the Catholic Church or the Protestant Church or the Mormon Church or the Church of God, or any other of the innumerable churches to have set up shop on Tarawa; if a family found itself unable to pay their monthly tithe to their church, which typically took 30 percent of their meager income, they were called up to the front of the church by their pastors and loudly castigated for their failure to pay God His due. And woe to the mother who decides to skip the four-hour service to stay home and tend to a newborn.

On a Sunday afternoon, after the churches had released their flocks, I was pleasantly surprised to see a woman approach the reef with her child's morning output, pause for moment to read the sign, and turn around, no doubt searching for someplace where she could be assured that her baby's poop would be spared the flame. That's right, lady. Not In My Back Yard.

J. Maarten Troost's essays have appeared in The Atlantic Monthly, Washington Post, *and* Prague Post. *The two years he spent in Kiribati inspired his book* The Sex Lives of Cannibals: Adrift in the Equatorial Pacific, *from which this story was excerpted. After living in Fiji for several years, he now resides with his wife and son in Northern California.*

21 JERRY MILLER

A FISH DRIVE IN WOLEAI

Going out with the locals is a privilege, especially when you're useless.

I WAS SITTING AT A DESK IN THE CONCRETE-WALLED, METAL-roofed shack that served as a combined storeroom, office, and teacher's lounge for Seliap Island's elementary school. It was a hot, sleepy day. I'd just eaten my lunch of boiled fish and taro and was drowsily getting some of my notes in order. Seliap had only four teachers, so I was able to work with each of them individually on each of my twice-weekly trips to the island. I'd finished three class visits and three conferences, and my final observation was scheduled to begin in ten minutes. Manno, the teacher who also acted as Seliap's principal, came into the office. He looked apologetic.

"Augustine just came over from Wotegai," he said. "They've spotted a big school of mackerel."

I was in my second year as a Peace Corps volunteer, so Manno didn't need to explain any further. My class observation had just been cancelled, and so had school. Wotegai and Seliap are small, neighboring islands, each with a population of about a hundred. When either island has a fish drive, all the men and boys from both islands are needed. Since mackerel won't wait, school does. The girls, and all the boys below the fourth grade, were already chattering homeward. The teachers and older boys were setting off for the men's house to load the community's nets and fish traps into the island's boats.

I looked for Matthew, the young Woleaian man who drove the school district's boat for me, and found him grinning with excitement. That was good. I wanted to go fishing, too. We grabbed a large fish trap, about five feet long by three and a half feet tall and wide, carried it out through the surf, and balanced it rather awkwardly across the front of our anchored boat. Then we went back and got another one. Once both traps were loaded, Matthew and I heaved ourselves out of the water and into the back of the boat. One of the teachers joined us and then five or six boys flopped on board the fourteen-footer and crammed into or balanced on top of whatever leftover space they could find.

Our boat was first choice among the boys because of the motor. We had forty horses—at least ten more than anyone else. All of this power naturally obliged us to race at top speed toward Wotegai. Unfortunately, the two islands are very close neighbors. At low tide, you can wade from one to the other in two or three minutes. For the boys, it was a disappointingly short trip.

I had come to Woleai Atoll eighteen months earlier, as a Peace Corps volunteer. The atoll is located within the Federated States of Micronesia, and is made up of nineteen tiny islands—all of them beautiful, and five of them inhabited. The total population is less than a thousand.

I lived on Falalop, the largest of the islands. My job was to provide additional training for the teachers. In my first year,

I had worked on my home island, which had the atoll's largest elementary school and the only high school for 400 miles. Now, in my second year, I was working with the small elementaries on Woleai's other inhabited islands.

It was a fascinating experience. Woleaians are among the few Pacific Islanders who still live a traditional South Sea life, but they have become fully functional in the modern world as well. They still build and use traditional outrigger canoes, but they also own fiberglass boats with outboard motors. Their economy is based on subsistence fishing and agriculture, but high school students are taught to use computers. Many Woleaians subscribe to *TIME* or *Newsweek*, but none wear anything but flowers above their waists. The men wear a combination breechcloth and skirt made of cotton cloth, and the women wear colorful wrap-around skirts they weave themselves.

Breadfruit, taro, coconuts, rice, and fish make up 90 percent of their diet, and fish is considered an essential part of any meal. For two years, my host family apologized to me every time we ate a fishless meal, whether it was breakfast, lunch, or dinner.

Fishing, in fact, is not only a Woleaian man's chief occupation, it is also his hobby and his obsession. He will sometimes get up at 4 A.M. to spend his morning fishing for tuna far out on the ocean, spend his afternoon servicing fish traps in the lagoon, and then, just for fun, go reef fishing that night.

The biggest catches on Woleai, however, are always the result of fish drives. These require so many men and boats that they are usually only worthwhile when a large school of fish has been spotted close to a shoreline. Today a school of migrating mackerel had been seen not far from Wotegai's western beach.

By the time we arrived, a small flotilla of outrigger canoes and motorboats from Wotegai were already beginning to line up in the lagoon about a long city block from Wotegai's western shore.

Four men on the beach were using hand signs to show us where the fish were and how we should arrange the boats. Matthew cut the motor. He stood up in the boat and peered across the water.

"Can you see them?" he asked me.

"No."

"That black water over there," he said, nodding his head vaguely toward the east. "That's the mackerel."

I tried hard. We were far out from shore, but the water was still shallow enough to be a pale, transparent emerald. I could see two darker areas, but those were cloud shadows.

"Over there," he said, pointing carefully.

I searched again. Among my other shortcomings, I do not have fishermen's eyes. It was all surf to me.

Fortunately, I didn't need to see them. I only needed to help with the fish traps. The boys were already in the water with their snorkels and masks, bobbing about like corks. It would be their job, along with some of the men, to straighten the nets in the water and hold them in position. The nets had been brought over in three boats. There were two long nets about four feet wide. They looked like endlessly extended tennis nets. There was a shorter, wider net that would be placed in the center, between the other two. Several fish traps would go beneath the center net. Those fish that dove to avoid the mesh would be caught in the traps.

It took a long while to get all the boats in position and start feeding out the nets. We spread them in a horseshoe shape, with the open end of the shoe closed off by the beach. Swimmers and waders were positioned along the net to hold it in place. When the entire "horseshoe" had finally been spread, we attached long ropes to the net ends nearest the shore. On the beach, the other ends of the ropes were circled around coconut trees so the trunks could act as pulleys. Two groups of men, looking like tug-of-war teams at a beach picnic, hauled on the ropes to tighten the nets around the mackerel school—and any other fish in the neighborhood. They hauled, moved their hands up on the ropes, hauled, moved their hands, hauled. They chanted songs and pulled in time to the rhythm.

It was slow work to pull the nets through the huge expanse of water they surrounded. For a long while little progress was made. The only excitement was an occasional shout of surprise when someone along the net was startled by an escaping fish darting through his legs or grazing his side.

Slowly, the nets narrowed until they formed a long corridor leading out to the large net and the fish traps. Things started to get lively. A number of fish panicked and bolted onto the beach, skipping and "swimming" over the sand. Small boys chased after them, scooping them up and dropping them into sacks. Everyone was shouting and splashing. The panicked fish tangled themselves in nets or dashed to freedom. Several of the men began driving the fish up the corridor toward the large net and the traps. The water boiled.

It was big all right. Big and ugly. It was mostly head, with fat, bulging eyes and a flabby, almost shapeless body.

I saw one man with a long-handled dip net scoop up a large fish. "He doesn't want the big ones to get away," I thought. But then he simply dropped the fish outside the net. He netted another large fish and tossed that into the open sea as well. His actions made no sense to me, but when I asked about it later, I was shown a fish of the same species that had evaded the dip net. It was big all right. Big and ugly. It was mostly head, with fat, bulging eyes and a flabby, almost shapeless body. The Woleaians won't eat them. The dip net man was getting them out of the way so their bulk wouldn't aid the escape of better fish.

As the "beaters" reached the end of the corridor, all the creatures that had not escaped were wriggling about in the nets or inside a fish trap. No one was concerned about the fish in the traps. They weren't going anywhere, and they could be dumped into the boats later. The netted fish were trickier. It's not easy to disengage a lively fish from a net without having it burst out of your hands and back into the sea.

Finally, all the fish had been harvested from the nets and traps and dumped into the boats, so we set off for the nearest men's house to count and distribute the catch. Each family on the two islands would get their share. There is a strict formula for this division between the island's families, based on the traditional prestige of each, and it is meticulously followed. The men carry out all the steps quickly, but the counting out of a large catch is a time-consuming business.

Since I lacked the proper knowledge to help with the distribution, I stayed in the boat and steadied the fish traps. The sun was low in the sky, and the soft breeze made bobbing about on the surf a very pleasant recreation. A dozen men did the counting. The rest selected one or two fish from the varieties Woleaians enjoy eating raw, and walked into the surf. Soon I was surrounded with men up to their waists in the sea. They had worked hard all afternoon, and they ate hungrily, cleaning the fish by ripping at them with their fingers and teeth, tossing away whatever was inedible. From time to time they dipped the rest into the sea.

It was one of those Perfect Peace Corps Moments. I could hear a group of women singing somewhere in the island's interior. I was rocking peacefully on the water, watching the sun sink low in the west. The emerald sea, the white sand, and the coconut trees were the stuff of tourist posters; and I was surrounded by half-naked men voraciously ripping stunned fish apart with their fingers and teeth and devouring them raw, with only the salt sea for sauce.

It had been a good day's work. Matthew and I were as exhausted as we were happy when we finally turned homeward with the bottom of our boat covered in fish. Since we had been guests from another island, tradition required that we receive an especially generous and choice share of the catch. As I looked back, I could see dark gray woodsmoke rising in a dozen places above the treetops of Seliap and Wotegai. The women would soon be smoking the mackerel to keep them from spoiling—the two islands had no electricity.

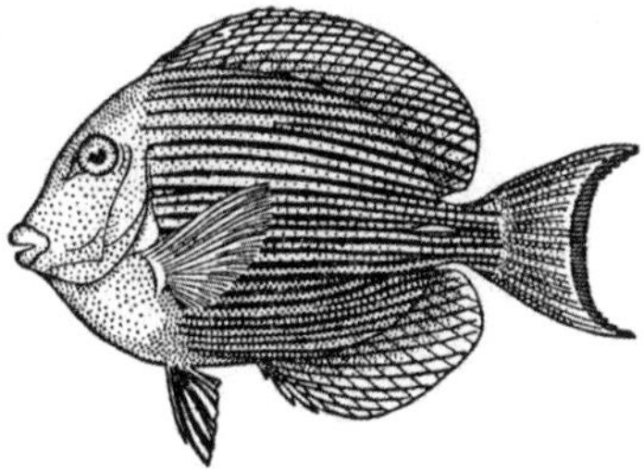

I sprawled across the boat seats while the twenty-year-old Matthew drove us home and told me about the old days. The nets were woven by hand in those times, from cord made of coconut fiber. Pieces of palm leaves had been attached to the nets to drive the fish better. People didn't do it that way now, but the old way was best. The ancestors knew more than the people of today. No one remembered any longer how to do things the right way.

Jerry Miller is a former English teacher and former public radio music host. He began his two years of Peace Corps service at the age of 58, and now lives in California where he is a freelance writer. "A Fish Drive in Woleai" has been adapted from his work-in-progress, Imperishable Summer.

22 JOE YOGERST

IN SEARCH OF THE LAST LEGEND

Are you a cargo god?

Isaak Wan sits beneath a tree in Namakara, cowry shells dangling from his neck, a hand-rolled smoke as thick as a finger tucked behind one ear. As chief of this village, he is lord and master of all he surveys. But Isaak is also a prophet, shaman, and historian for the several thousand islanders who comprise his flock—and one of the last links to a mysterious past that has brought me to his doorstep.

Lighting up with a twig from a campfire, he takes a deep drag and assesses me with wise eyes. *"Yu blong wea?"* he asks in Bislama, the pidgin English used throughout Vanuatu. *Where are you from?*

"America," I tell him.

Isaak smiles. *"Farawe long ia."*

You betcha *far away*. It took me thousands of miles

and what seems like ten thousand years to get from San Diego to the east side of Tanna, one of the remote islands that makes up the Pacific nation of Vanuatu, in my quest to find one of the last of the cargo cults.

Anyone who has spent much time in the antipodes has heard about cargo cults, but few have actually come face to face with any of these extraordinary groups. The cults were founded in the wake of World War II by Melanesians who came in contact with U.S. soldiers. According to one long-held theory, the islanders who developed these cults saw "giant silver birds" drop crates that floated down to earth with parachutes and burst open when they hit the ground. Most of the military hardware was useless in the jungle. But once in awhile the cargo was something special—like Spam—which more or less tasted like pork, a meat reserved for sacred ceremonies such as weddings and circumcisions. With no other explanation, the islanders concluded the airborne cargo must be gifts from the gods.

As quaintly as that legend plays out, a more likely explanation is that cargo cults were founded by islanders who worked at American bases and returned to their villages after the war with tales of amazing contraptions such as airplanes. When the troops and their fancy machines departed as abruptly as they had arrived, cults were created to explain the alien invasion and to lure the Americans back—with even more cargo.

New Guinea, the Solomons, and Vanuatu all had cargo cults. In some places, tribes built mountaintop landing pads and giant wooden airplane effigies to mark the spot where the Americans should return. Others built fake radio towers and fashioned tin cans into imaginary telephones on which they chatted with "the gods" in far-off Honolulu. Most of the cults have disappeared, overwhelmed by Christian missionaries or simply overcome by modern times. But I had heard that a group continued to flourish in Vanuatu—the mysterious John Frum cult—whose devotees worship the Stars and Stripes and await a "second coming" of the Americans. And it just so happens that Isaak Wan—the old man sitting across from me, toking on the fat hand-rolled cigarette—is the high priest of this strange little faith.

Vanuatu has always been an off-beat place, a tropical archipelago that dances to a much different tune than the rest of the Pacific. Captain Cook dubbed these volcanic islands between the Solomons and New Caledonia "the New Hebrides," although no one is quite sure why, because they bear little resemblance to Scotland. For nearly seventy-five years prior to their independence in 1980, they were ruled by both the French and British in a rather bizarre arrangement called the "condominium"—dubbed the "pandemonium" by those who had to endure the constant squabbling between the colonial rivals.

"Cannibalism was a way to feed everyone. Not necessary today."

The pink-skinned planters and missionaries never had more than a tenuous influence over the native islanders: dark-skinned Melanesians with a primitive lifestyle but a complex social structure that had developed over thousands of years. Many of the archipelago's sixty-nine inhabited islands have their own language, most of them unintelligible to their neighbors, and nearly every tribe has its own unique (and often bizarre) customs.

Poring over yellowed *Vanuatu Daily Post* articles a few days earlier in Port Vila, the nation's small but modern capital on Efaté, I felt like I was skimming *Ripley's Believe It or Not*. One story lauded the Monkey Men of Malekula, a tribe that lived in trees for so many years its members evolved curled toes for grasping the branches.

The Monkey Men are no longer around but other strange clans still exist—and adhere to their ancient ways and means. The Big Nambas, for instance, aren't especially large, but the men wrap their sexual organs in huge purple pandanus fibers—as opposed to the Small Nambas, who use much smaller penis wraps. The men on Pentecost Island were bungee jumping long before the modern-day outdoor-adventure types—"land diving" off fifty-foot towers with vines wrapped around their ankles—while over on neighboring Ambrym the islanders organize themselves into warlock covens.

Some customs spread throughout the archipelago, like kava drinking, a strong belief in mana (supernatural forces), and a taste for human flesh. According to an article published in 1923, human was considered more tender than pork. While not exactly defending cannibalism, Cifo Seimo, the oral historian for Ekasup village on the outskirts of Port Vila, did offer a logical explanation. "Many of the tropical fruits we have today were introduced by the Europeans. But our fathers say that in the eighteenth century, Vanuatu had 1 million people. Cannibalism was a way to feed everyone. Not necessary today. The last report of cannibalism was in 1969, in the northern part of Vanuatu."

Still, I come across a newspaper article from the late 1980s about local authorities constructing a high fence around the main cemetery in Port Vila to prevent people from digging up graves and sucking the bone marrow from dead bodies. And lest you think mana has faded in the wake of cell phones and satellite TV, consider the fact that just four years ago, half a dozen islanders were convicted of black-magic homicide.

Despite this gruesome legacy, the Ni-Vanuatu are among the friendliest people I've encountered. Sunday morning, strolling past a Presbyterian Church, I am beset by waves and handshakes from strangers. "Good morning!" "God bless you!" And a man who feels obliged to apologize for the rainy weather. "God gives us all sorts of days," he shrugs.

With a mixed bag of transplanted Polynesians, Asian shopkeepers, aging Europeans, and young Melanesians, Port Vila is a typical South Pacific melting pot. Several beach resorts, some of them fairly upscale, cater to the Aussie honeymoon and summer vacation market. More recently, the town was awash with Americans shooting the latest *Survivor* series—not on some remote desert island, where you might expect, but on the outskirts of the capital. Close enough for the crew to hit the local pubs each night.

The fellow sitting next to me on the plane to Tanna is an American missionary charged with the task of translating the Bible into an obscure island language. Shifting the bag of mozzarella cheese wedged between his legs (one of the few "luxuries" he allows himself in the wilderness), he assures me that God is making progress among the islanders. But moments later, he amends that statement. "All over Tanna," he laments, "people still believe that if you do the right magic, you'll get what you want or need. They use the kava god as a sort of telephone to talk to the other gods. You want the best bananas? You ask the kava god to ask the banana god on your behalf."

I get a similar riff from Bev Petterson, an Aussie who runs White Grass Ocean Resort. "I often get the feeling that while the locals embrace Christianity they still have a strong belief in their *kastom*, or traditions. People will stay at a hospital to get cured, but when they get home they'll have the *kleber*, or witch doctor, slash their back with a broken bottle to release the evil spirits. And there are villages in the interior where white people are still not welcome."

None of this is readily apparent on Tanna's west coast, where civilization has washed ashore in the form of soda pop, pickup trucks, and David Beckham t-shirts. But as you venture inland, time ticks backward, decades and centuries falling by the wayside.

At the top of a muddy track blocked by fallen trees, about an hour's drive from the coast, I stumble upon a village called Yakel, where the men wear little more than *nambas* and the women nothing but grass skirts. Coming from the land where a "wardrobe malfunction" sparked national debate, I find their nakedness—and total lack of shame—both startling and refreshing.

Tom Nowka—the only villager with any formal schooling and hence the only one who speaks English—takes me on a stroll through the assemblage of thatched huts set around muddy clearings. The women cultivate manioc, taro, and yams. The men hunt with spears or bows and arrows. Wild pigs and chickens are their primary game, although Tom admits (with a grin) that domestic cats are also pretty tasty. The villagers also raise pigs—their currency for trading with other *kastom* villages on Tanna.

Tom shakes his head in dismay. "A wife is so expensive! Maybe ten pigs! But I pay only *seven* for mine—two to the chief of her village and five to her family." He shrugs and adds, "She comes from the coast," as if that explains the cut-rate price. In other words, she was tainted by contact with the outside world rather than born into tradition. "But now she lives the *kastom* way," he says proudly.

Yet the village isn't totally removed from the world economy. Before I depart, the villagers show me baskets, boar-tusk necklaces, and other handicrafts they would like to trade for cash. Suddenly I'm skeptical. Is this just a show for tourists who occasionally make their way up to Yakel? I pull my driver aside and whisper into his ear: "Do they put clothes on again after we leave?" He gives me a look like I must be crazy. "They are *always* naked," he insists.

As the crow flies, Yakel is just over the hill from the village of

Sulphur Bay where the John Frummers allegedly dwell. But other than jungle trails, there is no direct route. To reach the far side of Tanna, I must backtrack along the coast and find a road that cuts across the White Grass Plains. Named after a snowy wildflower that once flourished among the grasses, the area is windswept and remote. There isn't a man-made structure in sight. Nothing but high grass and wild horses, the descendants of steeds imported during the colonial era but shunned by tribesmen who feared the strange beast.

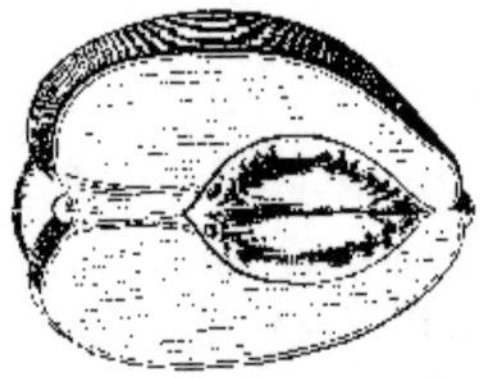

Beyond the grasslands, the road traverses a thick knot of jungle called Middle Bush, where coconut and kava grow in abundance. Tumbling toward the east coast, the route continues across the Ash Plain, a treeless lava wasteland created by Mount Yasur, one of the globe's most active volcanoes.

A road leads up to the volcano, where, I am told, I can watch an eruption. It is already late in the day and the cargo cult, I decide, can wait until tomorrow. Who would miss an erupting volcano? Up we go, parking about one hundred fifty yards from the crater's edge. Clouds swirl around me as I walk to the edge and peer into the great hole. *What's the big deal?* I think to myself. Moments later, a giant blast splits the sky and molten lava shoots into the air just a few hundred yards from where I'm standing. I duck for cover, almost tumbling backward, before I regain my footing. Like a witch's caldron, steam curls over the crater lip, the magma cooling in neon-red lumps. And then it happens again—another tremendous explosion, another shower of hot rock so close I can almost touch it.

I linger at the summit for close to three hours—through a thunderstorm and the ensuing rainbow, and the transition from sunset to starry sky—watching Yasur react to the atmospherics, brighter and brighter as the evening wears on. And when I finally tear myself away, stumbling down switchbacks in the dark, I notice a twinkle of lights in the distance. It is the village of Sulphur Bay—cradle of the quirky faith I have come so far to investigate.

The next morning at dawn, we leave our home base at Friendly Bungalows. The final leg of my journey leads across the deeply cracked floor of what used to be Lake Isiwi. A source of freshwater and a stopover for migratory birds for centuries, Isiwi vanished in June 2000 when torrential rains burst a volcanic dike that had held back the lake waters—an act that locals attributed to evil spirits. One last bend in the road and I'm on the edge of Sulphur Bay. The anticipation is killing me. Will I find the Frummers? And if I do, how will they react to the appearance of an American in their midst?

But it's a moot point. The cult, it seems, was done in by the flood. Not washed away, but superseded by a new group under a charismatic leader named Prophet Fred who allegedly predicted the flood. "He had a vision of apocalypse," says Maliwan Tarawai, who calls himself a lay pastor for the new group. "Many people did not believe. There was much confusion and much refusion. But six months later, the water came through the dike, and now people follow Fred."

Maliwan describes the new faith as a mix of Christianity, John Frum, and *kastom* traditions. While it definitely qualifies as a cult, there is nothing even remotely "cargo" about it. It seems my quest is over. The last of the great cargo cults has vanished for good. But as we stand on the black-sand beach at Sulphur Bay, Maliwan keeps talking...and talking...and talking. A rambling story that continues for more than an hour as he relates how "other chiefs" basically put out a hit on Prophet Fred, an assassination attempt that nearly sparked tribal warfare. The turmoil continued until last December when the Twelve Nakamal—an island-wide council of elders—brokered a peace treaty.

A thought occurs to me: If there was a peace treaty, there had to be two sides. And the other side was most likely...the John Frummers. Which means they're still around. But where? Maliwan's eyes drift toward Mount Yasur. "Up there," he says, pointing to a cluster of thatch about halfway up the volcano. Amongst the trees I spot a flash of red, white, and blue—Old Glory flapping from a wooden staff.

There has always been substantial doubt as to whether or not John Frum was an actual person. According to legend, he was a mystical black man who first appeared at Green Point on Tanna in the mid-1930s, telling a group of kava-drinking elders that all disease would disappear and material wealth would flourish if they expelled the Europeans from their homeland. Not long after, the Americans appeared with their inoculations and cargo, fulfilling the prophecy.

"He was real," Isaak Wan insists, through an interpreter, as we sit beneath the tree in Namakara, the village he founded after the feud with Prophet Fred. "He stayed with my father. He was present at my birth. He gave me this name—Isaak." But in the same breath the chief admits that Frum is also a spirit who drifts back and forth between Tanna and America, as well as a god who dwells in the bowels of Yasur with all the other deities. "We believe in many spirits," Isaak continues. "The yam spirit and the volcano spirit. Each kind of tree has its own spirit, and each animal. The wind, the sun, lightning, and thunder—they are all spirits."

When I ask about cargo, Isaak insists that the true aim of the cult has never been material wealth, but emancipation from foreign domination. "The missionaries changed our life, our customs, our culture. That's why John Frum came here—to help us change back." With a little help from the Yanks, who also left a few Stars and Stripes behind at the end of the war. "The Americans told us that flying these flags would stop the colonial powers from interfering with our customs and culture," Isaak explains. And sure enough, it happened—the archipelago eventually gained its independence from Britain and France. Another prophecy fulfilled.

But do these people actually worship the Yanks? As far as I can tell, I'm not being treated with more deference than anywhere else I've been the past ten days. The Frummers are fervently polite but not down on their hands and knees. Americans may be respected, but they're not venerated. Perhaps the Frummers are starting to have second thoughts about the second coming.

Isaak disappears into his hut and returns with a clear plastic bag. Inside is a pristine copy of *TIME* from the week after 9/11—a cover picture of an airliner crashing into one of the Twin Towers. "How can this happen?" Isaak asks me with genuine curiosity. "How can the world's most powerful building fall down?" I'm not sure how to answer. "If they are the top power," he continues, "how come they didn't know before and stop this?" In other words: Gods have premonitions. They can see into the future. They can alter events. Isaak shakes his head in dismay, troubled by the possibility that America is no longer omnipotent.

Despite Isaak's doubts, the Stars and Stripes still flaps above Namakara, beside Vanuatu's national flag. And every Friday night, devotees from all around Tanna gather to honor John Frum and expedite a return of the Americans.

As the volcano rumbles behind us—the sky lit by rocketing magma—I dance a jig around the village square with hundreds of Frummers, everyone clapping hands and stomping feet to a song whose pidgin words everyone knows by heart—"America is a lighthouse that shines on Tanna…" It doesn't matter if John Frum was real or merely a figment of someone's imagination. Their faith is rock solid, their devotion just as resolute now as it was sixty years ago when the big silver birds first flew this way.

Joseph R. Yogerst is a Fellow of the Royal Geographical Society in London who has written or edited several travel books, including the award-winning Land of Nine Dragons: Vietnam Today *and* Long Road South: The Pan American Highway. *His work has appeared in* Islands, Condé Nast Traveler, National Geographic Traveler, *and other publications.*

23

ANTHONY SOMMER

A GRAVEYARD FOR SHIPS

Astonishing debris litters this sea floor.

WELCOME TO THE POST-NUCLEAR ENVIRONMENT.

If you were expecting only a blackened pile of atomic rubble, prepare to be surprised. Picture instead a circular chain of stunningly beautiful tropical islands fringed by white beaches. And imagine the wrecks of massive warships virtually untouched and unexplored since they were sunk in that brilliant blue lagoon a half-century ago.

In 1996, for the first time since 1946, the Bikini Ghost Fleet, the most spectacular collection of shipwrecks in the world, was open to divers.

Swim onto the bridge of the Japanese battleship where the order to attack Pearl Harbor was given. Inspect the massive guns of an American battleship that shelled Normandy and Iwo Jima and Okinawa. Look into the cockpits of dive bombers parked beside a row of 500-pound bombs on an aircraft carrier.

Bikini—located in the most remote corner of the very remote Marshall Islands more than two thousand miles southwest of Hawai'i—became the focal point of world attention during Operation Crossroads in 1946, the first postwar tests of atom bombs.

The spectacular explosions inspired a French designer to call his new swimsuit the bikini, a name that still endures.

Equally enduring is the band of nuclear nomads the tests created. The 167 islanders living on the atoll in 1946 were convinced that they would benefit all humanity if they agreed to be temporarily relocated. Fifty years later, they were still waiting to be allowed to return home.

Crossroads was by far the single largest spectacle in history. Two atom bombs, each twenty-three kilotons, the size used at Nagasaki, were exploded. The Able shot on July 1, 1946, was detonated 518 feet above the lagoon's surface. The Baker shot on July 25, 1946, was fired ninety feet underwater.

Anchored in the lagoon were 100 unmanned target ships, including some of the most famous survivors of World War II. Outside the atoll, 175 ships carried 42,000 sailors, scientists, politicians, and journalists. Five dozen aircraft circled the lagoon with cameras and instruments.

The Able shot was something of a disappointment to observers on ships twenty miles away. The heavy tropical humidity absorbed the shock wave long before it could reach them. Observers expected to see warships flying through the air. Instead, only four ships were sunk.

The underwater Baker shot proved far more impressive: a thousand-foot-thick pillar of water erupted from the lagoon surface, then collapsed and crashed down on the ships with force great enough to rip away superstructures and crush decks.

The Baker shot sank only nine additional ships. But the

surviving ships were so dangerously radioactive that ultimately all were taken to deep water and sunk.

Shipwrecks are time capsules sealing everything inside at the instant they sink. Descending on the Bikini Ghost Fleet is dropping to the lagoon floor and touching history.

Attack Transport USS *Gilliam*: The target for the Able shot was the battleship USS *Nevada*, painted brilliant orange and clearly visible to the bombardier of the B-29 *Dave's Dream* as it approached from its base at Kwajalein, in the western Marshall Islands.

But the bomb drifted a half-mile west of the *Nevada* and exploded directly above the *Gilliam* instead. Today, the 446-foot *Gilliam* lies upright on the lagoon floor. The stern remains intact with an open container of shells standing beside the deck gun as though ready to be loaded. The rest of the *Gilliam* looks like a toy ship stamped on by an angry child. Deck levels are crushed together. The superstructure is a mass of twisted steel. Of all the Bikini wrecks, the *Gilliam* is the most mangled, looking more like a pile of naval scrap than a ship.

The *Gilliam* is also the only wreck heavily infested with sharks. Several six- to eight-foot gray reef sharks circled just below us when we entered the water, curious but not aggressive. Divemaster Scott Herman did not take us to the bow. "The sharks have chased me off of there too many times," he explained.

Destroyer USS *Lamson*: Inch for inch, the *Lamson* is the most heavily armed wreck in the lagoon, bristling with cannon, antiaircraft guns, torpedoes, and depth charges. The bridge and funnels are missing, and much of the superstructure is twisted. Like the *Gilliam*, the *Lamson* was near the zero point of the Able shot. Navy divers reported the destroyer on its side on the lagoon floor. But the force of the Baker shot pushed the ship back up on its keel, and it stands upright today.

The *Lamson* was no stranger to the Marshall Islands. In 1937 it had searched these same waters in vain for missing aviator Amelia Earhart.

Submarine USS *Apogon*: World War II fleet submarines were relatively small, and we were very deep before we could make out the outline of the *Apogon* below us. It first appeared as a dark, ghostly mass on the sandy bottom. As we continued to descend, details began to emerge: the conning tower, the deck gun on the bow, the anti-aircraft gun on the stern. The *Apogon* sits perfectly upright on the sea floor. The wood decks are gone, burned away by the bombs. The periscopes and guns are encrusted with coral and sponges. But on the bridge, an optical range finder has somehow survived intact. Even the metal flaps that shield its glass lenses still open and close.

It first appeared as a dark, ghostly mass on the sandy bottom. As we continued to descend, details began to emerge: the conning tower, the deck gun on the bow, the anti-aircraft gun on the stern.

Battleship USS *Arkansas*: The *Arkansas* was anchored closest to the Baker bomb, and there is some dispute about what happened to it in the first few seconds after the underwater explosion. Some eyewitnesses say that for an instant the ship was vertical, literally standing on its stern. They say a dark vertical blur, clearly visible in both still and motion pictures, shows this. Others say it didn't happen at all and the blur in the pictures is just a column of soot pushed out of the *Arkansas'* funnels by the force of the blast.

What was clear was that when the billowing cloud of radioactive spray and coral dust settled, the *Arkansas* was gone.

Completed in 1912, the *Arkansas* in 1946 was the oldest battleship in the U.S. Navy. The *Arkansas* carried President Taft to inspect work on the Panama Canal and escorted President Wilson to the Versailles Peace Conference following World War I.

It fired tens of thousands of rounds in support of amphibious landings—from Veracruz, Mexico in 1914 to the beachheads of both Europe and the South Pacific in World War II. Today, the *Arkansas'* massive guns, swung outboard as the battleship rolled over, all point to starboard from beneath the huge overturned hull. The bridge of the *Arkansas* was swept clear of the ship and had not been located prior to our visit. On our last dive, while searching in vain for the similarly unlocated Japanese heavy cruiser *Sakawa*, we accidentally came across the wreckage of the *Arkansas'* bridge and marked its location. By now it's probably a regular stop on the Ghost Fleet tour.

Battleship HMJIS *Nagato*: The largest warship ever built when completed in 1920, the *Nagato* was the only Japanese battleship or aircraft carrier to survive World War II. The *Nagato* was also the last symbol of the U.S. Navy's most humiliating defeat and could not be allowed to remain afloat after the war.

During the Pearl Harbor attack, the *Nagato* served as flagship for Admiral Isoroku Yamamoto, commander of the Japanese navy. It was from the *Nagato's* bridge that the *"Tora! Tora! Tora!"* signal was sent announcing the beginning of World War II in the Pacific.

The hull is upside-down, but the *Nagato's* distinctive pagoda-shaped superstructure was broken off and now lies flat on its side on the lagoon floor. The navigation bridge is easy to identify by its large square windows. Wartime films show Yamamoto peering at his fleet through binoculars from those same windows and studying navigation charts with his staff on that same bridge as the Japanese warships approached Hawai'i. Dropping to the 180-foot bottom, divers can swim under the shadows, the sixteen-inch guns seem impossibly oversize, almost surreal. At the ship's stern, the *Nagato's* four screws and two rudders dwarf divers. All these years after its sinking, the massive scale of the *Nagato* remains intimidating.

Aircraft Carrier USS *Saratoga*: The undisputed queen of the Bikini Ghost Fleet is the 880-foot *Saratoga*, standing upright and remarkably intact on the lagoon floor.

It was aboard the *Saratoga* and its sister ship USS *Lexington*, the United States' first true carriers, that U.S. Navy aviators in the late 1920s and 1930s developed the tactics used so effectively in World War II. The *Saratoga* fought in the Solomon Islands, Gilbert Islands, Marshall Islands, and finally at Iwo Jima, where on February 21, 1945, a kamikaze killed 125 sailors and put the carrier out of action for the rest of the war by badly damaging its flight deck.

Like the other target ships, the *Saratoga* was moored fully loaded for battle. Aircraft were lined up on the flight deck but all were blown overboard by the two atom bombs.

The Baker blast unleashed ninety-four-foot waves, the largest ever recorded, moving outward at fifty miles per hour, hitting the *Saratoga* broadside and pushing it 1,500 feet sideways. The *Saratoga* sank six hours after the explosion, with all 42,000 sailors on the support ships called on deck to witness its passing. Today, on the *Saratoga's* bow, two huge anchor chains reach halfway to the lagoon bottom. The impact of the waves lifted the *Saratoga's* bow forty-three feet, ripping off its massive anchors.

The aircraft elevators, once flush with the flight deck, both collapsed to the hangar-deck level, providing easy access for divers making a long free fall into the darkness.

In the aft hangar deck—a black dead-end tunnel where broken pipes and cables can easily ensnare the unwary diver—live torpedoes, bombs, and rockets are stored, some still in their racks, others in carts once used to carry them up to the flight deck to be loaded onto fighters and bombers, and many scattered loose on the silt-covered deck. Amid the wreckage an intact light bulb with its General Electric trademark clearly visible remains in its fitting.

The forward hangar deck is the final resting place for three dive bombers and a torpedo bomber, lined up in the deep shadows along the starboard bulkhead. All were hurled across the enclosed deck by the violent force of the bomb; engines snapped off, propellers bent, canopies cracked. Yet their rubber tires remain inflated, and in their cockpits, inches from twisted metal seat frames, delicate instruments survive with their glass covers unbroken.

Anthony Sommer has written for the Honolulu Star-Bulletin *and lives in Kauai.*

24 ROFF SMITH

AWAY FROM THE BEACH

The author gets a dose of cycling Fiji.

TWICE A DAY A TWIN-ENGINE TURBOPROP MAKES THE SHORT hop from Suva to Ovalau, flying over a breathtaking panorama of coral reefs. Levuka, a forty-minute drive from the Ovalau airstrip, is reached via a rough but scenic road that twists along the coast. I caught the dawn flight and arrived in town in time for breakfast, which I rustled up in the funky little Café Levuka on Beach Street. Eggs, bacon, fresh papaya slices, and juice, and a wicked little jazz number playing softly on the radio, while outside, the sleepy, sun-drenched seaport stretched and yawned.

Levuka seems to have dozed away much of the twentieth century. The false-front shops on Beach Street, with their shaded verandas and wooden sidewalks, look pretty much as they did in the bad old days when the harbor was crowded with tall-masted clippers, and scores of saloons, hotels, and brothels did brisk trade. Levuka's days as a godless, wide-open town came to an end in 1874, when Fiji's self-appointed king, Seru Cakobau, ceded his country to Britain as a way of getting England to cover some of his government's debts (incurred, by the way, on behalf of the U.S. consul). The bustling port of Levuka was proclaimed the new colony's capital. British authorities moved in, and Levuka was forced to clean up its act.

When the colonial administration shifted to Suva in 1882, Levuka went into a long and genteel decline but kept so many of its old buildings intact and retained so much of its old flavor that local leaders are now seeking to earn for the town World Heritage recognition as the last and best-preserved of the South Pacific's historic seaports.

This is a town to explore on foot, a watercolorist's dream of painted clapboard buildings squeezed between a sheltered harbor and steep mountains cloaked in emerald-green rainforest. It is still a maritime town, with its fishing trawlers and tuna cannery and the neon cross on the weathered stone tower of the Church of the Sacred Heart, which is lit up at night to guide incoming ships home. The stones where, in 1970, Prince Charles signed the Deeds of Cession on behalf of Queen Elizabeth (giving Fiji its long-awaited independence) are displayed on a manicured lawn on the south side of town, surrounded by a neat picket fence.

Roaming the town's back streets—muddy and bright with tropical flowers—I came upon surprises, such as the venerable Ovalau Club, which opened in 1904 as Fiji's first private club and today is an attractive reminder of Britain's tropical colonial days. A faded photograph of King George VI, apparently taken sometime in the 1930s, graced the entryway, and the plain wooden barroom was festooned with nautical flags and black-and-white photos of graceful schooners and vintage World War II Catalina seaplanes. There was even a letter written in 1917 by Count Felix von Luckner, a German adventurer who sank a lot of Allied ships in World War I.

Ceiling fans stirred the heavy tropical air. Feeling like I had stepped into the pages of a Somerset Maugham novel, I sidled up to the bar and ordered a beer—and considered the options.

There is only one real road on Ovalau, a rough and remote dirt track that makes a mountainous thirty-two-mile loop around the island. Intrigued, and imbued with a sense of old-style travel, I arranged to rent a bicycle the next morning, then took a room at the Royal Hotel. A rambling weatherboard structure build in the 1860s, the Royal is Fiji's oldest hotel and a relic of Levuka's wild days. The colonial atmosphere was still there: the high-ceilinged lobby with the palms, wicker, and fans; the old-fashioned billiard room; and the bartender who, I was told, had actually been born behind the bar, fifty-eight years earlier. It was as if one of my favorite Saturday morning Panama-hat adventure movies had come to life, in living color instead of black and white.

A fresh peal of thunder transported me back to my lonely jungle clearing . . .

The next morning I set out toward the wild north of the island. With my bulging knapsack, dilapidated bicycle, and that wholesomely naive combination of gameness and expectancy, I felt I was embarking on one of those Victorian excursions, the sort the old advertisements for the Royal Hotel used to plug (along with "the best bath in town" and "pure liquor"). An hour later I was splattered with mud, pushing my bicycle up a hideously steep jungle track, sweating in sauna-like heat between machine-gun bursts of rain while peals of thunder hinted at heavier downpours to come.

At the top of the grade, and before heading down the other side, I paused in a clearing to try to repair my useless front brake, which had failed so spectacularly on my last—terrifying—descent. As I fiddled with the mud-splattered cantilevers I glanced through the fronds across a rainy, gray sweep of Pacific, and there in the distance I saw it: a private island resort—$1,300 a day for all the pampering you can handle—bathed in its own exclusive shaft of sunlight. As I used the last vaguely clean bit of my shirt, under my left armpit, to wipe the mud from the lip of my water bottle, my mind conjured images of cool rum drinks served poolside, luxe deck chairs arrayed under the sun, and clean fluffy towels piled high.

A fresh peal of thunder transported me back to my lonely jungle clearing and the conundrum of the aging bicycle with the dodgy brakes. Three scraped knuckles later, and after the vengeful application of a size-fourteen sneaker, I was back in business, clattering down another treacherous grade, bouncing pothole-to-rock, eyes wide, feet splayed out like pontoons.

Seat-of-the-pants travel may have its perils and discomforts, but it also has its hidden joys, like experiencing things you would normally miss: the strange bright-winged jungle birds and brilliantly colored dragonflies darting among roadside flowers, the rich earthy fragrance of the rainforest. And there is the truculent independence of traveling from village to village, dodging the occasional pig, chicken, or cow, observing the world at your own pace.

It was Sunday, a big day in Fiji, and the valleys were filled with the sounds of hymns rising from the pastel-colored churches. Later, when church let out, I encountered families walking along the road. Peaceful, smiling, dressed in their Sunday finest—the men in crisp white shirts, newly pressed *sulus*, leather-bound catechism in one hand, umbrella in the other—they somehow managed to look as fresh as peeled eggs as they made their way back to homes tucked away in the forest.

By early afternoon the sun had burned through the clouds, magnifying the heat and humidity beyond anything that had come before. The hills had fallen away. Instead of toiling up slippery mountain slopes, I coasted past seafront villages, their wooden huts painted in coral pastels.

Children and dogs played along the beach; fishermen cast hand nets into the sea. Around four o'clock I pedaled back up Beach Street with a warm sea breeze at my back—tired, sunburned, and feeling (and probably smelling) like one of the past century's old salts coming into port. I dumped my bicycle in a shed behind the Royal Hotel, showered, and sauntered over to the Ovalau Club for a cold, well-earned beer. (Surely the sun was over the yardarm somewhere.)

As my aching thighs mellowed at the old colonial bar, I let my mind take a trip down memory lane, well beyond the miles of muddy jungle track I'd ridden that day, back thirty years to a New England porch and a stack of paperbacks brimming with tropical adventure. As my mind wandered, my eye caught a picture adorning the bar. It was a faded, framed pen-and-ink portrait of a classic character straight out of a *Boys' Own* novel. He wore a pith helmet, clenched a pipe in his strong white teeth, and stared into the 1930s as confidently as if he owned them. I raised my glass. "You and me both, mate."

Originally a Yankee, Roff Smith has lived most of his adult life in Australia. He worked as a reporter for the Sydney Morning Herald *and as a feature writer for Melbourne's* Sunday Age. *He was an award-winning senior writer for* TIME *magazine and now lives in Australia and freelances for a variety of international publications. He is also the author of* National Geographic Traveler: Australia, Life on the Ice: No One Goes to Antarctica Alone, *and* Cold Beer and Crocodiles: A Bicycle Journey into Australia.

25 CLEO PASKAL

SATURDAY NIGHT IN NAURU

Saving the world begins at home, especially when home is so small.

Mrs. Amram, the widow of the first home-grown Nauruan reverend, sits solidly in her living room chair as her world whirls around her. There are kids everywhere. Some are directly related to her. Others are not. But they all are contributing to mini disaster zones that are quickly merging into one enormous, spectacular mess.

Mrs. Amram forges on with our conversation regardless. She is one of those determined, immovable, wooden women carved into the front of a storm-tossed sailing ship. She has something to say and no mere sea of smashed Lego sets is going to stop her.

She wants people to know how her country, the Republic of Nauru, an island nation of eight square miles and 8,000 people in the Central Pacific, has managed to save itself.

It started, as most things do in Nauru, with bird droppings. Millennia ago, Nauru was the rest stop of choice on a migratory highway for birds crossing the Pacific. They came, did a little fishing, took a little bathroom break, and moved on.

Over the years, their squishy leavings petrified into some of the highest-grade phosphate in the world. By the late nineteenth century, their guano was perfect for fertilizing the growing agriculture industries in Australia and New Zealand.

From the turn of the century to the 1960s, various colonial overlords (starting with the Germans, then the British, Japanese, Aussies, and New Zealanders) mercilessly strip-mined Nauru's phosphate deposits. After independence, in 1968, the country was such an environmental disaster the Nauruans figured they might as well get out the last of the phosphate and use the money to eventually rebuild the island.

What they hadn't realized was that while the mining was literally eating away at their island, the money coming in from the mining was eating away at their culture. The sudden huge waves of cash (at one point Nauru had one of the highest per capita incomes on the planet) smothered traditional ways.

Nauruans abandoned local foods such as fish and breadfruit in favor of goods imported from Australia, such as Spam and chips. Suddenly no one cared how many fruit trees they owned; instead they bought TVs, VCRs, weed whackers, and, oddly, many, many trampolines.

But the biggest problem was alcohol. With their social structure eroding, the rootless youth of the country drifted into drink. Nightclubs sprang up everywhere.

According to Mrs. Amram, the situation was desperate, "They were skipping school and smoking and drinking and witless."

The kids would get drunk and head out along the country's one road, a circular route around the perimeter of the island. First they would drive clockwise, then counter-clockwise. Accidents and drunken brawls became regular events.

Finally Mrs. Amram and others had enough. "The women were very, very upset about their children," she says, "so we wrote a letter to the government."

And that was that.

Nauruan politicians, like most in very small countries, are deeply integrated into their communities. When the letter arrived they knew it was time to act or risk running into an irate Mrs. Amram at the grocery store. And the post office. And the church. And family dinners.

First, closing time for bars was changed from 4 A.M. to 2 A.M. Then midnight. And eventually, every nightclub on the island was shut down. Now, the only places you can drink are the staff bar at the Nauru Phosphate Company and the country's only hotel. And neither admit local teens.

The island is cleaner, accidents are down, school attendance is up, and, slowly, social structure is knitting itself back together. TVs lie broken and unmissed. Trampolines are used as beds. The void left by the disappearance of Stallone videos is being filled by a growing interest in traditional Nauruan culture. And, for the first time in years, they reintroduced traditional games on Nauruan Independence Day.

My inaugural field trip to see the New Nauru in action, decides Mrs. Amram, will be to the see the games. She summons her late husband's first wife's daughter, Woo-Woo, and dispatches the two of us to the celebrations.

Most national holidays the world over are pretty much the same. Set off fireworks, drink bad alcohol, get nationalistic, then try to pick a fight with some Americans.

Nauru is different.

Before the first Germans colonists came along to "set them

straight" in that special Teutonic way of theirs, Nauru was a matriarchy. There was a queen, a female god, the works. The Germans got rid of most of it, largely by locking the nation's twelve chiefs in a shed until they "saw reason."

> They continue to throw rocks at each other until one team calls it quits because many of its players are bleeding. *Itsibweb,* the world's most basic sport.

But, increasingly, bits of the matriarchy thing are starting to resurface, like delicate spring flowers. With *really* sharp thorns. To wit, Mrs. Amram and her prohibition.

Independence Day sporting events are also a good case in point. The main competitions are held in an open field in the shadow of the Nauruan Phosphate Company's mining works. Woo-Woo procures an official schedule and I consult it. There are a few run-of-the-mill events like sprinting and mat weaving. Then comes The Event We Are All Waiting For: *Itsibweb.* It is being covered live for Nauruan TV. Both the network's cameramen are there.

The canopied stands are full, with the comfortable chairs up front reserved for big shots. Lovely young lasses serve them drinks and snacks. We sit close enough to the comfy chairs to occasionally get mistaken for someone important. Never underestimate the allure of a free soggy sandwich.

The players assemble on the pitch. There are two teams, around ten players a side, all women, most barefoot or wearing flip-flops. They range in age from about twenty to about sixty. Their faces are smeared with brightly colored war paint and they all seem pretty cheerful, in spite of the fact that one of the teams is passing around a cannon-ball-sized rock loosely covered by a leaf. Around the edge of the field, frailer and older women sit cross-legged on the ground, practicing vicious Nauruan taunts. Woo-Woo goes and visits them. I stay near the sandwiches.

The game begins with the teams facing each other. Three women from the rockless team stand in front of their colleagues and make a defensive wall with their bodies.

No, they can't possibly intend to...YES!

A woman from the armed team runs towards them, bouncing the rock in her hand then swats it as hard as she can at the human wall. One of the women tries to catch it and fails. A cheer goes up. She goes down. One point for the rock thrower.

They continue to throw rocks at each other until one team calls it quits because many of its players are bleeding.

Itsibweb, the world's most basic sport.

According to a note in my Official Nauruan Independence Day Schedule, there is basically one rule. After the "ball" is hurled, "a player should either catch it, or leave it to hit the ground without moving any part of his body with the object of missing the ball." It is actually illegal to duck.

A note adds: "This sometimes brought about bloody misfortunes for some players."

According to my program, the traditional men's event, *Kariduga*, is next. It explains: "This sport was exclusively for men as some actions were considered tabu for the female of the species."

Considering what the women play, I settle in for a gladiatoresque orgy of violence.

The remaining *itsibweb* women are cleared off the field and two lackeys bring forth The Log. It is about fifteen feet long, and a foot thick. They lay it down.

A small clutch of men assemble about twenty feet away. And immediately start bickering. Seems no one can quite remember the rules.

They all agree that it is an individual sport and that it probably involves throwing sticks. After more arguing, it is agreed that the sticks are thrown at The Log. Then it is decided that the sticks have to skim off the The Log "just so." Extra points are to be awarded if you can get your stick to bounce off The Log in such a way that it rebounds straight up in the air.

For the next forty minutes, on the same spot that just before had hosted women deflecting mini-boulders for the sake of God and Country, grown men skip twigs off a log.

Mercifully, as soon as that is over, the women are back with competitive coconut husking. There are two varieties: skinning the coconut with a sharpened stick or impaling it on a branch. It depends on if you want to lacerate your leg or stab yourself through the arm.

No wonder the male politicians of Nauru didn't have a chance when Mrs. Amram set her sights on them.

When the celebrations end, flushed with excitement (or possibly blood splattered), I return to Mrs. Amram's with Woo-Woo. But the day isn't over, the Blessed Reverend's widow has arranged for yet another treat. That night, I am to go on a Legendary Noddy Bird Hunt with her son Maxwell. The Hunt is something Nauruans do without cameras. Without crowds. Without drink trays. Something private. Nearly sacred. And I'm going to get to go. Be still my beating heart.

That night, around dusk, Maxwell, his amiable friend Roy, and Roy's smiley wife Em, come to pick me up in a nearly dead Land Rover. There are two oversized butterfly nets sticking out the back and all the dials on the dash read zero.

To creaks and groans, mostly mine, we set off to find the near-mythic noddy bird.

Nauruans take their birds very seriously. With excellent reason. The national bird, the frigate, is such a nasty bastard that it doesn't actually fish itself, it just frightens other birds into disgorging their catch.

We clunk our way up into the interior, using mining paths, driving among the sixty-foot bleached white coral pinnacles that are the tombstones of the phosphate mines. We drive as far as we can, then take the nets out and set up sentries among the pinnacles, waiting for the noddies to return from their day's fishing.

Roy keeps his net out of sight and crouches low on a small rise, immobile, silent. Maxwell sits next to me in a small depression at Roy's feet. Em sits about ten feet away, but within net reach of Roy. It is dead still. Once upon a time, master noddy callers would summon the birds to their fate with complex vocalization. But now, the Nauruans just use digitally remastered noddy call CDs. Roy turns on his boombox and we wait for the birds to swoop down and check out the sound quality.

Soon a small, dark, suspiciously bat-like form dive-bombs the boombox. Roy bags it in his net, then passes it to Em.

I've fished and hunted and skinned rabbits. Hey, I'm Canadian, we learn that in grade school. But I've never seen an animal killed quite like this before.

At the beginning, I am actually worried for Em. The fist-sized noddy is viscously trying to peck the hand she holds it in.

"Em," I say, "aren't you scared it'll bite you?"

"Yeah," Em replies, "they bite. But I bite harder. They'll die."

And then, she laughs.

She flicks the bird. The fish it had just caught flies out of its beak. She stage whispers to me, "So it won't taste too bad."

Then she takes the bird's body in one hand, its head in the other and pu-u-u u-lls so its neck is stretched straight as a cable. Then she chomps down hard on the bird's neck. It twitches a little and she immediately starts plucking it.

I glance at Maxwell. To his credit, he looks like he is trying not to puke. But hey, his sister plays *itsibweb* so what does he expect from a night out with a Nauruan babe?

Soon the noddies are coming so fast and thick that Em doesn't really have time to properly chomp on them before she starts plucking. Apparently, that is a good thing because noddy "distress calls" (distress? More like bloody panic) result with other noddies showing up to see if they can help out. There's a clever survival mechanism.

Feathers are flying like flakes in a snow globe. I sit cross-legged on the ground next to Em. She is maniacally plucking convulsing noddies. She gestures for me to join in.

I am hesitant at first, delicately pulling out their tail feathers, apologizing to the noddies, explaining that it is nothing personal, that I am a journalist on a job. Their bodies are warm and their feet are still wet from the sea. The ripping out of the feathers takes little effort and sounds like velvet velcro.

Before I know it, I have the Fever. I am sucked into the frenzy and am trying to outstrip Em.

I start to learn which birds make the best distress calls. I pull back their wings "just so." And when I am through, I tie 'em together two-by-two by their wing tips.

I can feel the bloodlust pumping. More noddies. Thump-thump. More noddies. Thump-thump.

Over the next hour, we (O.K., Roy and Maxwell—all I caught was a shrub) bag thirty-one noddies. On the drive back to Roy's house I am in an euphoric daze.

Once there, we unload our catch while the local kids gather around in salivatory glee. The noddies are lined up on a rock ledge and the final pre-cooking touch is applied. Roy breaks out the blow-torch and sizzles the last remaining feathers off the now blackened birds. Then they are impaled on sticks and roasted like wieners at a barbecue. Yes, I tasted the flesh of noddies and. . .well... it tasted kind of like fishy pigeon, actually. But we make sure to bring home a few for Mrs. Amram.

She smiles benevolently as we come barreling in, adding to the noise and mess. She politely eats a few noddies and then it is time for bed. She has one last thing for me to do tomorrow. In her mind, it is the most important activity. And it requires rest. I sleep well and try not to dream of noddies.

The biggest event on the newly recovered Nauruan social calendar is the Choral Competition. Hundreds of Nauruans of all ages are members of dozens of choirs that sing in regular competitions and/or in church.

Mrs. Amram decides that the best way for me to understand what all this means is for me to sing as well. The next day, after lunch, she bellows for Woo-Woo to take care of the kids, takes me by the hand, and leads me to the nearby church.

We arrive in time for the regular afternoon service. The pews are full, with people of all ages. Mrs. Amram strides to the front and sits me down beside her in the section reserved for choir members.

For the next hour, we sing. Every now and then, Mrs. Amram looks at me and nods happily. The words are in Nauruan but the hymns are familiar. Voice quality is irrelevant. Sections of the choir delight in forging interlinking harmonies. *Itsibweb* players, noddy hunters, and politicians stand shoulder-to-shoulder and sing heart-to-heart. Every now and then, the pastor (who also happens to be Speaker of the Parliament) reads a few lines from the Bible, but that is mostly to give the choir time to find the next song in the hymn book. The feeling of community, of unity, is overwhelming.

And that is how the Nauruans are trying to save themselves.

Cleo Paskal has contributed stories to several anthologies, including Food: A Taste of the Road, Women in the Wild, *and* Travelers' Tales Japan. *Her work has also appeared in the British publications* Condé Nast Traveller *and* The Economist, *and Canada's* National Post *and* Weekly World News. *She wrote the Emmy-winning television series* Cirque du Soleil: Fire Within, *and she has hosted two BBC radio travel shows and taught at various universities in the U.K., Canada, and New Zealand.*

26 P. F. KLUGE

RUNWAYS TO HISTORY

Terrible forces were unleashed here.

IF SOMEONE SENDS YOU TO A BATTLEGROUND, YOU TAKE AN interest, even if the war's long gone. In 1967, I was a Peace Corps volunteer assigned to Micronesia, then called the Trust Territory of the Pacific Islands. It was there, with the remnants of World War II all around me, that I became a connoisseur of battlegrounds, a boondocks hiker, a snooping, crawling tomb-raider.

In Palau, on the island of Peleliu, I clambered over the Japanese cave complexes on Bloody Nose Ridge. In Truk I snorkeled over the remains of a sunken fleet. In the Marshalls I pondered the overturned German cruiser *Prinz Eugen*, used as a guinea pig in postwar nuclear tests. On Saipan, my home base in the Northern Marianas, tanks and landing craft rusted on the reef along the invasion beaches; gun emplacements, revetments, bunkers, and air-raid shelters sat neglected in the mean thickets of *tangan-tangan* brush that had been seeded by air after the war to halt erosion. I came across Japanese mess kits, canteens, canisters, sake bottles, and shoes. But memories were my only souvenirs.

I remember the sun that scorched me in the open, poached and drained me in the shade. I remember branches snapping and slapping, limestone cliffs that scratched and cut. I felt the utter discomfort of the war-littered landscape, the loneliness of left-behind places on left-behind islands. But the loneliest place of all, the saddest and the richest in history, was Tinian, three miles across a strait from Saipan.

I could see it every day, long before I visited—a flat, scrubby island with a rocky, take-no-prisoners coastline. Then, as now, Tinian was Saipan's satellite, its country cousin, sleepy and nondescript, a side trip in peacetime, a sideshow in war. It must have been heartbreaking: Tinian's 9,000-man garrison stood by while Saipan's 30,000 defenders went up in smoke. Only then did the Americans bother with Tinian.

"There was less apprehension about the outcome of Tinian than of any other battle of the war," wrote one historian. It was over in nine days. But Tinian's glory days were still to come.

On my first visit I stayed at the island's only hotel, a ramshackle wood structure that had been General Curtis LeMay's headquarters. At dawn I climbed into my rental car and headed north on Broadway. The Americans who captured Tinian noticed that it was the size and shape of Manhattan, so they named the streets they built after similarly positioned New York thoroughfares: 42nd Street, Riverside Drive, Eighth Avenue, and so forth. I headed up Broadway, Harlem-bound, passing through grassy rolling ranch lands. On my right I saw a Japanese communications building that had been converted into a slaughterhouse for a local cattle-ranching operation; on my left was a bullet-pocked Japanese shrine.

Before long, weeds snaked out onto the macadam, and ranks of *tangan-tangan* pressed against the road's shoulder, straining to touch overhead. I spotted an easy-to-miss track. It led me off the road on a bumpy axle-buster of a trip. Grass tickled the underside of the car; branches swiped at the roof and windshield and pressed the windows like a crowd of outraged demonstrators. Suddenly, though, the car lifted from the wretched road onto something that was wide and smooth and breathtaking; the first of four runways, each 8,500 feet long. I had come to a place that was a jewel, a scar, historic and haunted, an airfield that was once the biggest and busiest in the world, from which two B-29s departed every forty-five seconds. I was visiting the place the *Enola Gay* had called home.

To have that place to myself, the maze of runways, the laterals and parallels and service roads, was a gift. And at first I responded like a kid. I drove out onto the airstrips like an actor in the greatest chase scene never filmed, wandering at will, speeding down runway Able, then over to runway Charlie, feeling my way from one to the next.

In front of me was the vast, hot sky, filled with billowing clouds just begging for planes to fly through them. Forests of *tangan-tangan* rustled in an ovenlike breeze that blew down the runways. And there were the strips themselves, history's launching pads. Could I be blamed for speeding? Or, when I came back at night, for switching off the headlights and counting on the moonlight to guide me, just letting the place and the feeling of the past wash over me?

Eventually I found—or felt—my way to the A-bomb loading pits, where the weapons that destroyed Hiroshima and Nagasaki had been hoisted into the bellies of the *Enola Gay* and the *Bock's Car*. They sat in a cul-de-sac off runway Able. There I sometimes encountered visitors—returning veterans, Japanese priests. I didn't feel so buoyant then. But I valued the one-on-one encounter with history that Tinian afforded. It was history without guards, guides, matrons, docents, or rangers; without filmstrips, slides, sound-and-light shows, or interactive audiovisual gee-whiz stuff of any kind.

I returned to Tinian recently and discovered something about history: it keeps on happening. Tinian is now part of a U.S. Commonwealth. A Chinese casino underwrites an air-conditioned ferry that crosses over from Saipan. My jaunt down Broadway was halted by a Marine Corps guard post fitted out with sandbags and razor wire; hundreds of marines were down from Okinawa on maneuvers. Though I was permitted a visit to the A-bomb pits and a glance at runway Charlie, it wasn't the kind of free and easy reunion I was hoping for.

Marines, tourists, and gamblers come and go in the Marianas, but on Tinian, ghosts abide.

P. F. Kluge is writer-in-residence at Kenyon College and lives in Gambier, Ohio with his wife Pamela Hollie. He is the author of several novels and nonfiction books, including Final Exam, Alma Mater: A College Homecoming, The Edge of Paradise: America in Micronesia, *and* MacArthur's Ghost. *He served in the U.S. Peace Corps in Micronesia and has worked as a reporter for* The Wall Street Journal *and as an editor for* Life *magazine. He has also contributed to* Rolling Stone, Playboy, *and* Smithsonian, *and is a contributing editor at* National Geographic Traveler.

27 JON BOWERMASTER

TO THE TUAMOTU!

Life looks different at sea level.

UNDER CLEAR NIGHT SKIES AND BEFORE A CALM WIND WE LEFT Fakarava, hoping to make the 13.5-mile crossing to the tiny *motu* of Kiria before the waves kicked up. Our destination was not much more than a sand spit, broken by a wide pass, or *hoa*, through which the tide ebbed and flowed.

Rising just six feet above the surface of the South Pacific, the *motu* was dotted by coconut palms and haunted by soaring frigate birds. On the ocean side, a reef circled the island and was pounded relentlessly by big waves. The lagoon inside, however, was calm, crystal clear, and a perfect place for kayaks.

We were two weeks into a six-week exploration of the long chain of atolls in French Polynesia known as the Tuamotu Archipelago. Our days now had a rhythm: Break camp with the sunrise, under a cool morning breeze.

Push off into the lagoon before 8 A.M., heading for…well, usually we had no specific goal.

On Fakarava and the larger atolls, we circumnavigated the interior lagoons, plying calm waters, occasionally humping the boats over the rough, exposed coral into outer lagoons.

We were a team of five who had come to the Tuamotu hoping to cover the length of the 932-mile chain mostly by kayak.

Oceania was the last area on earth to be settled by humans, and the beauty of traveling the Tuamotu Archipelago by sea kayak is that it was similar-size boats—probably coming from the Society Islands and the Marquesas—that settled these tiny lumps about one thousand years ago.

The very remoteness of the Tuamotu—which means "distant islets"—is what has kept them clean and underpopulated, with few hotels or towns. The chain lies exactly halfway between Australia and South America, 3,500 miles from each continent. It was given the nickname "The Dangerous Archipelago" by French explorer Louis-Antoine de Bougainville, thanks to the shallow, sharp reefs that surround the seventy-six atolls that spread northwest-to-southeast between Tahiti and the Marquesas. Hundreds of navigators before us must have run aground here on this spiky, edge-of-the-world speed bump, no doubt cursing it as something other than paradise.

Ferdinand Magellan was the first European to discover the Tuamotu chain, spying Pukapuka in 1521. Some three hundred years later the atolls finally succumbed to the French Protectorate. Life since then has been mostly peaceful, except for a period when the French tested nuclear weapons on the atolls of Mururoa and Fangataufa. That ended in 1996.

Our route began in Rangiroa, the world's second-largest coral atoll, and we planned to travel by kayak to Toau, Fakarava, and Faaite. From there, we would jump aboard a Tahiti-based cargo boat, making its monthly deliveries of cigarettes and beer, cinder blocks and frozen chicken, and travel 600 miles farther to Pukapuka.

On Rangiroa, at the tiny port town of Avatoru, we slipped our kayaks into the northern rim of the island's giant, roughly fifty mile-by-fifteen mile lagoon. At day's end, we reached the shallows on the far southern side of the lagoon. Paddling in to shore, we had to skirt coral build-ups that resembled giant wagon wheels studded with clams that sparkled like jewels under a navy blue sky. We made camp on a virgin, no-name beach, alongside a *hoa*—a pass running from the ocean into the lagoon.

Access to the interior of these atolls comes, if it comes at all, through a single natural pass, maybe two. Lining the reef on the ocean side are prehistoric, sharply barbed fossilized spikes—some eight feet tall—known as *feo*, coral heads that rose as a result of pressure on the tectonic plates below the surface hundreds of thousands of years ago. Every time we crossed the coral reefs we thought back to those early navigators who arrived at this place surrounded by fearsome natural barbed wire. Would they have ventured ashore here? Or steered away, looking for a more friendly isle?

We were not the only ones staying on the remote beaches. On the far side of Rangiroa, opposite from the small town of Avatoru, we met Tuamotu native Hinano Murphy camping on the beach with her family. Now living in Tahiti, Hinano had brought her two children—ages six and four—for a vacation, their first visit to the Tuamotu. She told us the story of her birth out here, announced, miraculously, by a great frigate bird.

Hinano's mother, living on the tiny atoll of Nukutavake, was pregnant and unwed. When her time came, to avoid undue

Dark-eyed and dark-haired, she laughed infectiously while telling her story, all the while plaiting palm fronds into baskets and weaving white *tiare* flowers into coronas she wore each morning on the beach.

scrutiny, Hinano's great-grandfather paddled his granddaughter across the open ocean in a canoe to the nearby, deserted atoll of Vairaatea, where the birthing took place. With no formal way to make the birth public—thus official—great-grandpa wrote the date and name of his new princess on a piece of paper ripped from a sugar sack. Snaring a bird, he wrapped the note in paper money and tied the small bundle to its wing with a strand of coconut husk. The announcement was found weeks later on a neighboring atoll and the birth officially recorded.

"Then, when I was four, my great-grandfather insisted my mother take me away to Tahiti," Hinano explained. "There were no schools here at the time and, more than anything, my father wanted an education for me—as well as a husband outside my extended family."

Dark-eyed and dark-haired, she laughed infectiously while telling her story, all the while plaiting palm fronds into baskets and weaving white *tiare* flowers into coronas she wore each morning on the beach. We spent the day together as she caught and cleaned parrotfish and surgeonfish and built an oven under the sand, using dried coral to start the fire. She opened coconuts with a machete in five practiced whacks and grated the meat into salads of manioc, breadfruit, and poi. Kneeling in the shallows atop a micro-atoll, she dug clams out of the coral with a sharp knife, sharing them raw, drenched under squeezed lime.

Hinano and a smattering of other islanders hope to protect

what remains of the Paumotuan language and culture. The future is not particularly bright; the blend of influential cultures from the outside have already made a large dent in a way of life that goes back centuries.

"Whenever I return to the atoll, everything my great-grandfather and other relatives taught me comes immediately back," says Hinano. "It is very special here—the ocean, the air, everything feels different. I feel like I belong." She continued, "But care needs to be taken to preserve the life, the environment, the culture here. The language is already lost, in part due to a rush to learn French and English. My generation was punished in the French schools here for speaking Paumotuan."

Just as the cultural world is at risk here, so is the natural world, threatened by global warming and storms. With elevations just five to ten feet above sea level, the *motu* are susceptible to rising tides and storm surges. Some scientists suggest it will be only another 50 to 100 years before the Tuamotu will be swamped and unlivable, the 16,000 residents forced to move.

To make the 100-mile passage from Rangiroa to Toau we hitched a ride aboard a passing fishing boat—a violently rough, five-hour trip over open ocean. As soon as we docked, we unloaded our kayaks and paddled toward a seemingly vacant beach on the walnut-shaped atoll. Before we could pull the boats up on the sand, a voice shouted out of the plantation palms. "Hello, my friends!"

The bellowing voice belonged to Alicia Snow, one of the island's forty inhabitants. She has lived here all her fifty years, in a two-room, tin-roofed plywood shack with her sixty-two-year-old husband and one of her two grown sons, a twenty-year-old called "100 Kilos."

There are three ways to make a living in the Tuamotu: fish, copra, and black pearls. Alicia and her extended family—she's related to everyone within a 100-mile radius—were into them all. Pens of big parrotfish sat off the nearest pass. Burlap sacks of dried copra—the white meat of coconuts, used to make coconut oil—were stacked under a porch roof (the twice-a-month cargo boat that brings everything the islanders need takes them away). And in a hibiscus tree hung the black nets used to float pearl-bearing oysters thirty or forty feet below the surface of the deep lagoon. This last industry, black pearls, is the lifeblood of the chain. As a result, everyone now wants to have his or her own pearl farm, threatening the future market value of the shiny orbs that range in color from champagne to green, but rarely true black.

Alicia was dressed in a blue swimsuit and gray shorts, with sunglasses stuck into her thick black hair. Since she was the first person we had seen since Rangiroa, she got to hear the story of how we somehow managed to leave behind all our water. Five jerry cans brimming with 100 liters of the clear stuff. The only thing we truly needed here, the only irreplaceable item, and we left it sitting on a cement dock at Avatoru. Alicia listened, nodded her head, seeming to understand our dilemma, but in seconds waved good-bye and zoomed off into the sunset in her white plywood speedboat.

But Alicia returned early the next morning, accompanied by 100 Kilos. As the boat skidded to a stop in the sand, 100 Kilos handed a fat blue plastic jug of freshwater over the side and Alicia flashed us a gap-toothed smile. She carried another gift—a coconut puller. As long as there are coconuts, you will always have water. But the freshest and wettest are the green ones high in the trees. To reach them, you need a long pole with a metal hook. Since starting our voyage, our self-sufficiency quota had doubled. We could now open a coconut in ten or twelve whacks, recognize fresh mangoes from 100 paces, and open clams with nothing but a knife. Only our spearfishing was lacking. Peter had the only take so far, a fist-size parrotfish that required more work to clean than it was worth.

Every day—and most noticeably, at night—we heard falling coconuts thudding to the ground with regularity. I asked Alicia how many times she'd been hit by falling cocos. It seemed like an inevitability, statistically speaking. She looked at me as if I was crazy.

"Never, of course!"

"And why not?"

"Because, silly, coconuts have eyes. Look at them! They can see if you're underneath and, if you are a good person, they will not fall on you. I promise. In my family it has never happened!"

Between paddling and ferrying our kayaks via fishing vessel and cargo boat, we covered 3,000 miles round-trip, stopping at twenty-three atolls. While many *motu* looked alike, each had a different personality and a variety of characters.

On Makemo, there was Paulina, who made us palm frond hats and danced for us, remembering her days as an extra in Marlon Brando's *Mutiny on the Bounty*. On Raroia, we met the man whose father discovered Thor Heyerdahl's *Kon Tiki* when it washed ashore in 1947. On Amanu, William Perry told us his father had fifty-eight children—with several wives—and today Perrys inhabit many of the Tuamotu.

On Pukarua, Mayor Turio invited us in for a breakfast of lobster and Coca-Cola and showed off a monstrous shark bite on his calf. He was spearfishing outside the reef with a friend, when a lemon shark went after the line of fish taken by his buddy—and then after his buddy.

Turio shot the shark with his speargun and it turned on him. He freed his leg by kicking the shark forcefully with his other foot and swam to the reef. A plane carried him to Tahiti where he was in the hospital for three months. Today it's just a big ugly scar and a good story.

Most nights during our trip, I slept in a hammock, which swung lazily in the darkness pushed by a constant breeze, waving palm fronds providing a sing-song lullaby. Mornings I awoke to an azure sky and frigate birds hovering above—heads straight out, wings extended, pronged tails directly downwind.

We kayaked and explored the atolls until sunset, and I finished my days reading Gauguin, Stevenson, and Melville, all white men who came here in search of the same thing, motivated by the same urging, a "dream of islands."

Idyllic? Paradise? Tropical dream? All of that and more. But the most salient fact about this scene is that I will miss it a thousand mornings over.

Jon Bowermaster has spent the last twenty years writing about adventure, the environment, and exotic corners of the world for publications such as The Atlantic Monthly, Outside, National Geographic, *and* The New York Times. *He has sledded across Antarctica, sailed across the Atlantic, and made first descents of rivers from Chile to China, among other adventures. Most of his recent work has been done on behalf of the National Geographic Society. When not traveling, he lives in Stone Ridge, New York.*

28

JORDAN RANE

MY DAD IS YOUR DAD

"Six degrees of separation" has a special meaning in Tonga.

IT WASN'T A GOOD REASON TO FLY OFF TO A REMOTE ISLAND, BUT before leaving Tonga there was something I needed to do. I had to go to Ha'apai to see if Tevita Vaikona's dad really would be sitting outside his shop waiting to take me in like family.

The fact that I wasn't at all family apparently didn't matter on Ha'apai. If a total stranger (like me) ever visited, Tevita assured me, his father, Tu'ifua, would take me on the next boat to his village on the tiny island of 'Uiha, where I'd go fishing *faka Tonga* (Tonga style), drink kava, and spend some quality time with the whole clan. Maybe I'd been traveling for too long. All I knew was that a little family time on a warm island in remotest Polynesia sounded pretty good, no matter whose family it was.

Tevita Vaikona is a professional rugby player for the Bradford Bulls in the English leagues. He's a recognized name in the United Kingdom and a hero in Tonga—especially ‘Uiha (population 450)—where his family and childhood friends still live (without cars, roads, or phones). ‘Uiha lies in Tonga's Ha‘apai island group, a cluster of coral atolls and volcanoes strewn across miles of ocean like loose change.

I would never have visited these islands if I hadn't by chance sat next to Tevita during an evening performance at the Tonga National Center, on the country's main island of Tongatapu. While a troop of large, oiled-down Tongans danced the *lakalaka* and *ma‘ulu‘ulu* for the small audience, Tevita told me about his scholarship to study accounting in New Zealand, and his "fluke" draft onto the Junior Kiwi national rugby team, which led to his going pro in England. He was between rugby seasons, heading home to ‘Uiha with a huge suitcase of gifts.

"If you ever make it out to Ha‘apai," he said after the show, "my dad has a shop on the main island. His name's Tu‘ifua. Tell him you're a friend. He'll get you over to ‘Uiha and you'll go fishing with my brothers *faka Tonga*."

It seemed like one of those kind invitations handed out to stray travelers as a matter of course. Besides, the odds of my being in Ha‘apai someday were immeasurably slim. I was booked to leave Tonga in two days. The next flight to Ha‘apai was the day after that. But at the last minute, something made me decide I had to make that unlikely trip.

I was one of two out-of-towners on the tiny Royal Tongan Airlines plane rattling north into the country's sparse midpoint that day; the other was a Fijian sales rep who sat across the aisle. I asked him what he sold.

"Corned beef," he said, "in a can. It's very popular in Tonga. And you?"

"Just visiting friends," I said, even though it sounded absurd to me.

After miles of open ocean, Ha'apai's languid islands appeared, looking like mixed greens on turquoise plates. Looming off to the west was the volcanic crater of Tofua, where the mutiny on the *Bounty* had occurred a few centuries prior. It was still the region's top headline. Not many visitors came out this way, said the corned-beef broker. He was amazed that I had friends here. I guessed I would soon find out if I did.

The sedate village of Pangai is a breezy walk from the island's airfield. Trudging past a closed post office, a one-desk bank, a police station, and a round of sunburned churches, I was finally hit by the full weight of what an embarrassingly bad idea this was. What was I doing here? I'd gone out of my way to barge in on some Tongan family for no good reason.

I found Tu'ifua's shop without a problem, and Tu'ifua—or a man I figured for him—was right outside his store, just like Tevita had said, sitting on a tree stump and tearing into a loaf of bread.

"Are you Tu'ifua?" I asked the man.

"Yes," he said, "I am Tu'ifua."

"Is Tevita your son?"

"Tevita is my son," he replied, squinting up at me.

A small group of his cronies lumbered over to see what the sweaty *palangi* with the backpack was trying to pull. It was definitely time to leave.

Instead, I found myself launching into an explanation about how I didn't want to impose but happened to be in town and it was really nice to meet his son and now him...and on and on I went. A terrible silence followed. Tu'ifua sat there on his stump, unhurried, peering up at me and glancing over at his silent entourage. He ripped another hunk of bread from the loaf and gazed at the endless ocean. I seemed to fade from his view. Then he smiled up at me, as if I were an afterthought: Oh, right—you. Of course I was welcome on 'Uiha, he said. It was good I'd come all this way. Everyone would be happy to see me. A few cronies nodded. One of them grabbed my bag and waded into the ocean toward his little boat, then turned to me and shrugged. Was I coming or what?

Tevita was dozing in his parents' front yard when I pulled ashore out of the blue. He wasn't the least bit surprised to see me. During a round of introductions, I met his brothers and cousins and uncles and aunts and sisters and childhood friends, whom he also referred to as his brothers. It was decided that we'd all drink kava that night. Tomorrow we'd go fishing.

That was just what we did—we closed out the day eating yams and *ota ika* with our hands, and laughed over card games with a deck that included a 13 of hearts. We drank more kava the next night, lots more. Then, bloated on murky brown liquid, raw fish, starch, and good times, I had to leave Ha'apai for home.

Home? Where was that again?

On my way back, I found Tu'ifua right where I'd left him, holding court from the tree stump outside his shop, sitting with his buddies, eating his loaf of bread, sharing his hospitality. It flows in abundance on islands like Ha'apai, where lucky castaways might enjoy a good dose of family time.

Jordan Rane, formerly a senior editor for Escape *magazine, is a freelance writer who lives in Southern California.*

29

FRANCES FITZGERALD

THE SOLOMONS' SILENT WORLD

A diver explores a wonderland years before it became an underwater destination.

OUR DIVE BOAT, THE *BILIKIKI*, LAY AT ANCHOR IN THE LEE of Vangunu Island in the New Georgias. An extinct volcano rose sharply above us, its peak swathed in heavy, rain-filled clouds. The slopes were covered in jungle, which came right down to the water's edge. Across the lagoon a bright line of surf was breaking between two islets, and beyond, far in the distance, an underwater volcano's plume of steam billowed into the sky.

There was no sign of a village on Vangunu, but half a dozen dugouts were now tied up to the *Bilikiki's* stern. On the afterdeck, women in shapeless dresses were unpacking baskets filled with limes and coconuts and children were staring at our dive gear and listening quietly to the talk of the crew. In one of the dugouts a man was fishing, quite successfully, for bottom fish with a line weighted by stones tied in strips of palm frond. Each time he pulled up a fish, the stone would slip out and sink to the bottom. He would rebait his hook, tie on another stone, and throw out the line again.

We had come to this island to dive on the wrecks of three World War II ships, and had spent the morning exploring a Japanese transport ship in 120 feet of water. Four large groupers guarded the stocks of ammunition in her hold, and a tiny—and quite rare—hawkfish darted about the soft coral on her mast. But the visibility was poor, and rather than dive on another similar wreck, we decided to check out other waters.

Now we took one of *Bilikiki's* two motorboats to the outer edge of the turquoise channel between the two islets, where we dropped overboard. Below the surface there was no current at all, so we swam easily past the shallow coral ledge to a wall that dropped down straight as a plumb line into the ocean depths.

Leveling off at seventy feet, we swam toward the channel, seeing nothing at first except the blue expanses. Then a slight current picked up from behind us, and the visibility decreased. Rounding a point where ocean water entered the lagoon and stirred up nutrients, we found ourselves surrounded by schools of rainbow runners. Squid swam by us, followed by a school of fish that looked like sardines—until they opened their mouths; then their jaws dropped as if on hinges, and they looked like a thousand silver Pac-Men. A large barracuda idled in the current, and three small white-tipped sharks drifted by, ignoring us totally in their pursuit of a midday meal.

We worked our way upward along the reef and found ourselves in a coral garden alive with the dance of Moorish idols, butterfly fish, and emperor angels. Near a huge, white table coral, two tomato clownfish poked their heads out of a pale green anemone. When we finally surfaced, it was in a splutter of delight.

The Solomon Islands, which extend across 600 miles of ocean just east of New Guinea, contain nine major island groups and scores of small islands. The islands themselves are hot, humid, malarial, and beset by equatorial storms. And until the *Bilikiki* went into service, the only way to move around the islands was on a sloop belonging to a former salvage diver. Few sport divers came to the Solomons, and few of the hundreds upon hundreds of miles of reefs had been explored.

Formerly a British protectorate and now a sovereign nation, the Solomons are largely covered by jungle. Plantations established by nineteenth-century British trading firms produce a traditional South Seas harvest of copra, palm oil, cocoa, and timber. Most of the country's quarter of a million inhabitants continue to live either in isolated coastal villages—cultivating gardens, catching fish, and selling a bit of copra—or in isolated bush settlements—practicing slash-and-burn agriculture.

During World War II, Allied troops fought their way up the Solomons in a series of bloody battles, leaving the sea lanes littered with sunken ships. In the dense jungles on land, rusting planes and artillery pieces look curiously small and antique. Yet on many of the islands they remain the only real evidence of the twentieth century. In two weeks we rarely saw any lights at night, except for those on tuna boats and interisland freighters.

We arrived in the Solomons by plane, landing on Guadalcanal. My husband and I saw only six other people who might be ticking off "pleasure" on the immigration forms as the purpose of their visit, and, as we discovered in the Customs shed, all of them were bound for the *Bilikiki*.

The ship's proprietor, Rich Belmare, met us with a minibus and a truck for our gear. A Canadian dive master, he had come to the Solomons with his wife in the 1980s on a trip around the

South Pacific and, quixotically, had decided to stay and build a business. There was, he said with a grin, no competition because few tourists came to the Solomons.

During the drive into the town of Honiara, Belmare pointed out the beach where the Allies had landed on August 7, 1942, and the escarpment known as Bloody Ridge, above the airport, as well as memorials to both Japanese and Allied troops who had died on Guadalcanal. We did not stop in Honiara—a small town of government buildings and Chinese-owned dry goods stores—but instead made our way past warehouses and tuna canneries to the fishing wharf where the *Bilikiki* was berthed.

Stan Waterman—tall, bronzed, and silver-haired—was on the pier to greet us. Behind him, to our dismay, was an entire television crew ready to film our hot and bedraggled arrival. One of the pioneers of underwater cinematography and a legendary raconteur, Waterman had probably had more diving adventures than anyone except Jacques Cousteau. He had come to the Solomons once before to film the war wrecks. This time he was to be the host for our group—fifteen keen sports divers and amateur underwater photographers making our first trip to the Solomons—while a television crew made a documentary on him.

With all the gear, the *Bilikiki* looked something like a Steven Speilberg special effects lab. The sophisticated electronic equipment stood in some contrast to the ship itself. Three years earlier Belmare and a partner had salvaged the rusting hulk of a 121-foot interisland freighter and made her into a comfortable boat, with ten air-conditioned double cabins and efficient dive equipment. Yet the bridge had just one instrument—a compass. The captain, a canny Solomon Islander, seemed to navigate by some private system of his own.

The *Bilikiki* put out to sea that afternoon and made a night crossing to the Russells, a small cluster of volcanic islands some forty miles northwest of Honiara. We woke in a still, hot cove on the shore of an enormous coconut plantation. Beyond a jetty we could see some antiquated machinery and the roofs of copra drying sheds. The cove had been a PT boat base during World War II, Waterman said, possibly one that John F. Kennedy had visited. Some of us donned our wet suits and plunged in—only to discover that the sea was as hot, green, and still as the jungle itself.

In the Russells we dived on a wartime munitions dump, where huge sponges that looked like outsize calla lilies grew between rusting jeeps and piles of .50-caliber machine-gun rounds. (Ten days later, on our return trip through the Russells, we heard an underwater explosion so loud that each diver thought that his or her own air tank had blown up. From the radio we learned that an Australian ship had been exploding dangerous shells from that dump.)

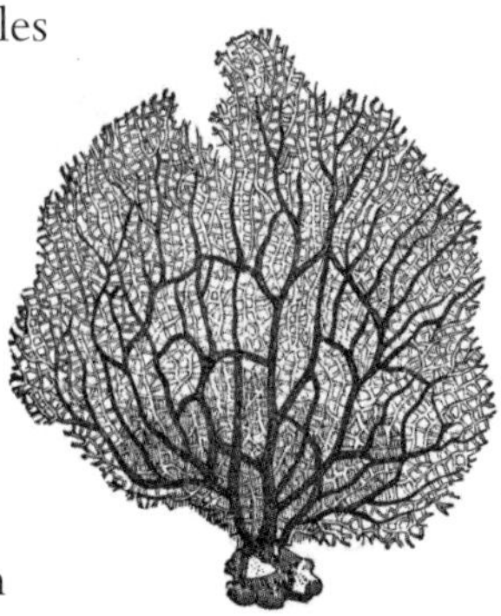

We also found several astonishing vertical walls in the Russells, walls descending hundreds, sometimes thousands of feet into the ocean. Huge sea fans were growing on the walls, some of them decorated with brilliantly colored crinoids. Turtles, tuna, and families of twenty-pound, bump-headed parrotfish swam surrealistically in around us.

One afternoon the ship's manager, Jim Light, dropped us off at the entrance to a narrow cave that extended hundreds of yards back into the limestone. Swimming the length of it, we came up in a small island pool dappled with sunlight streaming through a canopy of jungle. After returning to the cave's entrance, four of us caught a current that took us at dream speed past a series of coral outcroppings, each with collections of gorgeous aquarium fish. Mesmerized, we lost track of time.

When we surfaced, the boat was out of sight. It was a long swim back to shore, where a thatched hut sat in the shade of a mango tree. For a while, until the boat picked us up, I fantasized about staying there for good.

Our route took us from the Russells to a solitary island called Mborokua, or Mary Island, and from there to the New Georgias, another forty miles to the northwest. One of the major island groups in the Solomons, the New Georgias are composed of five large islands with steep volcanic mountains and dozens of smaller islands and islets around deep lagoons. The islands are sparsely populated, the reefs are pristine, and the lagoons filled with fish. On one dive we saw fifty or sixty lobsters in a single cave. On another we swam by three Tridacna clams that each must have measured five feet across.

Diving the Solomons is not like diving the Caribbean, or even the more temperate zones of the Pacific. Weather and currents are notoriously unpredictable. A few days into our trip, an out-of-season cyclone passed through the Solomons some distance away, sinking a yacht. We were never in any danger. But we had a couple of rough passages, and for some days we had to dive in poor visibility off the inner islands.

One morning, looking for calm water, we took the boats up a stream to a brackish lake, then turned down another stream to find ourselves in a small lagoon with a cut leading out into the ocean. Jim Light had been told that there was a beautiful cave below the cut, and because visibility in the lagoon was near zero, he led us down to find the entrance. At fifty feet he found himself in front of a black hole with water surging down, as if it were going down a drain.

Trusting that this torrent must be going somewhere, he went in. One other diver followed him, but the rest of us, fearful of the downward tug of a current in murky water, decided against it. A few moments later Light and the other diver were flushed out into the ocean, eighty feet below the surface.

Later, when the weather cleared, Light found that the storm had altered the dive sites he knew. Often we found only empty ocean in places where, he said, there had been many fish only two weeks before. But frequently we were lucky when we simply dropped overboard at a place that looked promising on the charts.

School upon school of rainbow runners, fusiliers, and jacks rushed past us while a torrent of surgeonfish and unicornfish dived downward and through them from the top of the reef.

On one such dive, as four of us were descending to ninety feet, I looked up and saw an eight-foot silvertip shark bearing down on me from the reef. It occurred to me that the shark might consider the reef his private preserve and my presence a disagreeable intrusion. But at the last moment the shark turned away and sped off into the ocean—with three photographers swimming after him as fast as they could.

One afternoon, in pouring rain off Kicha Island, we dropped off onto a wall. Sixty feet down, the water was perfectly clear. Then suddenly the visibility dropped, and we found ourselves in a maelstrom of fish. School upon school of rainbow runners, fusiliers, and jacks rushed past us while a torrent of surgeonfish and unicornfish dived downward and through them from the top of the reef.

Below us we caught glimpses of sharks in deep water. Just in front of us a school of 500 silver barracuda passed by and returned, swimming figure eights in perfect formation. Behind us, where the reef shelved upward, we could see three much larger barracuda with prominent teeth, hunting in a roiling mass of triggerfish, grouper, coral rock cod, and small reef fish. The sheer mass of fish was overwhelming. The photographers among us swam about distractedly, hardly knowing what to focus on.

Each day, late in the afternoon, the *Bilikiki* would put into a lagoon and find an anchorage, usually just off a village. We would gaze out toward the thatched houses on the beach and watch children netting bait fish or splashing in the shallows. Sometimes we would see the red flash of an eclectus parrot in the coconut palms. One Saturday evening, near a Seventh Day Adventist village, a procession of women in bright cotton dresses coming home from church filed down a path toward the beach, as graceful as women in Gauguin paintings.

We went ashore occasionally but did not stray very far from the beach. Walking through a village on these islands is as much an invasion of privacy as walking through someone's house without invitation. Always, however, the villagers came out to the ship in their narrow dugouts, the women with vegetables and fruit to sell and the men bringing fish or, if we were lucky, mangrove crabs.

In the New Georgias, where wood carving is a tradition, village carvers brought rosewood bowls, ebony masks, and sculptures of birds and marine animals. Displaying their wares, they bargained with us diffidently and with impeccable politeness, often accepting a dive knife or a snorkel in lieu of money.

This commerce with islanders was, Light told us, an important part of the *Bilikiki's* routine. By customary law the villages owned all the reefs in the Solomons, each village considering the closest neighboring reefs its "gardens" and jealously guarding its exclusive right to fish on them. Belmare had spent eighteen months negotiating with the chiefs on the islands, convincing them that divers were coming to photograph, not to fish. He had agreed to buy produce and fish from the islanders and to pay them a small sum for each dive. Now, two and a half years later, the *Bilikiki* had come to depend on the villages for water and vegetables—including lettuce and eggplant grown from seeds the ship itself had introduced. For their part the villagers now had cash to buy trade goods, from flashlights to outboard motors.

For us the evening visits from the islanders were one of the signal pleasures of the trip. They gave us a glimpse of a culture still largely isolated from the outside world—as well as a glimpse of ourselves.

I found myself negotiating with a carver for a replica of a mask his ancestors had used when going out head-hunting. Speaking English, he said that he needed cash for it, as he was paying school tuition for a nephew to become a teacher or a pastor. He spoke so earnestly that I asked him about the rest of the family; later he asked me a bit about the United States. Were there carvers in America? Did Americans live in the bush, as well as on the coasts? And why was it that America was so powerful—and always seemed to be fighting?

I responded as best I could, then changed the subject to religion. I had heard, I said, that while all the coastal villages of the Solomons had been Christian for many, many years, some villages of the interior had never converted. Why was this?

Well, the carver replied, this was a question he had puzzled over himself for some time. It certainly wasn't for lack of evangelizing, so the only answer he could come up with was that there was a strong devil in the bush who lost his powers when he approached the shore.

Perhaps, I thought, the missionaries had not quite completed their job, even in the villages of the coast.

We dined well on the *Bilikiki*—sometimes on fresh tuna we caught trolling out at sea—and by 9 P.M. sleep seemed almost irresistible. Yet at least some of us were always ready to suit up for a night dive.

The boat would anchor on a shallow reef, and we would swim down into a dark, warm sea as thick with phosphorescence as the night was full of stars. It was on these nights we saw the true curiosities of the reef: the flower corals, the cuttlefish, the scorpionfish, and all the creatures that came out to feed after dark.

One evening I found a crab with a gelatinous green hat that walked forward instead of sideways on feet that seemed to be made out of Velcro. Another time we saw a dwarf lionfish out hunting, as well as a family of translucent aquamarine needlefish—the needlefish so sleepy and so dazzled by our lights they bumped delicately into our masks.

Then as we surfaced through the phosphorescence, we would find ourselves in the equatorial night, once again as far away from the world of familiar things as we could be on the planet.

Author and journalist Frances FitzGerald received both the Pulitzer Prize and the National Book Award for Fire In the Lake: The Vietnamese and the Americans in Vietnam, *first published in 1972. She also wrote* Vietnam: Spirits of the Earth, Way Out There In the Blue: Reagan, Star Wars and the End of the Cold War, *and* Cities on a Hill. *She is a frequent contributor to* The New Yorker, *has written for the* New York Review of Books, The New York Times Magazine, Esquire, Rolling Stone, Islands, *and other publications. She also serves on the editorial boards of* The Nation *and* Foreign Policy, *and is vice-president of PEN.*

30 TARA AUSTEN WEAVER

ONE DAY IN A LIFE

It is good to melt into creation, and be reborn.

I LIE AWAKE IN THE DARK AND LISTEN TO THE SCRATCH-scratching of a crab as he tries to make his way through the bamboo slats that form the walls of my thatched *bure*. The noise blends with the lapping of the ocean and the cry of a million different Fijian insects. The crab is persistent and soon is crawling about the sand floor of my hut. By daybreak he is gone, leaving behind hundreds of tiny crab claw tracks in the sand.

I rise early and breakfast on papayas the size of melons. There are bananas as well, an entire branch of them hacked off the tree with a machete and hung to ripen in the outdoor kitchen. I sit at a table under the palm trees and watch gentle waves break on shore, the persistent rhythm now a backdrop to all that I do. I have not been out of range of the sound of the ocean for weeks now. I have ceased to hear it, as I cannot hear my own heartbeat.

There are four small islands lying offshore in a chain, like bits of earth flung off the mainland. I point my kayak towards them in the early morning light. It is not yet noon but the sun beats down with a tropical intensity as my boat slices through water clear as glass. Below me the coral, distorted by the waves, looks like a miniature magical forest. The third island out has a small sandy beach and I pull the boat ashore. It is my island for the day—three trees, a few bushes, rocks, and sand. I throw off my clothes, don my snorkel, and immerse myself in a magical kingdom under the sea.

Starfish are purple, rocks are green and yellow, and tiny blue fish hover around a peach-colored coral, like bluebirds perched in a tree. Snakes are striped black and white like zebras, and sea anemones extend tentacles of green and gold. It is like a dream, a hallucination, stranger than imagination, yet as real as the salt on my skin and the sun on my back. I sink into warm sand and savor my world. I can hear the laughter of a pack of local schoolboys echoing over the water. They laugh like all Fijians laugh, a cascade of sound unrestrained and joyous, utterly entrancing. I have laughed more in these islands than ever before. Laughed more, and heard more laughter, than anywhere else I have ever been. Though I am here alone, I never feel lonely. Friendly eyes watch over me and people I have not yet met call out my name, rolling the pronunciation so that it sounds like an invitation, an incantation, a bond between us.

Afternoon finds the kayak heading back to the mainland. The magic kingdom will wait for another day, another explorer. For me it is a long walk down the dirt road, into a flaming crimson island sunset. Later I lie in the dark—tired, invigorated, mystified, and satisfied. I listen to the lapping of the waves, the faint crash of the surf as it breaks on offshore reefs, and the scratch-scratching of a crab trying to get through the bamboo slats of my seaside hut.

Tara Austen Weaver is a San Francisco-based writer and developmental editor specializing in travel, cultural issues, and adventure sports. She is the coeditor of two Travelers' Tales anthologies, Tuscany *and* Provence, *and lead author for the guidebook* Art/Shop/Eat San Francisco. *She has lived in five countries on three continents, but Fiji remains one of her very favorite places. She can be reached through www.taraweaver.com.*

INDEX

A

B

C

D

E

F

G

H

I

K

L

M

T

U

V

W

Y

ACKNOWLEDGMENTS

We would like to thank our families and friends for their usual forbearance while we are putting a book together. Many thanks also to Susan Brady, Stefan Gutermuth, Cynthia Lamb, Judy Johnson, Christy Harrington, Sarah Jolley, Ashley Pickering, Alexandria Brady, and Kelly and Jonathan Knowles. And special thanks to Lisa Gosselin and Nancy Maul of *Islands* magazine, Jonathan W. Reap of Tahiti Tourisme North America, Susan Bejeckian of Susan Bejeckian Public Relations, Melissa Hinderman at Graham and Associates, David Stanley, Frank Chan, and all the wonderful staff and management team at the Jean-Michel Cousteau Fiji Islands Resort.

"*Vive le Surf*" by Aaron Perry reprinted from the December 1994 issue of *Islands*. Copyright © 1994 by Aaron Perry.

"Dreamland" by James C. Simmons excerpted from *Castaway in Paradise: The Incredible Adventure of True-Life Robinson Crusoes* by James C. Simmons. Copyright © 1993 by James C. Simmons. Reprinted by permission of Sheridan House, Inc., Dobbs Ferry, New York.

"Looking for Bali Ha'i" by Thurston Clarke originally appeared as "Searaching for Bali Ha'i" in Volume 18 Issue 4 of *Islands*. Copyright © 1998 by Thurston Clarke. Reprinted with permission from the author.

"A *Fale* with a View" by Tony Perrottet published with permission from the author. Copyright © 2005 by Tony Perrottet.

"Freighter to the Fabled Isles" by Lynn Ferrin published with permission from the author. Copyright © 2005 by Lynn Ferrin.

"The Heart of the Dance" by Laura Florand published with permission from the author. Copyright © 2005 by Laura Florand.

"Listening to Lullabies" by Kathryn J. Abajian published with permission from the author. Copyright © 2005 by Kathryn J. Abajian.

"The Black and the White" by Eugene Burdick excerpted from *The Blue of Capricorn* by Eugene Burdick. Copyright © 1961 by Eugene Burdick. Reprinted by permission of Houghton Mifflin, Inc.

"Last Old Boys' Club in the Pacific" by Rick Carroll published with permission from the author. Copyright © 2005 by Rick Carroll.

"Marked by the Marquesas" by Bob Payne reprinted from the January 1999 issue of *Islands*. Copyright © 1999 by Bob Payne. Reprinted with permission from the author.

"Petticoat Juncture" by Linda Hagen Miller published with permission from the author. Copyright © 2005 by Linda Hagen Miller.

"Mama Rose's Coconut Bread" by Celeste Brash published with permission from the author. Copyright © 2005 by Celeste Brash.

"Yap Magic" by Lawrence Millman originally appeared as "Micronesian Idyll" in the May/June 1999 issue of *Islands*. Copyright © 1999 by Lawrence Millman. Reprinted with permission from the author.

"Cross-Dressing in Paradise" by Tony Perrottet published with permission from the author. Copyright © 2005 by Tony Perrottet.

"Paddling a Chain of Pearls" by Jeff Hull originally appeared as "Paddling Through Paradise" in the July/August 2005 issue of *Islands*. Copyright © 2005 by Islands Publishing Company. Reprinted by permission.

"Faces of the Past" by Bob Payne reprinted from the September/October 2001 issue of *Islands.* Copyright © 2001 by Bob Payne. Reprinted with permission from the author.

"Heaven Is Not What You Think" by J. Maarten Troost excerpted from *The Sex Lives of Cannibals: Adrift in the Equatorial Pacific* by J. Maarten Troost. Copyright © 2004 by J. Maarten Troost. Used with permission from Broadway Books, a division of Random House, Inc.

"A Fish Drive in Woleai" by Jerry Miller published with permission from the author. Copyright © 2005 by Jerry Miller.

"In Search of the Last Legend" by Joe Yogerst originally appeared as "In Search of the Last Legend of the South Pacific" in the May/June 2005 issue of *Islands*. Copyright © 2005 by Islands Publishing Company. Reprinted by permission.

"A Graveyard for Ships" by Anthony Sommer originally appeared as "History Haunts Bikini" in *The Arizona Republic.* Copyright © 1996 by The Arizona Republic. Reprinted by permission.

"Away from the Beach" by Roff Smith originally appeared as "Adventures in Paradise" in the February 2000 issue of *Islands*. Copyright © 2000 by Roff Smith. Reprinted with permission from the author.

"Saturday Night in Nauru" by Cleo Paskal published with permission from the author. Copyright © 2005 by Cleo Paskal.

"Runways to History" by P. F. Kluge reprinted from the March 2004 issue of *Islands*. Copyright © 2004 by P. F. Kluge. Reprinted with permission from the author.

"To the Tuamotu!" by Jon Bowermaster reprinted from the January/February 2005 issue of *Islands*. Copyright © 2005 by Islands Publishing Company. Reprinted by permission.

"My Dad Is Your Dad" by Jordan Rane reprinted from the May/June 2004 issue of *Islands Magazine*. Copyright © 2004 by Islands Publishing Company. Reprinted by permission.

"The Solomons' Silent World" by Frances FitzGerald reprinted from the May/June 1992 issue of *Islands*. Copyright © 1992 by Frances FitzGerald. Reprinted with permission from Lescher & Lescher.

"One Day in a Life" by Tara Austen Weaver published with permission from the author. Copyright © 2005 by Tara Austen Weaver.

ABOUT THE EDITORS

Sean O'Reilly is director of special sales and editor-at-large for Travelers' Tales. He is a former seminarian, stockbroker, and prison instructor who lives in Virginia with his wife Brenda and their six children. He's had a lifelong interest in philosophy, theology, and travel, and recently published the groundbreaking book on men's behavior, *How to Manage Your DICK: Redirect Sexual Energy and Discover Your More Spiritually Enlightened, Evolved Self* (www.dickmanagement.com). His most recent travels took him through China, Thailand, Indonesia, and the South Pacific.

James O'Reilly, president and publisher of Travelers' Tales, was born in England and raised in San Francisco. He graduated from Dartmouth College in 1975 and wrote mystery serials before becoming a travel writer in the early 1980s. He's visited more than forty countries, along the way meditating with monks in Tibet, participating in West African voodoo rituals, living in the French Alps, and hanging out the laundry with nuns in Florence. He travels extensively with his wife, Wenda, and their three daughters. They live in Palo Alto, California, where they also publish art games and books for children at Birdcage Press (www.birdcagepress.com).

Larry Habegger, executive editor of Travelers' Tales, has been writing about travel since 1980. He has visited almost fifty countries and six of the seven continents, traveling from the Arctic to equatorial rainforests, the Himalayas to the Dead Sea. In the early 1980s he co-authored mystery serials for the *San Francisco Examiner* with James O'Reilly, and since 1985 their syndicated column, "World Travel Watch," has appeared in newspapers in five countries and on WorldTravelWatch.com. As series editors of

Travelers' Tales, they have worked on more than eighty books, winning many awards for excellence. Habegger regularly teaches the craft of travel writing at workshops and writers' conferences, and he lives with his family on Telegraph Hill in San Francisco.

Women's Travel

A WOMAN'S EUROPE $17.95
True Stories
Edited by Marybeth Bond
An exhilarating collection of inspirational, adventurous, and entertaining stories by women exploring the romantic continent of Europe. From the bestselling author Marybeth Bond.

WOMEN IN THE WILD $17.95
True Stories of Adventure and Connection
Edited by Lucy McCauley
"A spiritual, moving, and totally female book to take you around the world and back."
—*Mademoiselle*

A MOTHER'S WORLD $14.95
Journeys of the Heart
Edited by Marybeth Bond & Pamela Michael
"These stories remind us that motherhood is one of the great unifying forces in the world."
—*San Francisco Examiner*

A WOMAN'S PATH $16.95
Women's Best Spiritual Travel Writing
Edited by Lucy McCauley, Amy G. Carlson & Jennifer Leo
"A sensitive exploration of women's lives that have been unexpectedly and spiritually touched by travel experiences.... Highly recommended."
—*Library Journal*

A WOMAN'S WORLD $18.95
True Stories of World Travel
Edited by Marybeth Bond
Introduction by Dervla Murphy

Lowell Thomas Award
—Best Travel Book

A WOMAN'S PASSION FOR TRAVEL $17.95
True Stories of World Wanderlust
Edited by Marybeth Bond & Pamela Michael
"A diverse and gripping series of stories!"
—Arlene Blum, author of *Annapurna: A Woman's Place*

Food

ADVENTURES IN WINE $17.95
True Stories of Vineyards and Vintages around the World
Edited by Thom Elkjer
Humanity, community, and brotherhood compose the marvelous virtues of the wine world. This collection toasts the warmth and wonders of this large extended family in stories by travelers who are wine novices and experts alike.

HER FORK IN THE ROAD $16.95
Women Celebrate Food and Travel
Edited by Lisa Bach
A savory sampling of stories by the best writers in and out of the food and travel fields.

FOOD $18.95
A Taste of the Road
Edited by Richard Sterling
Introduction by Margo True

Silver Medal Winner of the Lowell Thomas Award
—Best Travel Book

THE ADVENTURE OF FOOD $17.95
True Stories of Eating Everything
Edited by Richard Sterling
"Bound to whet appetites for more than food."
—*Publishers Weekly*

HOW TO EAT AROUND THE WORLD $12.95
Tips and Wisdom
By Richard Sterling
Combines practical advice on foodstuffs, habits, and etiquette, with hilarious accounts of others' eating adventures.

Travel Humor

SAND IN MY BRA AND OTHER MISADVENTURES $14.95
Funny Women Write from the Road
Edited by Jennifer L. Leo
"A collection of ridiculous and sublime travel experiences."
—*San Francisco Chronicle*

HYENAS LAUGHED AT ME AND NOW I KNOW WHY $14.95
The Best of Travel Humor and Misadventure
Edited by Sean O'Reilly, Larry Habegger & James O'Reilly
Hilarious, outrageous and reluctant voyagers indulge us with the best misadventures around the world.

LAST TROUT IN VENICE $14.95
The Far-Flung Escapades of an Accidental Adventurer
By Doug Lansky
"Traveling with Doug Lansky might result in a considerably shortened life expectancy...but what a way to go."
—Tony Wheeler, Lonely Planet Publications

NOT SO FUNNY WHEN IT HAPPENED $12.95
The Best of Travel Humor and Misadventure
Edited by Tim Cahill
Laugh with Bill Bryson, Dave Barry, Anne Lamott, Adair Lara, and many more.

THERE'S NO TOILET PAPER ON THE ROAD LESS TRAVELED $12.95
The Best of Travel Humor and Misadventure
Edited by Doug Lansky

***
Humor Book of the Year Independent Publisher's Book Award

***
ForeWord Gold Medal Winner—Humor Book of the Year

WHOSE PANTIES ARE THESE? $14.95
More Misadventures from Funny Women on the Road
Edited by Jennifer L. Leo
Following on the high heels of the award-winning bestseller *Sand in My Bra and other Misadventures* comes another collection of hilarious travel stories by women.

Travelers' Tales Classics

COAST TO COAST $16.95
A Journey Across 1950s America
By Jan Morris
After reporting on the first Everest ascent in 1953, Morris spent a year journeying across the United States. In brilliant prose, Morris records with exuberance and curiosity a time of innocence in the U.S.

TRADER HORN $16.95
A Young Man's Astounding Adventures in 19th Century Equatorial Africa
By Alfred Aloysius Horn
Here is the stuff of legends—thrills and danger, wild beasts, serpents, and savages. An unforgettable and vivid portrait of a vanished Africa.

THE ROYAL ROAD TO ROMANCE $14.95
By Richard Halliburton
"Laughing at hardships, dreaming of beauty, ardent for adventure, Halliburton has managed to sing into the pages of this glorious book his own exultant spirit of youth and freedom."
—*Chicago Post*

UNBEATEN TRACKS IN JAPAN $14.95
By Isabella L. Bird
Isabella Bird was one of the most adventurous women travelers of the 19th century with journeys to Tibet, Canada, Korea, Turkey, Hawaii, and Japan. A fascinating read.

THE RIVERS RAN EAST $16.95
By Leonard Clark
Clark is the original Indiana Jones, telling the breathtaking story of his search for the legendary El Dorado gold in the Amazon.

Spiritual Travel

THE SPIRITUAL GIFTS OF TRAVEL $16.95
The Best of Travelers' Tales
Edited by James O'Reilly & Sean O'Reilly
Favorite stories of transformation on the road that show the myriad ways travel indelibly alters our inner landscapes.

PILGRIMAGE $16.95
Adventures of the Spirit
Edited by Sean O'Reilly & James O'Reilly
Introduction by Phil Cousineau

ForeWord Silver Medal Winner
—Travel Book of the Year

THE ROAD WITHIN $18.95
True Stories of Transformation and the Soul
Edited by Sean O'Reilly, James O'Reilly & Tim O'Reilly

Independent Publisher's Book Award
—Best Travel Book

THE WAY OF THE WANDERER $14.95
Discover Your True Self Through Travel
By David Yeadon
Experience transformation through travel with this delightful, illustrated collection by award-winning author David Yeadon.

A WOMAN'S PATH $16.95
Women's Best Spiritual Travel Writing
Edited by Lucy McCauley, Amy G. Carlson & Jennifer Leo
"A sensitive exploration of women's lives that have been unexpectedly and spiritually touched by travel experiences.... Highly recommended."
—*Library Journal*

THE ULTIMATE JOURNEY $17.95
Inspiring Stories of Living and Dying
James O'Reilly, Sean O'Reilly & Richard Sterling
"A glorious collection of writings about the ultimate adventure. A book to keep by one's bedside—and close to one's heart."
—Philip Zaleski, editor, The Best Spiritual Writing series

Special Interest

THE BEST TRAVELERS' TALES 2004 $16.95
True Stories from Around the World
Edited by James O'Reilly, Larry Habegger & Sean O'Reilly
"This book will grace my bedside for years to come."
—Simon Winchester, from the Introduction

TESTOSTERONE PLANET $17.95
True Stories from a Man's World
Edited by Sean O'Reilly, Larry Habegger & James O'Reilly
Thrills and laughter with some of today's best writers, including Sebastian Junger, Tim Cahill, Bill Bryson, and Jon Krakauer.

THE GIFT OF TRAVEL $14.95
Inspiring Stories from Around the World
Edited by Larry Habegger, James O'Reilly & Sean O'Reilly
"Like gourmet chefs in a French market, the editors of Travelers' Tales pick, sift, and prod their way through the weighty shelves of contemporary travel writing, creaming off the very best."
—William Dalrymple, author of *City of Djinns*

DANGER! $17.95
True Stories of Trouble and Survival
Edited by James O'Reilly, Larry Habegger & Sean O'Reilly
"Exciting...for those who enjoy living on the edge or prefer to read the survival stories of others, this is a good pick."
—*Library Journal*

365 TRAVEL $14.95
A Daily Book of Journeys, Meditations, and Adventures
Edited by Lisa Bach
An illuminating collection of travel wisdom and adventures that reminds us all of the lessons we learn while on the road.

THE GIFT OF RIVERS $14.95
True Stories of Life on the Water
Edited by Pamela Michael
Introduction by Robert Hass
"...a soulful compendium of wonderful stories that illuminate, educate, inspire, and delight."
—David Brower, Chairman of Earth Island Institute

FAMILY TRAVEL $17.95
The Farther You Go, the Closer You Get
Edited by Laura Manske
"This is family travel at its finest."
—*Working Mother*

LOVE & ROMANCE $17.95
True Stories of Passion on the Road
Edited by Judith Babcock Wylie
"A wonderful book to read by a crackling fire."
—*Romantic Traveling*

THE GIFT OF BIRDS $17.95
True Encounters with Avian Spirits
Edited by Larry Habegger & Amy G. Carlson
"These are all wonderful, entertaining stories offering a *bird's-eye view!* of our avian friends."
—*Booklist*

IT'S A DOG'S WORLD $14.95
True Stories of Travel with Man's Best Friend
Edited by Christine Hunsicker
Introduction by Maria Goodavage
Hilarious and heart warming stories of traveling with canine companions.

Travel Advice

THE PENNY PINCHER'S PASSPORT TO LUXURY TRAVEL (2ND EDITION) $14.95
The Art of Cultivating Preferred Customer Status
By Joel L. Widzer
Completely updated and revised, this 2nd edition of the popular guide to traveling like the rich and famous without being either describes, both philosophically and in practical terms, how to obtain luxurious travel benefits by building relationships with airlines and other travel companies.

SAFETY AND SECURITY FOR WOMEN WHO TRAVEL (2ND EDITION) $14.95
By Sheila Swan & Peter Laufer
"A cache of valuable advice."
—*The Christian Science Monitor*

THE FEARLESS SHOPPER $14.95
How to Get the Best Deals on the Planet
By Kathy Borrus
"Anyone who reads *The Fearless Shopper* will come away a smarter, more responsible shopper and a more curious, culturally attuned traveler."
—Jo Mancuso, *The Shopologist*

SHITTING PRETTY $12.95
How to Stay Clean and Healthy While Traveling
By Dr. Jane Wilson-Howarth
A light-hearted book about a serious subject for millions of travelers—staying healthy on the road—written by international health expert, Dr. Jane Wilson-Howarth.

GUTSY WOMEN (2ND EDITION) $12.95
More Travel Tips and Wisdom for the Road
By Marybeth Bond
Packed with funny, instructive, and inspiring advice for women heading out to see the world.

GUTSY MAMAS $7.95
Travel Tips and Wisdom for Mothers on the Road
By Marybeth Bond
A delightful guide for mothers traveling with their children—or without them!

Destination Titles

ALASKA $18.95
Edited by Bill Sherwonit, Andromeda Romano-Lax, & Ellen Bielawski

AMERICA $19.95
Edited by Fred Setterberg

AMERICAN SOUTHWEST $17.95
Edited by Sean O'Reilly & James O'Reilly

AUSTRALIA $18.95
Edited by Larry Habegger

BRAZIL $18.95
Edited by Annette Haddad & Scott Doggett
Introduction by Alex Shoumatoff

CENTRAL AMERICA $17.95
Edited by Larry Habegger & Natanya Pearlman

CHINA $18.95
Edited by Sean O'Reilly, James O'Reilly & Larry Habegger

CUBA $18.95
Edited by Tom Miller

FRANCE $18.95
Edited by James O'Reilly, Larry Habegger & Sean O'Reilly

GRAND CANYON $17.95
Edited by Sean O'Reilly, James O'Reilly & Larry Habegger

GREECE $18.95
Edited by Larry Habegger, Sean O'Reilly & Brian Alexander

HAWAI'I $17.95
Edited by Rick & Marcie Carroll

HONG KONG $17.95
Edited by James O'Reilly, Larry Habegger & Sean O'Reilly

INDIA $19.95
Edited by James O'Reilly & Larry Habegger

IRELAND $18.95
Edited by James O'Reilly, Larry Habegger & Sean O'Reilly

ITALY $18.95
Edited by Anne Calcagno
Introduction by Jan Morris

JAPAN $17.95
Edited by Donald W. George & Amy G. Carlson

MEXICO $17.95
Edited by James O'Reilly & Larry Habegger

NEPAL $17.95
Edited by Rajendra S. Khadka

PARIS $18.95
Edited by James O'Reilly, Larry Habegger & Sean O'Reilly

PROVENCE $16.95
Edited by James O'Reilly & Tara Austen Weaver

SAN FRANCISCO $18.95
Edited by James O'Reilly, Larry Habegger & Sean O'Reilly

SPAIN $19.95
Edited by Lucy McCauley

THAILAND $18.95
Edited by James O'Reilly & Larry Habegger

TIBET $18.95
Edited by James O'Reilly & Larry Habegger

TURKEY $18.95
Edited by James Villers Jr.

TUSCANY $16.95
Edited by James O'Reilly & Tara Austen Weaver
Introduction by Anne Calcagno